D1591614

1 & 2 CORINTHIANS

1&2 CORINTHIANS

A Commentary for Bible Students

KENNETH SCHENCK

Copyright © 2006 by Wesleyan Publishing House
Indianapolis, Indiana 46250
Printed in the United States of America

ISBN-10: 0-89827-309-9
ISBN-13: 978-0-89827-309-0

WESLEYAN BIBLE COMMENTARY SERIES

GENERAL PUBLISHER
Donald D. Cady

EXECUTIVE EDITOR
David W. Holdren, D.D., S.T.D.

EDITORIAL ADVISORY COMMITTEE

Joseph D. Allison, M.Div.
Publishing Manager
Evangel Publishing House

Ray E. Barnwell
General Director of Sunday School
and Discipleship Ministries
The Wesleyan Church

Barry L. Callen, M.Div., M.Th., D.Rel.
University Professor of Christian Studies
Anderson University

Ray Easley, M.Div., Ed.D.
Vice President of Academic Affairs
Wesley Biblical Seminary

Dorothy Hitzka
National Consultant for Christian
Education
The Salvation Army

Arthur Kelly
Coordinator of Christian Education
and Congregational Life
Church of God Ministries

Stephen J. Lennox, Ph.D.
Professor of Bible and Chair, Division
of Religion and Philosophy
Indiana Wesleyan University

Bonnie J. Perry
Director
Beacon Hill Press of Kansas City

Dan Tipton, D.Min.
General Superintendent
Churches of Christ in Christian Union

John Van Valin
Free Methodist Pastor
Indianapolis, Indiana

EDITORS
Lawrence W. Wilson, M.Div.
Managing Editor

Stephen J. Lennox, Ph.D.
Theological Editor

Darlene Teague, M.Div.
Senior Editor

To my godly parents, Lee and Helen Schenck,
Who raised me in the "nurture and admonition of the Lord."
They have modeled for me and all who know them
lives fully devoted to Jesus Christ.
To know them is to know the absurdity of doing
anything but God's will.

CONTENTS

Contents

EXECUTIVE EDITOR'S PREFACE

ife change. That, we believe, is the goal of God's written revelation. God has given His written Word so that we might know Him and become like Him—holy, as he is holy.

Life change is also the goal of this book, a volume in the Wesleyan Bible Commentary Series. This series has been created with the primary aim of promoting life change in believers by applying God's authoritative truth in relevant, practical ways. This commentary will impact Bible students with fresh insight into God's unchanging Word. Read it with your Bible in hand.

A second purpose of this series is to assist laypersons and pastors in their teaching ministries. Anyone called to assist others in Christian growth and service will appreciate the practical nature of these commentaries. Writers were selected based on their ability to soundly interpret God's Word and apply that unchanging truth in fresh, practical ways. Each biblical book is explained paragraph by paragraph, giving the reader both the big picture and sufficient detail to understand the meaning of significant words and phrases. There results of scholarly research are presented in enough detail to clarify, for example, the meaning of important Greek or Hebrew words, but not in such a way that readers are overwhelmed. This series will be an invaluable tool for preaching, lesson preparation, and personal or group Bible study.

The third aim of this series is to present a Wesleyan-Arminian interpretation of Scripture in a clear and compelling fashion. Toward that end, the series has been developed with the cooperative effort of scholars, pastors, and church leaders in the Wesleyan, Nazarene, Free Methodist, Salvation Army, Church of God (Anderson), Churches of Christ in Christian Union, Brethren in Christ, and United Methodist denominations. These volumes present reliable interpretation of biblical texts in the tradition of John Wesley, Adam Clarke, and other renowned interpreters.

Throughout the production of this series, authors and editors have approached each Bible passage with this question in mind: How will my life change when I fully understand and apply this scripture?

Let that question be foremost in your mind also, as God speaks again through His Word.

DAVID W. HOLDREN

1 CORINTHIANS

INTRODUCTION TO
1 CORINTHIANS

AUTHORSHIP

The apostle Paul was born in Tarsus (Acts 9:11, 22:3), a city on the southeast coast of Asia Minor (modern-day Turkey). As such, he was certainly fluent in Greek (Acts 21:37). But he also knew Hebrew, the language of the Old Testament, and spoke Aramaic, the language primarily used by Jews in Jerusalem (Acts 21:40). Since Greek was the best known language throughout the Roman Empire, it is no surprise that God inspired Paul to write all his letters in Greek.

POSSIBLE TIMELINE OF PAUL'S EARLY MINISTRY

A.D. 30	Christ crucified/resurrected
A.D. 33–34	Paul comes to Christ (Acts 9)
A.D. 36–37	Paul escapes from Damascus, visits Jerusalem (Gal. 1:18)
A.D. 48–49	Paul's first missionary journey (Acts 13–14)
A.D. 49	Jerusalem Meeting (Acts 15; Gal. 2:1)
A.D. 49	Paul begins second journey (Acts 15:41)
A.D. 50–51	Paul in Corinth (Acts 18:11), writes 1 Thessalonians
A.D. 51–52	Paul begins third journey (Acts 18:23)
A.D. 52–55	Paul in Ephesus (Acts 19:8, 10), writes 1 Corinthians (1 Cor. 16:8)
A.D. 55	Paul in Macedonia (Acts 20:1–2), writes 2 Corinthians (2 Cor. 7:5–6)

The book of Acts tells us he was born a Roman citizen, a high status but very rare among Jews, which suggests his family was somewhat wealthy or at least had high status in Tarsus (16:37, 22:25–29, 25:10–11). Acts also tells us he worked as a "tent-maker" on his journeys (Acts 18:3).

At some point in his early life he went to Jerusalem, probably to train as a rabbi. Acts implies that he had family there at one time (Acts

23:16–22). It is at least possible that Paul went to live with family in Jerusalem during this part of his life. Acts 22:3 tells us Paul was trained in Jerusalem "at the feet" of Gamaliel, an extremely famous Pharisee we also meet in Acts 5. During this period Paul was educated in the Jewish law and became "zealous for God" (Acts 22:3; Phil. 3:6).

PHARISEES

Paul became a Pharisee (Acts 23:6; Phil. 3:5). Pharisees were a relatively small group of Jews who nevertheless exerted considerable influence over the Jewish masses. Their chief characteristic was the way they kept rather extensive oral traditions ("traditions of the elders") on how to observe the Old Testament laws (Mark 7:3). For the Pharisees and many other Jews these traditions spelled out the details of what it meant to keep the commandments in specific life situations.

For example, the fourth commandment says not to work on the Sabbath (Exod. 20:8–11). But what constitutes work? How far would someone have to walk before he or she had worked on the Sabbath? Different groups of Jews had different answers to these questions. Among these groups, the Pharisees tended to have a somewhat strict view of what you could and could not do.

We can tell from Jesus' strong indictment in Matthew 23 that some Pharisees missed the point of the law. Jesus had strong words to say to anyone who made the law an end in and of itself. He spoke against those who would make someone go hungry because of the Sabbath law (Mark 2:23–3:6) or who would use a technicality to get out of caring for their parents (Mark 7:9–13).

Paul makes an interesting comment in Philippians 3:6 about his life as a Pharisee. He says he became "blameless" as far as the righteousness in the law is concerned.[1] Paul probably felt as confident of his righteousness as the Pharisee in the parable of Luke 18:9–14.

But everything changed on a road to Damascus around the year A.D. 33. Our gracious God stopped Paul the persecutor and pointed him in a different direction. In an instant God turned his whole view of life and the world upside down. Paul had thought God hated Christians; it turned out they were the ones who understood His will. Paul had thought God was all-concerned with the details of the Jewish law; it turned out He was more interested in bringing lost sheep back into His fold.

In all this change it is important to realize that Paul never stopped being an Israelite (2 Cor. 11:22; Phil. 3:5).[2] "Saul" was not Paul's pre-Christian name, as if he suddenly became "Paul" when he turned to Christ. Acts continues to call Paul by his Jewish name (Saul) almost fifteen years after he became a Christian (Acts 13:9). Nor did Paul change religions when he came to Christ. He did not give up his Jewish faith, but discovered Christ as the gracious fulfillment of the Judaic law that he had studied as a Pharisee.

We also have every reason to believe Paul applied the same vigor to his preaching of the gospel that he had earlier dedicated to its destruction. Less than three years after he came to Christ, people were trying to arrest and kill him for his preaching (2 Cor. 11:32–33). While the apostles were able to remain alive in Jerusalem, Paul's persecutors forced him out of the city (Acts 9:29–30).

Paul increasingly exercised strong (overbearing?) leadership in the church. On his first missionary journey in Acts we increasingly find him the lead speaker, even though Barnabas may originally have led the mission (Acts 13:2; 14:12). He and Barnabas came into so much conflict after this journey that they went their separate ways, with Paul now the clear leader of his own mission (Acts 15:39–40; Gal. 2:13).

Just as God had called Peter to minister to Jews, Paul understood that God had called him as the apostle of the non-Jews or Gentiles (Gal. 2:7). Paul's strategy was thus to preach in places that had not yet heard the good news, to go with spiritual boldness where no preacher had gone before (Rom. 15:20). So it was on this so-called "second missionary journey" that Paul first visited Corinth.

In what increasingly became the pattern of his ministry, he found himself drawn to a big city. Acts tells us he spent a year and a half here before he moved on again (Acts 18:11). Before he was martyred, he would visit this city at least two more times and write them at least four letters. God preserved two of these for us in the collection of inspired writings we now know of as 1 and 2 Corinthians.

RECIPIENT

Corinth was a big city with a long history by the time Paul arrived there in the first century.[3] In Greece's Golden Age it was considered one of the most promiscuous cities in the world, the "sin-city" of its day. The

Greek playwright Aristophanes even coined the term "to corinthianize," meaning to be sexually immoral, and the geographer Strabo claimed that the Temple of Aphrodite had a thousand sacred prostitutes at one time.[4]

But the Corinth of Paul's day was not the same city as the one to which these writers referred. The Romans destroyed the city in 146 B.C., obliterating the old Corinth. Julius Caesar re-founded it in 44 B.C., just weeks before he was assassinated. No doubt the city's location soon pushed it in the same seedy direction that it had gone in a previous generation. But it was probably no more promiscuous than any other port town.[5]

Corinth was located just south of a narrow strip of land or "isthmus" between southern Greece and the northern part with Athens. At its narrowest, this isthmus was about four miles wide. This location was an ideal shortcut for trade and commerce since the trip around the south of Greece took six days and involved sailing through difficult waters. This shortcut, called the *diolkos*, made it possible to pull a smaller boat over land from one side to the other. A larger ship could unload its cargo on the one gulf and have it reloaded on another ship in the other gulf.

The Isthmian Games were held in the area of Corinth every other year.[6] These games were of the same sort as the more famous Olympic Games

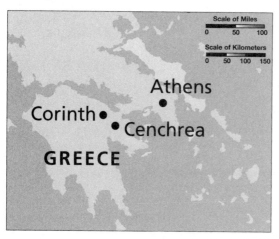

to the southeast. Paul was in fact in Corinth when the games of A.D. 51 were celebrated. No doubt this fact played into his use of athletic imagery in the letter (1 Cor. 9:24–27).

The city walls of Corinth covered an area roughly three miles wide and two and a half miles north and south. Two additional long walls protected the road north from Corinth about a mile and a half to the port village of Lechaeum. Eighty thousand inhabitants called Corinth home, with twenty thousand more or so in the surrounding area.[7] Only a relatively small portion of the city is currently unearthed, chiefly the center area where the most important public buildings were located.

Towering over the city is the over 1,880–feet-high Acrocorinth or "high Corinth." It was on this hill that the famous Temple of Aphrodite had stood in the classical period. But the temple in operation at the time of Paul was much smaller and probably did not include temple prostitutes.

A number of relevant sites stand on the plateau below. Today you will still find the ruins of the *bēma* (BEE-mah) where Paul may have stood before the Roman prefect Gallio in A.D. 51 (Acts 18:12).[8] You will also find the remains of several temples, including the dominating temple of Apollo; it was already archaic by the time Paul was there. Less accessible to the tourist are the ruins of the temple of Asclepius, which was just inside the northern city walls. These are the kinds of places where one might have obtained the meat offered to idols (1 Cor. 8–10).

You can also find ruins of more than one marketplace (1 Cor. 10:25) as well as those of various shops. Paul may have set up a tent-making booth in one of these and used it as a way of introducing people to the gospel. We have not yet unearthed a synagogue from Paul's period, but no doubt Corinth had such a building (Acts 18:7).[9] The city clearly had a significant Jewish population there.

Another artifact of significance is an inscription found near the remains of Corinth's theater. Here you will find a stone that reads "Erastus laid this pavement at his own expense in return for his *aedile-ship*." An aedile was a Roman political official in charge of city maintenance and public festivals. It made a good starting point for those wishing to climb the political ladder. Rom. 16:23 mentions an Erastus who was the "city's director of public works," very likely the same individual who paid for this stone. We begin to realize that the Corinthian church not only had slaves and individuals of relatively low status, but also at least a few who were wealthy and well connected.

Corinth was a Roman colony and the chief city of the region (Achaea)—even more important than Athens at that time. As a Roman colony its citizens were exempt from Roman taxation, and the city's official language was Latin. The city thus tended to have a strong Roman orientation even though it was located in Greece.

Julius Caesar re-founded the city mostly with former soldiers and freed slaves. Some scholars have argued that this background led to a situation in which the city had a number of "empowered" individuals with wealth who nevertheless did not have the kind of "noble status" that usually went along with it.[10] Such a "status inconsistency" might help explain some of the things going on in the church at Corinth, where boasting was so prevalent and several groups seemed to be using Christianity as a way to gain status.

DATE OF WRITING

It is difficult to date the events of Paul's life with great certainty. Thankfully, we have at least one firm date for Paul's activities. A stone inscription discovered at Delphi, Greece, indicates that a man named Gallio governed the region where Corinth is located in the years A.D. 51–52, although he returned to Rome early due to sickness. Paul appeared before this Roman proconsul late in the time he was first at Corinth (Acts 18:12–17). We can thus date Paul's first visit to Corinth with relative certainty to the years A.D. 50–51.[11]

Paul did not write 1 and 2 Corinthians *from* Corinth—he wrote them *to* Corinth, not during his *second* missionary journey while he was in Corinth, but later on his *third* when he was in Ephesus. After leaving Corinth on his second missionary journey in late A.D. 51, Paul briefly visited Ephesus, made his way to Jerusalem and then up to Antioch (Acts 18:18–22).

Then after "some time" in Antioch he started his third missionary journey, traveling through the churches of Galatia and Phrygia he had previously founded (Acts 18:23). It is hard to know how much time all these travels took. It is at least plausible that Paul did not arrive in Ephesus (Acts 19:1) until somewhat late in A.D. 52.

Paul would stay in Ephesus at least two years and three months (late 52–early 55; Acts 19:8, 10). Some time in mid-53, Paul received a report of immorality in the church at Corinth. At that point he wrote them a letter that has not survived (1 Cor. 5:9). So 1 Corinthians is not really his first letter to the Corinthians; it is the second.

Paul wrote 1 Corinthians probably right around the first of the year in A.D. 54. His ministry in Ephesus was blossoming (1 Cor. 16:9; Acts 19:11–12), although it is also possible that he had already been arrested once (1 Cor. 15:32). Paul planned to stay in Ephesus until the Feast of Pentecost (1 Cor. 16:8), so he probably wrote the book sometime in the first half of the year.

On the other hand, Paul departed from Ephesus around the turn of the year 55, just a little over two years after he had arrived. We must allow for some time between the writing of 1 Corinthians and Paul's final departure from Ephesus. From various comments Paul makes, his plans apparently did not turn out quite the way he had originally planned. Paul did make a visit to Corinth—one that Acts does not mention (2 Cor. 2:1, 13:1). He then promised them another visit that he in the end did not make (2 Cor. 1:16). Instead, he sent them a harsh letter that apparently has not survived.

He must have done all these things between the time he wrote 1 Corinthians and his departure for Macedonia in early 55. He would then spend some time in Macedonia, write 2 Corinthians, and spend three months in Greece.[12] He would celebrate the Passover in Philippi and rush to get to Jerusalem before the Feast of Pentecost fifty days later.

We might thus date the writing of 1 Corinthians to early 54 and 2 Corinthians to early 55.

PURPOSE

The period between Paul's first visit to Corinth (A.D. 50–51) and the writing of 1 Corinthians (early 54) saw some changes in the church's situation. After Paul left, a man named Apollos became a Christian and ministered to the church there (Acts 18:24–19:1). Apollos was from the Egyptian city of Alexandria, the second largest in the empire and home to the most famous library in the world. If we are to judge by Paul's opening comments in 1 Corinthians (1 Cor. 1:17, 20), Apollos must have brought with him an eloquence and education superior to Paul's (1 Cor. 2:1, Acts 18:24–25), at least by the secular standards of that day. First Corinthians gives us hints that these two great men, Paul and Apollos, may have differed slightly in their approaches to things. Some of those who thought on an earthly rather than spiritual level exploited these differences to their advantage.

Sometime after Paul arrived in Ephesus, perhaps in mid-53, Paul became aware of sexual immorality in the Corinthian church. As a result, Paul wrote a letter to the church telling them not to associate with Christians who were sexually immoral (1 Cor. 5:9–11). Unfortunately, we have lost this letter to time. But sexual immorality remained an issue at Corinth; it is just one among many issues that gave rise to 1 Corinthians (chaps. 5–6 in particular).

However, the fundamental problem that gave rise to 1 Corinthians was undoubtedly the disunity of the community. First Corinthians 1:10 gives us the key verse of the entire letter, the "proposition" of 1 Corinthians: "I appeal to you, brothers, in the name of our Lord Jesus Christ, that all of you agree with one another so that there may be no divisions among you and that you may be perfectly united in mind and thought." We find this same sentiment echoed in 11:18: "I hear that when you come together as a church, there are divisions among you."

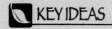 KEY IDEAS

DISUNITY

The fundamental problem that gave rise to 1 Corinthians was undoubtedly the disunity of the community.

Scholars have spilled a good deal of ink discussing the exact nature of the divisions at Corinth. In general, we can boil these divisions down to (1) a group that saw itself as more "spiritual" and "wise" than the other group and probably aligned with Apollos, (2) a second group who largely remained loyal to Paul and his teaching.

A number of different factors seem to have coalesced in these two groups. We can at least wonder whether the Corinthians were using some of Apollos's teaching to argue that they could eat meat sacrificed to idols. Did Apollos teach them that "an idol is nothing at all in the world" (1 Cor. 8:4) and thus that it really did not matter whether they ate meat offered to one? Paul did not necessarily disagree, but he would lead them away from knowingly eating such meat.

This "spiritual" group was also probably a little more affluent than others in the community. On the whole, "not many" in the community were "wise," "influential," or "of noble birth" (1 Cor. 1:26). But the way Paul words this statement hints that some apparently were. It is likely this group that had the resources to buy meat at the marketplace (10:25) and to get drunk at the Lord's Supper (11:21).

The church at Corinth was probably not a very large church. Paul most often uses the word *church* to refer to a group that actually meets together. Thus in Romans, Paul greets the church that meets in the house of Priscilla and Aquila (Rom. 16:5). Later in that same chapter, we hear that the whole church at Corinth enjoyed the hospitality of a man named Gaius (Rom. 16:23). For this reason many scholars have suggested that the church at Corinth could fit in his house when they met together as a whole. The nearby village of Cenchrea also had its own church there (Rom. 16:1). This would suggest the entire church numbered between 40–50 people.

We know at least fifteen of these by name at the time Paul was writing: households of Chloe (1 Cor. 1:11) and Stephanas (1:16); Crispus and Gaius (1:14); Fortunatus and Achaicus were perhaps members of Stephanas's household (1 Cor. 16:17). We learn several additional names of Corinthians from the greetings they send in Romans 16: Erastus, the city's director of public works, as well as Quartus (Rom. 16:23); Paul's relatives Lucius, Jason, and Sosipater (16:21); and Tertius who served as Paul's scribe (1 Cor. 16:22). Acts mentions Titius Justus (Acts 18:7) and Sosthenes (18:17).

In addition to these fifteen individuals, we know of a man sleeping with his step-mother (1 Cor. 5:1), perhaps someone who entered the community after Paul had left. We also know the community must have had any number of women associated with it (1 Cor. 7:10–11, 11:5–6, 14:34–35). As we might expect, most of the names are Latin, reflecting the fact that Corinth was a Roman colony largely re-founded with Roman transplants. Some of them, like Erastus, Crispus, Gaius, and Sosthenes, were apparently individuals of some means, given what we know of them.

It stands to reason that most of the individuals whose names we know were part of the "Pauline group," the group in the church that submitted to Paul's authority. The leadership of the church also seems to have come from this group. Clement, writing from Rome in the mid-90s, would remind the Corinthians of the leadership Paul had established there at the very beginning.[13] Of course we cannot deny the possibility that some of the more powerful in this list were culprits in the problems at Corinth.

The immediate occasion of Paul's letter was news from Chloe's household about disunity in the community (1 Cor. 1:11). This information was perhaps the main source behind the kinds of things Paul addressed in the first six chapters, including reports about the sexually immoral man (1 Cor. 5) and the lawsuits in the community (1 Cor. 6). It may also have included reports about the Lord's Supper, the problem with head coverings (1 Cor. 11), and the disbelief of some in the resurrection (1 Cor. 15).

Perhaps while Paul was even in the process of writing 1 Corinthians, a delegation of sorts from the Corinthian church arrived with a letter from the Corinthians themselves. This delegation consisted of men by the name of Stephanas, Fortunatus, and Achaicus (1 Cor. 16:17). Apparently the individuals of this household were the first to come to Christ in Corinth (1 Cor. 16:15).[14] Most of the content of 1 Corinthians is Paul's response to this letter, which he may have sent back with these men.

The typical ancient letter consisted of three main parts: (1) a greeting or "prescript," (2) the body of the letter, and (3) closing greetings called a "postscript." In addition, many ancient letters had a "thanksgiving" section or blessing that followed the greeting and preceded the body of the letter. The letters often "wind down" with closing remarks of a more personal or incidental nature. Paul's letters generally follow

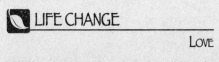

LIFE CHANGE

LOVE

If disunity was the central problem in the Corinthian church, the fundamental solution was love.

this basic pattern with some typical modifications he makes. The outline that follows the Introduction shows how Paul did so in 1 Corinthians.

If disunity was the central problem of the Corinthian community (1 Cor. 1:10), the fundamental solution was love. In many ways, 1 Corinthians 13, the "love chapter," sums up Paul's response to the Corinthians. Love would resolve the divisive spirit that led various groups to think they were better than everyone else in the church (1 Cor. 1–4). Love would solve the problem of the Corinthians taking each other to court (1 Cor. 6). The Christians at Corinth would not insist on their rights at the expense of others if they were acting in love (1 Cor. 8–10), nor would the women uncover their heads immodestly in front of the other men and women in the community (1 Cor. 11:3–16). Finally, love would put to an end the selfish way they were acting at their community meals (1 Cor. 11:17–34). The love chapter relates most directly to the subject of spiritual gifts (1 Cor. 12–14), which apparently some used to claim superiority over others in the community.

Of all the books in the Bible, 1 Corinthians reads the most like a catalog of issues in the church today. Human sexuality, divorce, tongues, disputable matters, church unity—these issues are as pressing today as they have ever been. The Corinthians also remind us of our own struggle to get along with each other in the church. Unfortunately, things only got worse after 1 Corinthians, and 2 Corinthians does not end on a positive note. Indeed, we do not know if this church ever got its act together.[15] We lament their problems, but their loss is an incredible gain for us. How much less we would know about the early church if we did not have these letters—and how much more we know about how to live today!

ENDNOTES

1. The Jewish Sabbath is from sundown on Friday to sundown on Saturday, the seventh day of the week.

2. While Acts 22:3 refers to Paul as a Jew, Paul generally avoided calling himself one (1 Cor. 9:20).

3. It was originally founded in the eighth century B.C.

4. *Geography* 8.6.20. The archaeological evidence does not support these wild claims. Scholars now agree that Strabo's numbers were exaggerated.

5. So C. K. Barrett, *A Commentary on the First Epistle to the* Corinthians (New York: Harper & Row, 1968), 3.

6. Archaeologists debate whether the games were actually held in Corinth at that time or whether they had already moved back to Isthmia, just a few miles east of Corinth. We can say with some certainty that they had at least moved back to Isthmia within ten years of Paul's first visit to the city.

7. For demographic information of this sort, see D. Engels, *Roman Corinth: An Alternative Model for the Classical City* (Chicago: University of Chicago, 1990) and J. Murphy-O'Connor, *St. Paul's Corinth: Texts and Archaeology* (Wilmington: Glazier, 1983).

8. For other possible locations see O. F. A. Minardus, *St. Paul in Greece* (Athens: Lycabettus, 1972), 77–79.

9. Not all synagogues or Jewish "gatherings" took place in free standing buildings; some must have met in homes. But Corinth clearly had such a building, since Paul could go to the house next door. A synagogue has been found from a later period.

10. The main proponent of this idea is W. Meeks, *The First Urban Christians: The Social World of the Apostle Paul* (New Haven, CT: Yale University, 1983).

11. Acts indicates that Paul was there for about a year and a half on this visit (Acts 18:11). It was likely during this period that he wrote 1 Thessalonians and perhaps 2 Thessalonians.

12. On this third visit to Corinth he apparently wrote Romans, early A.D. 55.

13. 1 Clement 47.

14. The way 1 Cor. 1:16 jogs Paul's memory, in contrast to his ready memory in 16:15–18, makes us wonder if Paul had already started the letter when the delegation arrived. The classic treatment of these kinds of issues is J. C. Hurd, *The Origin of 1 Corinthians* (London: SPCK, 1965).

15. Thirty years later we will find this church trying to oust its leaders (1 Clement 47).

OUTLINE OF 1 CORINTHIANS

I. **Greetings (1:1–3)**
II. **Thanksgiving (1:4–9)**
III. **The Body of the letter (1:10–16:18)**
    A. **Responding to things heard (1:10–6:20)**
        1. Rumors of divisions (1:10–4:21)
            a. The general principle: Christ is not divided! (1:10–17)
            b. The principle in practice (1:18–4:21)
                (1) The foolishness of cross (1:18–2:5)
                (2) True wisdom and spirituality (2:6–3:4)
                (3) Applying the principles (3:5–23)
                (4) Don't be arrogant (4:1–21)
        2. Rumors of body problems (5:1–6:20)
            a. The man with his step-mother (5:1–13)
            b. Taking each other to court (6:1–11)
            c. Visiting prostitutes (6:12–20)
    B. **Responding to things written (7:1–16:18)**
        1. Question 1a: Should Christians have sex? (7:1–24)
            a. Husbands and wives (7:1–7)
            b. Getting and staying married (7:8–16)
            c. Paul's bottom line: Stay as you are (7:17–24)
        2. Question 1b: Should virgins get married? (7:25–40)
        3. Question 2: What about meat sacrificed to idols? (8:1–11:1)
            a. The general principle: Eating with others in mind (8:1–13)
            b. Paul uses himself as an example (9:1–27)
            c. Back to the subject of idolatry (10:1–11:1)
                (1) The danger of idolatry (10:1–13)
                (2) Paul's final answer (10:14–11:1)
        4. Interlude: Christian traditions and worship (11:1–34)
            a. Tradition 1: There is no longer "male and female" (11:3–16)
            b. Tradition 2: The Lord's Supper (11:17–34)

5. Question 3: What about spiritual gifts? (12:1–14:40)

    a. General discussion: Spiritual gifts in the church (12:1–31)

    b. The love chapter: Solution to the Corinthian problem (13:1–13)

    c. Particular discussion: Unedifying use of tongues in worship (14:1–40)

        (1) Basic point: Better to prophesy (14:1–5)

        (2) Prophecy better than tongues in worship (14:6–25)

        (3) Specific guidelines for the use of spiritual gifts in worship (14:26–40)

        (4) An aside: 1 Corinthians 14:34–35

6. More rumors: some reject the resurrection (15:1–58)

    a. Paul reminds them of Christ's resurrection (15:1–11)

    b. Paul's argument for a future resurrection (15:12–34)

    c. What kind of body will we have? (15:35–57)

    d. Conclusion (15:58)

7. Question 4: What about the collection? (16:1–4)

8. Paul's plans (16:5–18)

IV. Farewell (16:19–24)

GREETINGS AND THANKSGIVING

1 Corinthians 1:1–9

1. PAUL'S GREETINGS (1:1–3)

The typical ancient letter greeting or "prescript" had three elements: (1) the name of the author, (2) the name of the recipients, and (3) the word "greetings" (*chairein*). Paul's letters follow this basic pattern, although he added his own characteristic touches. In particular, Paul sometimes described himself and his audiences in ways that were appropriate to the letter he was writing, and he also developed his own special way of saying "greetings."

Paul identifies himself in the way he does so often: as an **apostle** (1:1).[1] An apostle (*apostolos*) was someone sent with a special purpose or commission. In the case of the early church, Jesus had designated certain individuals as apostles to carry his message and authority into the world. We remember that many did not view Paul as an apostle and that the church at Jerusalem may even have had some questions about his approach and theology.[2]

In contrast, Paul indicates that his apostleship came in accordance with God's will and call. Paul believed that God had "set me apart from birth and called me by his grace . . . that I might preach him among the Gentiles" (Gal. 1:15–16). His commissioning came with his vision of the risen Christ on the road to Damascus (1 Cor. 9:1). Paul did not think himself one bit inferior to any other apostle (2 Cor. 11:5; Gal. 2:6, 9). Just as Peter was the apostle to the Jews, Paul saw himself as God's apostle to the Gentiles (Gal. 2:8).

It is easy for us in the Wesleyan tradition to read past Paul's language of calling here and elsewhere. We over-react to those who teach that God has already determined the eternal destiny of each person and deny clear language of selection. We probably remain most faithful to Paul when we affirm both God's election and our responsibility without trying to work out the philosophical problems.

The New Testament teaches in some paradoxical way that both God and we choose. Here is the typical Pauline paradox of calling and freedom: Paul affirms God's control and guidance of the universe while also holding humans free and responsible for their choices. To eliminate one or the other seems to negate an important part of the mystery that is our God, whose ways are past understanding.

The mention of Sosthenes is a bit more puzzling, as Paul never mentions him again in the letter. It is quite possible that he was the same Sosthenes who was a synagogue leader during Paul's stay in Corinth (Acts 18:17). If so, he was the individual the prefect Gallio had beaten in front of his judgment seat (*bēma*), probably in A.D. 51 (see Fig. 2 in the Introduction).

Two primary possibilities exist for Sosthenes's role in the writing of 1 Corinthians. The first is that he was the secretary who actually wrote down the words of this letter. We know that the ancients, including Paul, typically used an *amanuensis* or secretary to write down their letters. For example, the amanuensis of Romans identifies himself as Tertius (Rom. 16:22). We know that Paul used such a scribe to write 1 Corinthians, because Paul picks up the stylus to write a greeting in his own hand in 16:21.

A second possibility is that Paul entrusted this Sosthenes to take the letter to Corinth, perhaps even to read it aloud to the congregation. If he was the former synagogue leader mentioned in Acts 18, then it would make sense that he would have connections and reasons to go there. We should remember that there was no empire "postal service" to carry letters to their destinations. Individuals had to make their own arrangements for the transportation of such messages.

We cannot know for certain whether Paul gave instructions to his letter carrier on how to read it to the Corinthians, but we should keep in mind some significant differences between the way we read a book like 1 Corinthians and the way the original audiences would have. First, we are a "literate" culture—we read and are oriented around written words. We thus refer to 1 Corinthians as a book or even better, think of it as a letter. However, we should think of Paul's letters as oral documents meant to represent his physical presence and be read among their recipients. The vast majority of Christians everywhere would have been illiterate and would have "heard" rather than read these books (Rom. 2:13). They were thus "audiences" far more than readers.

It is perhaps significant that Paul says to **the church of God in Corinth** (1:2), not "to the churches" in Corinth. For example, the letter to the Galatians addresses the churches (plural) in this large region. In at least his earlier letters, Paul typically uses the word "church" in reference to a group of Christians meeting in an individual home, thus as mentioned earlier, the church in Corinth was relatively small (fifty or less members).

It is worth pausing to remind ourselves just who was the original audience of this letter. As Christians we believe God inspired this book *for* us, but the letter tells us that it was not written *to* us—it was written to a group of Christians who lived in the ancient city of Corinth. In other words, if we take the Bible seriously, we will reckon with the fact that these words were not written to us in the first instance. So often we are programmed to "read and apply" the meaning of the Bible directly and literally to today. But we should be careful about this practice, because doing exactly the same things they did then will not always *mean* the same thing today.

Given the great differences between the way the ancients thought and the way we do, there are no doubt countless places where we do not even realize we are reading the words of the Bible differently than the original audiences did. God's commands to them often had a great deal to do with the particulars of their situations and cultures. The principles behind those commands do not always play out the same way in different times and places. Nevertheless, God speaks to believers through the words of the Bible wherever they might be in their pilgrimage to understand its original meaning. He makes its words come alive to those who know little of the ancient meaning and yet also speaks to those who know a great deal about it. He gives us communities of faith and spiritual common sense to help us figure out how these words might play out today.

GREAT THEMES

EARTHLY SAINTS

Paul considered all Christians to be "saints," "sanctified," "holy ones." They were God's property and had the Spiritual power of God on their lives.

Paul now expands on the nature of the Corinthian church: **to those sanctified in Christ Jesus and called to be holy** (1:2). While Christians from other traditions are prone to read right past the word *sanctified*, it jumps out at those of us in the Wesleyan tradition. We believe that God has led our community of faith to emphasize a life fully devoted to Jesus Christ, something we call "entire sanctification." The Wesleyan tradition uses this phrase to refer not only to the complete consecration of a person's life to God, but also to a work God does in the believer's heart to make them victorious over the power of sin.

In its original meaning, it is clear that the word "sanctified" in 1 Cor. 1:2 did not refer to an experience of "entire sanctification" or the "Christian perfection" of which John Wesley wrote. Indeed, Paul considered many of the Corinthians he was addressing as "carnal" or "worldly," as the NIV puts it (3:1–3). Paul's letter to the Corinthians leads us to consider meanings for this term that not only include Christians who were still thinking with their "flesh," but to include individuals who were not even believers! (7:14).

Sanctification in this instance refers to being set apart as belonging to God, to the sphere of the sacred rather than the secular. Without negating terms like "initial," "progressive," or "entire sanctification," we will need to make some new categories to "get into Paul's head." On the one hand, sanctification here is "positional" in a sense—it relates to the side of "God's line" we are standing on. Do we belong to God and thus to the holy, or are we ordinary, belonging to the sphere of the merely human?

We should not limit the meaning of this term to an individual experience, and we should not limit the meaning of 1:2 to some "initial sanctification" that takes place when a person first comes to Christ. Paul can apply the "sanctifying work" of God to everyone from the unbelieving spouse of 1 Cor. 7:14 to a group like the Gentiles (Rom. 15:16) to the person God sanctifies "through and through" in 1 Thess. 5:23.

We can also translate the phrase "called to be holy" as "called to be saints." Paul considered all Christians to be "saints" or "holy ones." In other words, when Paul said they were "called to be holy" he was focusing on God's calling rather than on holiness as something they needed to strive for. In short, Paul does not use the words *holy* or *to sanctify* here in the sense of entire sanctification.

The Corinthians shared the fact that they were holy, set apart to God, **with all those everywhere who call on the name of our Lord Jesus Christ—their Lord and ours** (1:2). Here we see an aspect of the New Testament church that we often miss today—the fact that God's church is much bigger than any lone individual or even a particular denomination. Paul will drive us again and again to read the truths of 1 Corinthians together as a body of Christians rather than as individuals. So many times we take the "you" of Scripture to be "me" personally when in fact more often than not Paul was addressing an entire church.

One of the most important truths of 1 Corinthians is the unity of God's church. It is not that it is wrong for there to be different denominations or different church buildings. What is wrong is if we in some way mistake our denomination or church for the broader body of Christ. Two thousand years later, with over twenty thousand different Christian groups, it may be hard for us to discern who is truly "in" and who is not.

But we must remember that all those who truly "call on the name of the Lord" are our brothers and sisters, no matter which visible church they may attend. As Ephesians says, there is "one body and one Spirit" (Eph. 4:4), a body that Ephesians elsewhere equates with the church (1:22–23). First Corinthians gives us one basis for this unity: all Christians share the same Lord in common, "both theirs and ours" (1 Cor. 1:2, 8:6).

Paul ends the opening greeting of 1 Corinthians in a way that is typical of all his letters: **Grace and peace to you from God our Father and the Lord Jesus Christ** (1:3). The typical ancient letter simply said "Greetings" at this

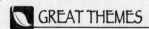

GREAT THEMES

BROTHERS AND SISTERS

All those who truly call on the name of the Lord are brothers and sisters in Christ, no matter what visible church they attend.

point. But the word *greetings* (*chairein*) was just too close to the word *grace* (*charis*) for Paul to pass up. Paul thus began all his letters with a wish for God's grace to be on his audience.

Paul then added a wish for peace to this wish for grace. "Peace" was the Jewish way of greeting another person (*shalom*). By joining these two—"grace and peace"—Paul created a greeting that combined the Greek and Hebrew ways of saying hello. In other words, his very way of greeting was a reflection of his belief that in Christ there was neither "Jew nor Greek" (Gal. 3:28). Both were now one in Christ Jesus.

Paul told the Corinthians that the sources of these blessings were God the Father and the Lord Jesus. We have often heard grace defined as "unmerited favor," a good starting point for understanding it. For Paul and the original audiences of his letters, this unmerited favor was likely understood from within the categories of what we might call "patron-client" relationships. The "have-nots" of that day (clients) often relied on the "haves" (patrons) for their survival and well being. The "haves" gave to the "have-nots," not because the "have-nots" deserved or merited such favor, but because the "haves" received honor from their act of giving.

God gives to us because He loves us as much as to receive honor from us. But no ancient would have understood these gifts to come with "no strings attached." Just because we do not merit or earn God's favor does not mean that He does not expect something from us in return. As we will see, the idea of God as our heavenly patron likely lies behind Paul's language of grace (*charis*) as well as behind his concept of the spiritual gift (*charisma*). Understanding these categories will lead us to see that both the notion of eternal security and the traditional faith versus works debate are quite foreign to Paul's way of thinking.

2. PAUL'S THANKSGIVING (1:4–9)

Almost all of Paul's letters have an opening section in which Paul gives thanks to God for something related to the audience of the letter.[3] We should not think of these words as just a part of Paul's "form letter." We can assume that Paul really did pray for his congregations and thank

God for them. He is a model for pastors and church leaders in the way he regularly brought those under his ministry before God in prayer.

Yet it was also fairly typical of ancient letters to begin with a thanksgiving or prayer section, in the same way that we usually exchange a few pleasantries today before "getting down to business" in our letters. "I hope everything is going well at your house," we might say to "break the ice." In Paul's case, his thanksgiving sections also prepared in one way or another for some of the main topics he then went on to discuss. Such is the case with his first letter to the Corinthians. He thanks God for some of the things he will later advise them about in the letter.

The first thing he mentions is the **grace given you** (1:4). We hinted above that God's grace is His willingness to give to us even though we cannot earn His gifts. It is God's willingness to serve as our divine "patron." A patron is someone with wealth or power who gives to others in exchange for honor or favors. If we look for a model in Paul's world that might explain how he understood grace, this model seems the most likely. The early Christians likely understood God to be their ultimate Patron, the one who provided for them expecting only their honor and obedience in return. Paul will again mention the many gifts God had given the Corinthians (1:9), a comment Paul will develop further in chapters 12 to 14.

Paul expands on God's graciousness to them: **enriched in every way** (1:5). Paul again hints at topics he will soon discuss in the body of the letter. For example, he will discuss their claims to **knowledge** in chapter 8. **Speaking** could refer to tongues (1 Cor. 14) or to the eloquence they think Paul lacks (2 Cor. 10:10). The word can also mean "reason," so Paul could also allude to the fact that they think are wise (1 Cor. 4:10).

The remainder of the thanksgiving section looks back to evidence God had already provided of His work in them (1 Cor. 1:6), evidence He was currently providing (1:7), as well as to the fact that God would later accept them when Christ returned (1:8–9). **[O]ur testimony about Christ was confirmed in you** (1:6) by the fact that **you do not lack any spiritual gift** (1:7). The way Paul words the second comment seems to tell us that the presence of so many "gifts" in the community was confirmation that the message he presented to them about the Messiah had taken root among them.

Given some of the current discussion of spiritual gifts, we should clarify what Paul was saying here. First of all, the word *spiritual* in "spiritual gifts" is not in the Greek. Certainly Paul is alluding to the discussion of spiritual gifts he will have later in chapters 12 to 14. But it might be helpful to hold off reading our current "definitions" and discussions about spiritual gifts as we read this verse. For example, we should not restrict his meaning here to tongues, prophecy, or the other gifts Paul will mention in chapter 12.

Gifts (*charismata*) are instances of God dispensing His grace (*charis*). The knowledge and wisdom the Corinthians had were some of these gifts. Their use of prophecy and tongues were also instances. All these demonstrations of God's grace provided confirmation that the Corinthians had truly accepted Paul's message about the Christ, the Messiah.[4]

Our current culture pushes us to think of these gifts in terms of individuals. Our tendency is thus to jump immediately to the question of what *my* gift is. But the *you* in 1 Cor. 1:6 is normally plural, and a better translation sees God confirming the message "among you." God's gifts are not private empowerments that belong to us as individuals. Rather, God gives gifts to individuals so that they can enhance *communities* of faith.

The signs of God's gracious working among them continued in the present. They **eagerly wait for our Lord Jesus Christ to be revealed** (1:7). Here we have a reminder of how focused the early church was on the second coming of Jesus to the earth. With so much time past, we have come to think much more in terms of going to heaven and hell when we die. But Paul and these Corinthians really lived in the expectation that Christ would soon return, probably within their lifetime. Paul believed that they would be **blameless on the day of our Lord Jesus Christ** (1:8). This comment indicates Paul thought it a real possibility that these individuals at Corinth might be living when Christ returned. Paul believed God would continue to confirm their place in His grace **to the end** (1:8).

The Day of the Lord was the Day of Judgment. The phrase itself comes from the Old Testament, where it refers to those occasional points in time where God judged His people in a momentous way. Thus the prophet Amos foretold the day when God would judge the northern kingdom of Israel: "Woe to you who long for the day of the LORD! Why do you long for the day of the LORD? That day will be darkness, not light" (Amos 5:18).

But after Christ the phrase had taken on a very specific Christian meaning as the Day of Judgment for the world. However, it was at the same time the Day of Salvation for those in Christ.[5] It was the point when Christ would return to save those called **into fellowship with his Son Jesus Christ our Lord** (1:9).

It is significant for those in the Wesleyan tradition to notice the importance Paul places on being "blameless" on that day. Paul is not using these words as some "legal" shenanigan God pulls to consider us innocent although we are really "guilty as sin." God really wants us to live above sin both as communities and individuals.

The basis for all these expectations remains the fact that **God is faithful** (1:9). The thanksgiving section thus both begins and ends with God's graciousness. It is the gracious God who has enriched the Corinthians in speaking and knowledge (1:5). It is the gracious God who has dispensed gifts on the community, confirming their calling (1:7). This same gracious God would be faithful to see them through to the end so that by His power they would be blameless when Christ returned to the earth. God has accomplished all these things by bringing the Corinthians **into fellowship with his Son Jesus Christ** (1 Cor. 1:9). It is our identity in him, the fact that we "have been crucified with Christ" (Gal. 2:20) that makes the dispensing of God's grace possible.

ENDNOTES

1. He identifies himself this way in many of his earliest writings (1 Cor. 1:1; 2 Cor. 1:1; Gal. 1:1). "Apostle" also appears in Eph. 1:1, Col. 1:1, 1 Tim. 1:1, and 2 Tim. 1:1. Elsewhere he identifies himself as a "servant of Christ Jesus" (Rom. 1:1; Phil. 1:1; Titus 1:1) and a "prisoner" (Phlm. 1). 1 and 2 Thessalonians simply identify Paul as author without description.

2. For example, Paul did not fit the criteria to be a "top level" apostle according to the criteria of Acts 1:21–22.

3. Galatians is the most noticeable exception—Paul was rather upset at the Galatians at the time he was writing (Gal. 5:12).

4. It is perhaps noteworthy that Paul refers to "*the* Christ" here, something he rarely does, possibly highlighting the fact that the Corinthians accepted Jesus as the Messiah.

5. Many will want to integrate Paul's teaching on the "end times" with that of Revelation. But Paul and the other New Testament authors give us no sense that they are aware of Revelation's two resurrections and millennial reign. Further, Revelation never mentions a seven year period of tribulation; this idea is usually pieced together by reading Daniel out of context and then imposing its language on Revelation.

In the end, God may have revealed some of these interpretations to certain prophecy teachers, even if they are not the meanings these writings originally had. But it is also important for us to be faithful to Paul's writings on this topic and to listen to what *he* has to say before imposing the categories of Revelation—and of modern prophecy teachers—on him. Paul only tells us of one return of Christ and one day of judgment that takes place at that time.

2

THE GENERAL PRINCIPLE:

CHRIST IS NOT DIVIDED!

1 Corinthians 1:10–17

1. THE KEY VERSES OF 1 CORINTHIANS (1:10–17)

These eight verses (1 Cor. 1:10–17) introduce the basic concept Paul will drive home in the next four chapters (1:18–4:21) and indeed in the rest of the letter: Christ is not divided like the Corinthian community is. The way they are "choosing sides" is inappropriate. We can thus think of 1 Cor. 1:10 as the key result Paul wishes to achieve by writing, namely, unity in the church.

Paul appropriately begins with a charge for the church to be **united** (1:10). This verse is arguably the "proposition" of 1 Corinthians, the key verse of the letter. If the Corinthians would put this charge into practice, Paul's mission would be accomplished.

Unfortunately the community was divided, and word of its problems had reached Paul from some in the church, individuals with whom he apparently had close contact. It is reasonable to see these unnamed individuals from **Chloe's household** (1:11)

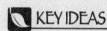 KEY IDEAS

UNITY SOLVES PROBLEMS

1 Corinthians 1:10 is arguably the "proposition" of the letter, the basic point Paul was trying to make. If the church would only learn to be united in their attitudes, their problems would be solved.

as Paul's main source of information for the first six chapters, as well as perhaps the material in chapter 11.

We mentioned in the introduction that the entire church seems to have met in the house of a man named Gaius (Rom. 16:23). At other times smaller groups may have met in the houses of other Christians like Chloe (1 Cor. 1:11) and Stephanas (1:16). It is reasonable to see some of the divisions in the community in terms of these smaller clusters of Christians in the community. Chloe's household must have had clout in the community for Paul to mention it. It is interesting that this household had a woman at its head, perhaps indicating that her husband was dead or perhaps not a Christian. We wonder if Crispus, Gaius, or both were from this household (1:14). Of course we have no real evidence to conclude one way or another on such matters.

One of you says, "I follow Paul"; another, "I follow Apollos"; another, "I follow Cephas"; still another, "I follow Christ" (1:12). Apparently, the divisions largely fell along the lines of those who were loyal to Paul and those who claimed to be superior because they favored some other Christian leader. Scholars debate whether Corinth actually had a distinct party for each of these names. For example, they ask whether there was really a "Peter group" at Corinth (Cephas is the Aramaic form of Peter's name).[1] And it is not even clear what a "Christ group" would be, since as Paul himself asks, **"Is Christ divided?"**(1:13).

Paul's discussion throughout the rest of this section (1:10–4:21) makes it clear that the focal point of division was between those loyal to Paul and those who looked to Apollos as a way of claiming superiority. When Paul returns to these divisions in the section, he usually refers only to Apollos and himself (3:4–5, 4:6). When he is concluding this unit of thought he indicates that he has been applying principles to "myself and Apollos" (4:6). He never alludes to a Christ group after this opening and only mentions Peter one more time thereafter (3:22). We can rightly conclude that the divisions he addresses in 1 Corinthians largely fell in terms of an Apollos vs. Paul conflict.

On the other hand, he does bring up Peter again once (3:22), and we could interpret some of the things he says in the letter as indications that some challenged him from a different angle than the Apollos group would have. Apollos likely reflects a challenge to Paul from a more "liberal" Jewish direction. Peter would represent a challenge from a more "conservative" Jewish position. We see the conservatism of Peter in Gal. 2:11–14, where Peter withdraws himself from eating with Gentile Christians over the purity regulations of the Old Testament. Even Barnabas disagrees with Paul on this issue at that point. While we might think the Jerusalem Council would have solved such issues, it is interesting that Paul never mentions the letter of Acts 15:24–29 in any of his writings. Paul could have easily invoked this letter in 1 Corinthians to settle issues over whether Christians should eat meat offered to idols. Instead, he not only does not mention it; his teaching stands in some tension with it.

We also remember that Paul and Barnabas went their separate ways at the start of the second missionary journey. We cannot speak definitively, but we have enough evidence to wonder whether the Jerusalem church viewed Paul with some disagreement and suspicion (Acts 21:21). We can at least say with some certainty that many in the early church did not view Paul as an apostle as they did Peter (1 Cor. 9:5–6). Some at least seemed to question whether he was genuinely an apostle (9:1–2). It is not clear that those of this persuasion formed a distinct or divisive group in the community, but this way of thinking probably did exist there.

Some have suggested that Paul is being sarcastic when he suggests there might be a group claiming to be "of Christ." But his follow up questions seem to point in a different direction: **Is Christ divided? Was Paul crucified for you? Were you baptized into the name of Paul?** (1:13). The fact that Paul asks if Christ was divided could indicate that some in the early church might have actually claimed to be of Christ in a way that set them apart from other Christians.

The apostles and those who were privileged to follow Jesus while he was on earth are the main candidates for such a claim. Is this comment a subtle corrective to those "who seemed to be important"—apostles like Peter, James, and John? (Gal. 2:6). Certainly it is also possible that some of those who had heard Jesus while he was on earth had come to live in Corinth. After all, there were apparently some in Ephesus where Paul was who had been baptized under John the Baptist (Acts 19:1–7). In any case, Paul never takes up this idea clearly in the rest of the letter.

Let us return to 1 Cor. 1:14. We have already mentioned **Crispus and Gaius** in the introduction. Crispus was a synagogue ruler in Corinth whose entire household came to Christ at a point where Paul was forced to leave the synagogue (Acts 18:8). This was a person of some means who provided important material support for the synagogue. Gaius was the individual in whose home the entire church would eventually meet (Rom. 16:23).

It is significant that Paul also corrects those who are saying that they **follow Paul** (1:12). He asks them if he was the one who was crucified for them (1:13) and shudders to think some might gloat that they had been baptized in his name (1:15). We will find plenty of places in Paul's writings where he seems to draw attention to his own significance and importance, but we should always keep in mind in those instances what he has to say here. He is just a servant of Christ (3:5), the one who planted (3:6). God gives the increase, and Christ was the one who died for our sins.

The way in which Paul adds the comment about baptizing **the household of Stephanas** (1:16) is interesting, since he has just said that he only baptized Crispus and Gaius at Corinth (1:14). It seems like an afterthought, like something Paul forgot and then remembered in the course of writing. He later mentions that the members of Stephanas's household were the first converts in the area of Corinth (16:15). These are the sort of people you mention first. It is hard to resist the impression that Paul wrote 1:14 and then only later remembered or was reminded about Stephanas. Indeed, perhaps it was Stephanas himself who reminded Paul, after Stephanas' delegation arrived at Ephesus with a letter from the Corinthian church (16:17). Perhaps Paul had already started the letter on the basis of reports from Chloe's house when Stephanas arrived.

Questions like these are of little importance in the light of eternity, even if they are fun to ask. But they also raise the more important matter of what we mean when we say that 1 Corinthians is both inspired and inerrant. Christians have always worked hard to balance the full humanity of Christ with His full divinity. Perhaps in these words of Paul we are also reminded of our need to balance the human and the divine aspects of revelation as well. The Bible's words are fully inspired and yet also fully delivered in the human clothing of its original authors and contexts. This wonder, like the nature of Christ, is a mystery to our fallible minds.

Paul ends this general exhortation to unity with a pointed comment that must have undermined the argument at Corinth. The Corinthians were claiming superiority on the basis of who baptized them, and were apparently claiming that Apollos was much wiser and more eloquent than Paul. Paul counters that these preoccupations are not ultimately the heart of the matter. **Christ did not send me to baptize, but to preach the gospel** (1:17). What is important is the cross of Christ, the means by which we are reconciled to God. The Corinthians were judging him by secular standards, that is **human wisdom** and not from God's point of view.

ENDNOTES

1. We know Peter as Peter because this is the Greek translation of his name. Jesus probably called him "Cephas," the Aramaic word for "rock," rather than "Peter." His given name was Simon.

3

THE PRINCIPLE IN PRACTICE:
THE FOOLISHNESS OF THE CROSS

1 Corinthians 1:18–2:5

If 1 Cor. 1:10–17 gives us the general principle that Christ is not divided, then 1:18–4:21 plays this principle out. Paul begins by showing that the world does not think like God does—God's wisdom seems foolish to it. Paul unashamedly proclaims in this first part the "foolishness of the cross" (1:18–2:5). The next four chapters of this commentary explore this part of 1 Corinthians.

Paul binds the train of thought in this section by beginning and ending with reference to the power of God (1:18, 2:5). This way of setting off this section helps us see what his central concern is in these paragraphs. Paul wishes the Corinthians to know that God's normal way of operating is to use the weak and the foolish to highlight His superior strength and wisdom. In contrast, some of the Corinthians were emphasizing their own power and wisdom.

He begins the section with the word **For** (1:18), which tells us that Paul is now going to explain and substantiate the claim he has just made in 1:17 about the power of the cross. He has pleaded for the Corinthians to find unity among themselves (1:10–17), emphasizing that his preaching did not focus on things like baptism or human wisdom (1:17). Rather, he preached about Christ's death on the cross. He will now explain what he meant by this comment and defend it in the next three and a half chapters (1:18–4:21).

[T]he message of the cross is foolishness to those who are perishing, but to us who are being saved it is the power of God (1:18). Throughout this section Paul will indicate that God's way of thinking is different from the way most people think, particularly those who are wise according to the standards of the non-Christian world. He will underline the mysteriousness of God's will and plan—it is not the kind of plan we would have devised.

In particular, the message of the cross no doubt must have seemed ridiculous to many of those to whom Paul preached. For us, the cross is an immensely positive symbol of God's grace. We sing hymns that celebrate it, decorate our churches with it, and wear it as jewelry.

But in Paul's day, it was an instrument of capital punishment, used by the Romans to rub their power in the noses of anyone who might oppose them. Would you wear a hangman's noose or guillotine around your neck? What about a syringe to symbolize death by injection or a tiny model electric chair? It must have seemed ludicrous to the "wise" of Paul's day to suggest that the capital punishment of a Jewish "criminal" on a cross by the Romans was symbolic of Christ's victory or God's grace!

But for Paul, the capital punishment of Jesus on the cross by the Romans was an atoning sacrifice for sin and the path to reconciliation with God. Christ had become like a Passover lamb (1 Cor. 5:7), a sin offering (Rom. 8:3), and an atoning sacrifice in general (Rom. 3:25). For Paul the atoning, sacrificial nature of Christ's death was one of the mysteries of God's plan. It might seem "foolish" to those who will perish on the Day of God's wrath. But it is the "power of God" that results in salvation on that day to those who trust in it.

Different New Testament authors emphasized different aspects of Christ's work in their proclamation of the gospel. For example, Luke focused on Christ's resurrection as the heart of the good news.[1] For Paul, the cross stood at the heart of the gospel. The degree to which this symbol of defeat has become a symbol of God's grace and power testifies to the victory of God over earthly and worldly wisdom.

Paul defends the mysteriousness of God's wisdom from the standpoint of human wisdom. First he gives a Scriptural justification: **For it is written: "I will destroy the wisdom of the wise; the intelligence of the intelligent I will frustrate"** (1:19). God's plans often unravel the plans of those who think themselves wise. We remember once again that Paul's opponents at Corinth thought they had arrived spiritually and were wiser than Paul. They perhaps looked to Apollos as a truly wise person by the standards of that day.

In contrast Paul asked, **"Where is the wise man?"** (1:20). They were not hard to find in Paul's day. But by and large they were not a part of the Christian movement. Paul could legitimately ask why the Corinthians valued secular wisdom so much when the "wisest" individuals by those standards could not see the truth of Christianity. If such non-Christians were really the true measure of wisdom, then why were they not Christians?

We should be careful not to use verses like these as an excuse for ignorance. In the past some have argued these as an anti-educational agenda. We should remember how much worldly wisdom and secular training Paul himself brought to the table; he was no dullard. The very fact that he could read put him among the most educated of his day. Indeed, Acts 17:28 shows us Paul quoting secular philosophy, and he cites a Greek poet in 1 Cor. 15:33. Surely God can use our minds as well as our hearts and emotions.

But we should also remember that human "wisdom" has a way of coming and going. How many Stoic or Epicurean philosophers have you met recently? How many Platonists or Peripatetics? Belonging to groups like these was like having a PhD from Harvard or Yale today. But so many of the things they taught now seem ridiculous to us, even if some of their errors are still around today in groups from our own time. It is not that we cannot find gems of truth in the thinking of these ancient groups, but their schools have closed. Christianity has survived.

Given the incredible diversity of Christian groups, we must also suspect that a great deal of the "wisdom" we hear even in the church must be all too human. Just because a minister says something from a pulpit and mentions a few words from the Bible does not mean that he or she truly has the mind of God. If the Spirit of God inhabits the body of Christ, the church, then spiritual wisdom is more accurately heard the more we are in contact with the rest of God's people.

God's actions in Christ turned worldly wisdom on its head (1:20). Worldly wisdom would think that since God is all-powerful and in control, He should force the world to submit to His rule. But God strangely did not force a sinful world to submit or conform to His will. The wisdom of God did not entail overt strength.

Somehow it was **in the wisdom of God** that the world would not know Him **through its wisdom** (1:21). Rather, **God was pleased through the foolishness of what was preached to save those who believe** (1:21). God chose to woo the world to Him, not to force it to follow Him. No doubt the Romans stood as a powerful symbol of worldly wisdom with their might and ability to force the world of their day to conform to their desires and laws. God has much greater power than they did.

But God in His "foolishness" chose preaching and invitation as His preferred method of evangelism. Here are some lessons for us as individuals and nations. Certainly God does model overt strength from time to time. But His preferred method is to invite, to court. Sometimes the easy route as a parent or nation is to force our children or enemies to submit to what we believe is right. There is a time for such strength.

We may win many battles with our children by force, but we win the war when we actually convince them to do right as part of their own conviction. Many Christian individuals and organizations seem wired to "catch the sinner," to force those within their walls and influence to live a certain way. Even more profitable would be to win others to our way of life by modeling God's power in our lives. Even nations can think they are acting on God's behalf by forcing other nations to stop their wrongdoing. Perhaps there is a time for such actions. But it is not God's first option or the way He chose to win the world.

God's approach was neither human power nor human wisdom. We have already mentioned how ridiculous the preaching of **Christ crucified** (1:23) must have seemed to the non–Christians of Paul's day. Did Paul really mean to say that the capital punishment of a Jewish "criminal" was the path to God? What foolishness, so many must have thought.

If the Greeks found such talk of crucifixion unwise, many Jews found it offensive. The Romans hoisted their opposition up naked in a public area so that everyone could see what happened to those who dared stand against them and their rules. This was the fate of so many Jews who led revolts against the Roman occupation of Israel.

In contrast, many Jews thought the true messiah would be victorious in battle over the Romans. One sign of the truly anointed one, the one God sent to reestablish and rule Israel, would be military and political victory. Did Paul really mean to suggest that God's messiah showed His victory by dying on the Roman tool of shame and humiliation? Those would have been fighting words, the kind of things people might kill you for saying.

But Christians see the power and wisdom of this powerless foolishness. **For the foolishness of God is wiser than man's wisdom, and the weakness of God is stronger than man's strength** (1:25). We may not always understand what God is doing in our lives and in the world. At times it may seem like we are in a position of weakness and that we are defeated. It is at this point we must remind ourselves of God's priorities. As God later told Paul, "My grace is sufficient for you, for my power is made perfect in weakness" (2 Cor. 12:9).

Paul has spent verses 18–25 setting out the principles of God's wisdom and power. In 1 Corinthains 1:26–31 he applies these principles to the Corinthian problems. **Not many of you were wise by human standards . . . influential . . . of noble birth** (1:26). In other words, the vast majority of the Corinthian church consisted of ordinary people from the disempowered masses of the ancient world, probably including a number of slaves.

Just as God showed His power in crucifixion, **God chose the foolish things of the world to shame the wise; God chose the weak things of the world to shame the strong.** (1:27). No one can boast before God that they are truly wise or truly powerful (1:29). When the Corinthians—or we—think we are wise or in control, we truly deceive ourselves. As Paul will say later, "when I am weak, then I am strong" (2 Cor. 12:10).

It is the gift of God **that you are in Christ Jesus** (1 Cor. 1:30). Paul has already told us that Christ is the wisdom of God (1 Cor. 1:24). Now Paul tells us how that wisdom comes to us as **righteousness, holiness, and redemption**. When we are baptized into Christ, we put on Christ (Gal. 2:27), participate in His crucifixion (Gal. 2:20), and are buried with him through baptism (Rom. 6:4). He becomes our right-ness before God (Phil. 3:9). We become holy and find redemption from the slavery of sin through him.

Paul turns to Jer. 9:24 for the inevitable conclusion: **Let him who boasts boast in the Lord** (1:31). Those who boast in their own wisdom or power reveal that they are not the true representatives of God. The "wise" at Corinth thus revealed their foolishness by the very fact that they thought themselves wise.

The Corinthians were looking for worldly eloquence and wisdom. But in 2:1–4, Paul says he did not **come with eloquence or superior wisdom** (2:1). One generation's eloquence is another generation's verbosity or boredom. The standards of these kinds of skills change from time to time.

Abraham Lincoln's Gettysburg Address was not thought to be a great speech by the standards of his day. It was far too short and to the point. A long, flowery speech with lots of allusions to classical literature was much to be preferred. Similarly, just because the Corinthians did not think Paul was eloquent does not mean he was really a bad speaker. Indeed, his writings probably reflect that he had actually had some rhetorical training at some point.

But Paul was not concerned to be eloquent or wise. **I resolved to know nothing while I was with you except Jesus Christ and him crucified** (2:2). You will sometimes hear people say that this approach represented a change in Paul's philosophy of evangelism. They argue that he had taken a more "intellectual" approach at Athens with sparse results, so he decided to stick to a more spiritual message at Corinth.

While this scenario is possible, we should observe carefully that Acts and Paul's writings do not actually tell us such things. For example, Acts tells us nothing about Paul having any kind of change of mind after leaving Athens. Indeed, Acts does not depict Paul's preaching in Athens as a failure (Acts 17:34), even if it did not yield the results of a Corinth or Ephesus.

Paul says nothing about a change of mind in 1 Cor. 2:2, only his resolve to focus on the crucified Christ. He does not mention his previous ministry in Athens, and we do not see any change or hint of such a change elsewhere in Paul's writings. Even in 1 Corinthians he quotes the Greek playwright Menander (15:33), showing that he was still not averse to drawing on secular literature.

Paul ends this section where he began it: with a reminder that the Christian gospel is about **God's power** (2:3–5) and wisdom, not ours.

Some of the Corinthians were so arrogant that they were in danger of forgetting God's grace. It seems likely that some of the Corinthians were demeaning Paul by saying he was not as **wise and persuasive** (2:4) as Apollos. We know from Acts 18:24–28 that Apollos was a highly educated person and an eloquent speaker. Paul reminds the Corinthians that it is not eloquence or philosophical wisdom that counts, but the power of God. A few chapters later Paul will underline the same thing: "I will come to you very soon, if the Lord is willing, and then I will find out not only how these arrogant people are talking, but what power they have" (1 Cor. 4:19).

ENDNOTES

1. Except for Stephen's sermon, the fact that God raised Jesus from the dead is the centerpiece of the sermons of Acts.

4

THE PRINCIPLE IN PRACTICE:
TRUE WISDOM AND SPIRITUALITY
1 Corinthians 2:6–3:4

In 1 Cor. 1:18–2:5 Paul lays down his central claims about what matters, namely, reliance on God's power through the cross rather than through human power or wisdom. In 2:6–3:4 he will expand on what true wisdom and true spirituality is. This train of thought leads him right back to where he began this discussion: the divisions at Corinth (3:4).

We do, however, speak a message of wisdom among the mature, but not the wisdom of this age or of the rulers of this age, who are coming to nothing (2:6). We have to be very careful as we read Paul's comments in 2:6–16 because he seems to be taking up the claims of his opponents in Corinth and using it against them. We know that they claimed to be wise (3:18, 6:5) and to have knowledge (8:1, 13:2). It seems likely that they also claimed to be spiritual (3:1, 14:37) and perhaps perfect, since the word translated as "mature" in 2:6 can also be translated "perfect" or "complete."

First Corinthians 2:6 contrasts the wisdom of the truly mature Christian with the wisdom of this age. By implication, the Corinthian trouble makers are not mature. As he will say in 3:1, they are merely "infants in Christ." In contrast to true wisdom, the wisdom to which they might lay claim is rather the wisdom of this age.

The wisdom of this age and of the rulers of this age is a wisdom of strength and power. When Paul says that the rulers of this age are "coming to nothing" (2:6), he uses the same word (*katargeō*) he used in the previous chapter to say that God chose "the things that are not—to *nullify* the things that are" (1:28). In that chapter, Paul was talking about how most of the Corinthians were not influential, of noble birth, or wise by human standards (1:26). Paul indicates that these are the characteristics of this age's wisdom, not God's wisdom.

While it is possible that Paul had demonic powers in mind when he speaks of the **rulers of this age** (2:8), the immediate context more likely suggests he is speaking of earthly rulers, probably the Romans in particular. Such earthly powers had no idea of the power they were unleashing when they crucified Christ, a power that would eventually signal the reign of Christ and the end of worldly authorities like them.

Paul modifies and expands Isa. 64:4 in 1 Cor. 2:9–10. Christians often think of heaven when they read this verse—certainly Christ has prepared something wonderful for us in heaven (John 14:2–3). But here Paul is referring to the salvation made possible by the cross. This is the mysterious, secret wisdom of the cross that brings salvation to those who love God. Because we have the Spirit, we recognize the true wisdom of the cross.

While as Christians we are accustomed to read the Old Testament with Christian glasses on, we should remember that the Jews of Paul's day by and large did not see Christian meanings in its words. The same is true of non-Christian Jews today. You probably will not convince many Jews today that the verses in the Old Testament we think relate to Christ were really about Christ. It was through spiritual eyes that Paul and other Christians saw prophecies and messages in the Old Testament. These eyes came to them largely after Christ, not before him—even Jesus' disciples apparently were not anticipating His death.

In 2:10–16 Paul lays the basis for countering the Corinthian claim to be spiritual. In so doing, he used some peculiar words that the Corinthians were probably using to describe themselves in contrast to others in the church. Paul's basic point in these verses is that the person with God's Spirit is truly spiritual and truly knows the mind of God.

Paul is not giving us the details of God's psychology when he says, **For who among men knows the thoughts of a man except the man's spirit**

within him? (2:11). He is laying the groundwork for the argument that follows. His basic point is that God's Spirit knows the **thoughts of God**.

This observation leads him to his next claim: **We have not received the spirit of the world but the Spirit who is from God, that we may understand what God has freely given us** (2:12). Again, Paul is not providing us with the details of how the human mind works. He is explaining the basis of true wisdom—having God's Spirit inside us. Because God's Spirit knows God's thoughts, we can know the mind of God—particularly as it relates to the cross—from God's Spirit inside us.

It is important to remember that Paul did not think you could even be a Christian if you did not have God's Spirit inside you. As he says in Rom. 8:9, "if anyone does not have the Spirit of Christ, he does not belong to Christ." The Spirit is God's "seal of ownership on us," "a deposit guaranteeing what is to come" (2 Cor. 1:22). All Christians have God's Spirit inside them whereby they can know the mind of God with regard to the cross.

The message of what God has freely given **is what we speak, not in words taught us by human wisdom but in words taught by the Spirit, expressing spiritual truths in spiritual words** (2:13). Remember that the wisdom of God is the foolishness of the cross (1:24). It is not rhetorical eloquence, human philosophy, worldly influence, or earthly status, but based on God's gracious power that He bestows on those of us who have His Spirit within.

It is at this point that Paul most likely takes up some of the language that the Corinthians have been using. **The man without the spirit** [*psychikos* person] **does not accept the things that come from the Spirit of God, for they are foolishness to him, and he cannot understand them, because they are spiritually discerned** (2:14). This verse is notoriously difficult to translate. The King James Version translates it as a verse about the "natural man." A more literal translation might be the "soulish" person, but this translation does not really make Paul's meaning any clearer to us.

First Corinthians 2:14–15 and 15:44–46 both contrast a "soulish" (*psychikos*) person with a "spiritual" (*pneumatikos*) person. This contrast is odd, since more often the soul and spirit of a person were viewed as very similar to one another. Since Paul never uses it elsewhere, it is reasonable to conclude that he was taking the language of some of the Corinthians themselves and turning it on its head. They claimed to be spiritual, in contact with heaven in a way others—even their fellow Christians—were not. By the time Paul is done, he will tell them they are none of the sort.

We will explore in more detail what they might have thought when we get to 1 Corinthians 15. Suffice it to say we often find Christians today who think themselves more spiritual than others, "holier than thou." It is exactly this attitude that Paul was combating at Corinth. As soon as you have this attitude, you are beginning to think according to the wisdom of the world, for it is worldly thinking that thinks in terms of superiority and higher status. Paul will emphasize in 1 Corinthians 12 that we are one body in Christ, and we should not exalt ourselves above the other parts.

Paul's use of Isa. 40:13 in 1 Cor. 2:16 confirms that Paul is meeting the Corinthians at their own argument. When Paul refers to this verse in Rom. 11:34, he will emphasize the mysteriousness of God's will and the unsearchableness of His judgments. In other words, he will use this verse to emphasize the unknowable nature of God's plans.

But in 1 Corinthians, Paul is emphasizing that we can at least know some things about the mind of the Lord, namely, the things relating to Christ and the cross. Through the Spirit we know that the foolishness and powerlessness of the cross is God's wisdom and power, not the kind of wisdom and power in which some Corinthians took pride. Paul will implicitly include himself within this group of the truly spiritual later on when he tells the Corinthians that he is not subject to their judgment or the judgment of a human court (4:3). Yet he also makes spiritual judgments, such as when he pronounces the appropriate verdict on the sinner of 1 Cor. 5:3.

Paul's Corinthian opponents might have agreed with him thus far. The spiritual person has the Spirit and knows the mind of God. They might also agree that the "soulish" person of their philosophy could not truly understand spiritual truths. But in 3:1–4 Paul gets to his point, the critique toward which he has been building throughout 2:6–16.

Brothers, I could not address you as spiritual (*pneumatikos*) but as fleshly (*sarkinos*)—mere infants in Christ. I gave you milk, not solid

food, for you were not yet ready for it (3:1–2). Paul now turns their own claims to be spiritual and call other Christians "soulish" against them. They may have claimed to be "perfect" or "mature." They may have put others down by claiming to be the ones on solid food, unlike the Christian "babies" around them. This last image was a common metaphor that philosophers used to describe the stages of coming to deep understanding.

But Paul tells them that they are in fact the ones who are **infants** and immature. After using their language (spiritual vs. soulish) he now uses his own imagery (spiritual vs. fleshly). In Paul's estimation they are not spiritual; they are "carnal" or

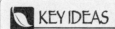

KEY IDEAS

"FLESHLY" VS. "SPIRITUAL"

The Corinthians thought of themselves as spiritual and looked down on others in the church as "soulish." Paul counters that they are not spiritual but "fleshly."

fleshly. They think with their bodies on a human, earthly plane—nowhere near the heavenly, spiritual plane where they think their minds roam.

Those who know Romans and Galatians will find this language very familiar. Paul regularly contrasts the spirit with the flesh. For example, Paul contrasts the "works of the flesh" with the "fruit of the Spirit" in Gal. 5:19–23. He clearly teaches that Christians should walk in the Spirit, not in the flesh. Such individuals do not "gratify the desires" of their flesh (Gal. 5:16). Paul similarly teaches in Romans that we used to be controlled by the flesh before we came to Christ, controlled by "the sinful passions aroused by the law" (Rom. 7:5). But now as Christians "the Spirit of life set me free from the law of sin and death" (Rom. 8:2). The result is that we can now keep the righteous requirement of the law (Rom. 8:4), namely, God has made it possible for us to love each other (Rom. 13:8–10).

While the NIV regularly translates the word *flesh* (*sarx*) as "sinful nature," this translation is somewhat misleading. Paul never talks about the flesh as a "nature." We rather have St. Augustine in the 400s to thank for this slight shift in meaning. The most literal meaning of flesh is the skin on our bodies. Paul viewed our bodies as the part of us most susceptible to sinful desires and passions. So when he speaks of "being in the flesh" or the "works of the flesh" he was referring to that aspect of our bodies that starts us out in life as a slave to sin's power.

However, when we are in the Spirit, sin ceases to have this power over our bodies. A Christian is set "free from the law of sin and death" (Rom. 8:2). Christians are no longer "slaves to sin" (Rom. 6:20). They "have been set free from sin and have become slaves to God" (Rom. 6:22). Christians are not supposed to fulfill the desires of their flesh, and "those who are in the flesh cannot please God" (Rom. 8:8, NASB).

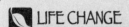

LIFE CHANGE

"FLESH" VS. "SPIRIT"

Paul viewed our bodies as the part of us most susceptible to sinful desires and passions. But when we are in the Spirit, sin ceases to have this power over our bodies. If you find yourself living in slavery to your flesh, trust God today to give you power over sin,

On the one hand, the problem Corinthians were Christians and had received the Spirit (2 Cor. 5:5). Paul even referred to them as sanctified (1 Cor. 1:2). They should be walking in the Spirit. Yet Paul told them **you are still fleshly** (*sarkikos*) (1 Cor. 3:3, NASB). These individuals were thus in a spiritual "no man's land." They should have been spiritual, but they were still living in the flesh. They were thus living inconsistently with who they were supposed to be in Christ.

This section of 1 Corinthians is a classic preaching text for entire sanctification. The typical sermon draws three types of individual from this passage: (1) the natural person of 1 Cor. 2:14, (2) the carnal person of 3:1–3, and (3) the spiritual person of 2:15 and 3:1. In this interpretation, the natural person is the one who is not even a Christian. The carnal person is the Christian who is saved, but not entirely sanctified. The spiritual person is then the one who has gone on to be entirely sanctified.

By now we can see that these are not exactly the categories by which Paul was operating. While the passage remains an excellent text from which to preach this doctrine of the Wesleyan tradition, Paul was addressing Christians who were still fleshly, even though they were in Christ. This was a problem and an inconsistency.

So it is today. Even if, in theory, Christians should walk fully in the Spirit from the moment they receive Christ, experience tells us that it frequently does not happen that way. There is always a need for us to be reminded of who we are in Christ and of the grace of God to live victorious over sin. Our generation is particularly sensitive to the fact that we are constantly changing as individuals. Complete surrender to God's Spirit is thus something we must reaffirm throughout our entire lives, not just in one moment in time.

For Paul, the divisive spirit of the Corinthian church was a tell-tale sign of its carnality and fleshly mind (3:4).[1] They probably claimed to reach the heavens in their spirituality, the realm of the divine. In contrast, Paul says they are acting on a human level. We can see some of the pitfalls of the holiness tradition in this verse. In the past, holiness was sometimes equated with particular ways of looking and dressing, as well as with strict standards of behavior. In themselves, these kinds of standards are not necessarily legalistic, for there is nothing wrong with living in the way you believe pleases and gives glory to God.

The problem was that some of those who most valued and prized the "spiritual" level of entire sanctification were sometimes those with the most vindictive and divisive spirits. Paul reminds us that the foremost criterion for discerning whether or not someone has the Spirit is love. Love is the fruit of the Spirit par excellence (Gal. 5:22), and love was the antithesis of how the Corinthians were behaving (1 Cor. 13). Their divisive, separating spirit was in fact the greatest indication of their carnality, their "fleshly," unspiritual behavior.

He ends this section with the underlying problem, leading him right back to where he began back in 1:10–17: **For when one says, "I follow Paul," and another, "I follow Apollos," are you not mere men?** (3:4). The fact that Paul only mentions himself and Apollos here confirms that the real point of conflict is between a group pitting Apollos against Paul as a way of undermining Paul's authority and influence at Corinth. But Paul will have none of it, not even an "I follow Paul" group. Christ is not divided, and the divisions at Corinth were proof of carnality.

ENDNOTES

1. The NIV reads "unspiritual" rather than "carnal," as I have substituted here to bring out Paul's precise meaning better.

THE PRINCIPLE IN PRACTICE:
APPLYING
THE PRINCIPLES

1 Corinthians 3:5–23

In 1:8–3:4 Paul established that the wisdom and power of God are not the same as the wisdom and power of the world or its thinking. Earthly wisdom and power would not represent themselves by the crucifixion of their king. The wisdom of the cross was foolishness to the world, and the power of the cross was weakness to the world. In contrast, God's wisdom is a hidden wisdom discerned by the Spirit. The truly spiritual grasp the wisdom of the cross and the power of weakness. Our weakness underlines God's strength. The factionalism at Corinth indicated that the problem Corinthians were not spiritual at all, but carnal, mere infants in Christ.

Paul will now take these truths and apply them to the division at Corinth between those who are loyal to him and those who are using Apollos as an excuse to undermine his authority and teaching. **What, after all, is Apollos? And what is Paul?** (3:5). Paul once again rejects even a division caused by loyalty to him. In the end, he and Apollos are only servants. It is the king who matters.

As king, the **Lord has assigned to each his task. I planted the seed, Apollos watered it, but God made it grow** (3:5–6). God often does great things in the world through us. As the song goes, "God uses people, ordinary people." When God uses us to do great things, we must always remind ourselves that it is in fact God who is doing them. It is all too tempting for the pastor of the large church or the successful Christian businessperson to begin subconsciously to congratulate him or herself for the success. Many times the rest of us push them in this direction because we ourselves have come to look at them this way. We love a hero to worship. Paul's comments are a strong warning for those of us who are tempted to take credit for the good things God is doing through us.

We should also keep in perspective that Paul was not primarily talking about numerical growth. The church of Corinth may only have had about fifty people at this time. Suffice it to say, it is not at all certain that we would invite him to speak at our church growth conferences (although we might let him speak about church planting). Indeed, Paul might very well look at our current preoccupation with church size as yet another example of worldly wisdom, the wisdom of power and strength.

We should also keep in mind that the roles of planting and watering to which God has assigned us are best seen in retrospect, as we look back on what God has done through us. We should not put God into a box by thinking that there are a fixed number of well-defined roles to which God assigns or that God uses. Indeed, God may have many roles for each one of us to play in our lifetime. God is far more profound than the limitations we often put on Him.

While the word **purpose** (3:8) is not actually in the Greek, it expresses the sense that both the planter and the water-er both have the same function: to facilitate the growth of the field. They are **God's fellow workers** (3:9). Paul may give himself a slight edge over Apollos in calling himself the planter. But it is helpful to think of them both as field hands. God is the owner of the **field**, the farmer himself. In the end, neither Paul nor Apollos are the ones who own the land or have ultimate authority over the field. They are working for someone else.

LIFE CHANGE

GOD GETS THE CREDIT

Paul gives a strong warning to anyone tempted to take credit for the good things happening in our lives. We do not do them ourselves, but God does them through us.

Paul did imagine rewards in the coming kingdom of God. Paul is not saying that we can earn our way into God's grace—then it would not truly be God's graciousness saving us. But Paul does seem to indicate that God will reward us according to our labor, not in this age, but presumably in the next. Jesus says similar things in Matthew: "your Father, who sees what is done in secret, will reward you" (Matt. 6:4, 6, 18).

First Corinthians 3:10–15 is sometimes used to argue for a "once saved, always saved" position. But a number of factors militate against this interpretation. For one, Paul is really talking about building the church more than about the way we live our individual lives as Christians. He is indirectly talking about his and Apollos' ministry at Corinth, as he makes clear later on in 4:6.

I laid a foundation as an expert builder, and someone else is building on it (3:10). This statement may simply be another way of saying that he planted and Apollos watered. Clearly the building he has in mind is the church at Corinth, as he has mentioned in 3:9. The word for **expert** here is actually "wise." In other words, Paul reminds the Corinthians that he is the one who truly has spiritual wisdom, unlike their carnal wisdom.

Paul now issues a warning either to Apollos or to whoever is now leading the congregation in an inappropriate direction.[1] **But each one should be careful how he builds** (3:10). If this statement is not a thinly veiled warning to Apollos, it is certainly directed at those at Corinth who were pushing the church in inappropriate directions. **For no one can lay any foundation other than the one already laid, which is Jesus Christ** (3:11).[2] Paul is primarily speaking of the church as a whole when he speaks of this building, although this comment applies to us as individuals as well. Jesus is the only true foundation for any Christian "building."

Again, despite the fact that we cannot earn salvation and do not deserve God's grace, clearly what we do in life matters to God. Some of our "construction projects" (built **using gold, silver, costly stones, wood, hay or straw,** 3:12) are better than others, and some ways of building the church are better than others. Here Paul is thinking of the way in which various Christians and Christian leaders have been building the church at Corinth. No doubt he thought of his own contributions more in terms of the categories of gold, silver, and costly stones. He had no difficulty in telling his churches to imitate him (Phil. 3:17) or in using himself as an example (1 Cor. 9:12–27). We can wonder if he thought Apollos' work was of the same quality, especially if some of the issues he is addressing in 1 Corinthians are by-products of Apollos' teaching (for example, meat offered to idols).

In any case, he clearly placed the attitudes and teaching of the "proud" Corinthians in the hay and straw category. Later on in this chapter (3:18–23) he will make it clear that the so-called wisdom of these Corinthians is none of the sort. Christ will make this fact all too clear when he returns to earth. The **Day** Paul mentions here is the Day of the Lord, the Day of Judgment when the Lord will come back. This day will reveal that the quality of their **work** is sub-standard.

If what he has built survives, he will receive his reward. If it is burned up, he will suffer loss; he himself will be saved, but only as one escaping through the flames (3:14–15). These are the verses some use to argue for "eternal security," the idea that once you have truly come to Christ, you will be saved no matter what you do from then on. The analogy Paul is using here directly addresses the Corinthian situation. He believes that these proud Corinthians will be saved in the end, even though they will face some correction from Christ when He returns.[3] The "human wisdom" room they added on to the back of the house will not make it through the fire of Christ's return.

One key to understanding these verses is to remember that although these Christians are carnal and off track, they still have Christ as a foundation. What they have built will burn, but at a fundamental level they are still a part of God's people. Some commentators suggest that Paul's language refers to the payment a contractor received for good construction (**reward**) and the fines for a builder whose work was sub-standard (**suffer loss**).[4] The builders Paul has in mind have not built the church wisely with the materials God gave them, but they will escape the burning house because of their foundation.

Clearly Paul believed a Christian could do worse than these individuals and be lost in the fire. We will see him express this possibility even of himself in 1 Cor. 9:27. The temple metaphor he now makes reflects similarly strong language. **If anyone destroys God's temple, God will destroy him; for God's temple is sacred, and you are that temple** (3:16–17). If you actually *destroy* God's temple, then God will *not* save you through the flames. He will destroy you.

Paul has compared the Christian congregation at Corinth to a field (3:6–9) and then to a building (3:10–15). Now he compares them to a temple (3:16–17). Modern English unfortunately has only one word for "you," making it impossible to know whether you are referring to a single "you" or referring to a group of "you."[5] In contrast, Greek distinguishes one "you" from more than one "you." Characteristically, Paul usually refers to more than one person when he says "you"—the whole congregation, in other words, not a single individual. When Paul says, **you yourselves are God's temple**, he means the whole Corinthian church.

Paul's warning to this point has been directed at those building up the church with inferior materials. Now he addresses those who would actually tear down or destruct the church. His warning here is even more severe: God will not save this person; He will destroy him or her. This language is no doubt stronger because he is no longer talking about just any house. He is talking about God's house, the temple made up of all true Christians. God's Spirit lives in this body of Christ.

In 1 Cor. 3:18–4:5 Paul returns from his warnings about "bad construction" at Corinth to the fundamental problems he is addressing: the false claims of certain Corinthians to wisdom and their improper attitudes toward him and Apollos. **Do not deceive yourselves. If any one of you thinks he is wise by the standards of this age, he should become a "fool" so that he may become wise** (3:18). Paul's earlier comments in chapters one and two were somewhat general as he discussed the foolishness of the cross and true spiritual wisdom. It is easy to lift them from their context and discuss them abstractly. However, when Paul gets to 3:18, it becomes quite clear that he has had the boasting Corinthians in view all along.

Some of the Corinthians thought they were really wise and claimed that Apollos was wiser than Paul as well. But as Paul has argued, their wisdom is not true wisdom. It is a wisdom of this age. The path to true wisdom is to become a fool in the eyes of worldly wisdom. **For the wisdom of this world is foolishness in God's sight** (3:19), as Paul has already demonstrated at length. Paul defends this claim once again with two quotations from the Old Testament. First he cites a verse from Job

5:13, **"He catches the wise in their craftiness"** (3:19).[6] Then he turns to Ps. 94:11: **"The Lord knows that the thoughts of the wise are futile"** (3:20).

Paul uses both of these quotations to put the "nail in the coffin" on this issue: worldly wisdom and prestige have nothing to do with God's values. **So then, no more boasting about men!** (3:21). They must stop touting Apollos as the "wise" one and boasting in secular wisdom. **All things are yours** (3:22). This comment probably entailed not a little irony on Paul's part, for many philosophers in Paul's day taught that everything belonged to the wise person.[7] In other words, with a twinkle in his eye, Paul says the same thing as some secular philosophers—all things are the wise person's—but applies it to the person who is wise in Christ (whom the secular philosophers would think a fool).

We notice that Paul once again comes back to himself and Apollos, and thus alludes to the two main groups in contention in the church. He also mentions Peter here as well, leading us to believe that at least some in the church may have favored Peter against Paul in some of the issues over which these two disagreed (Gal. 2:11–14). Notice that Paul has reworded the Corinthian claims. If they were saying, "I belong to Paul," "I belong to Apollos" (1:12), Paul now substitutes "Paul belongs to you; Apollos belongs to you" (3:22).

Paul's final comment in this chapter puts everything into proper perspective. He and Apollos are only workers; the Corinthian Christians are only a field. The true landowner is God. The true subordination is ultimately not them to Paul or them to Apollos or even Paul to them. Rather, **you are of Christ, and Christ is of God** (3:23). The whole church is under the authority of God and Christ, not under Apollos' authority.

God had not yet unpacked the details of the Trinity for Christians yet, so Paul here thinks of Christ (God the Son) in subordination to God the Father. Christians would later come to believe that none of the persons of the Godhead are subordinate to one another. Some early Christians explained this verse in terms of Christ's human nature. In other words, it was Christ's humanity that is subordinate to God the Father; Christ's divine nature remains equal in divinity to the other persons of the Trinity. Regardless of Paul's precise meaning, God has clarified for us what we should believe about the Trinity through the Christians of the ages: there is one God, one divine substance, yet at the same time three distinct persons, Father, Son, and Holy Spirit.

ENDNOTES

1. Some scholars have suggested that Peter had come to Corinth after Apollos left and that Paul refers to him here, thus explaining Paul's earlier reference to some saying "I am of Cephas" in 1:12 and Paul's comment in 9:5. But this interpretation seems doubtful. Paul seems to have himself and Apollos primarily in view (4:6). Why would he not actually mention Peter if that is who he is really thinking about?

2. Contrast Ephesians' later expansion of the foundation to include the "apostles and prophets" (Eph. 2:20). The prospect of Paul's death and the death of the early apostles no doubt impressed the early Christians with the need for standards of correct teaching and practice they could follow when there were no apostles around (2 Tim. 1:13).

3. Paul is not thinking of hell or purgatory here. His discussion relates to Christ's return to the earth at the time of the second coming.

4. For example, R. B. Hays, *First Corinthians* (Louisville: John Knox, 1997), 56.

5. Here is one advantage the King James Version had over most modern versions. "Thou" and "thee" were references to one "you," while "ye" referred to more than one "you."

6. Paul does something here that he could do because he was inspired, but that we should be very careful about doing. He is quoting verses from Job that were spoken by Eliphaz, one of Job's so called "comforters." Since God clearly did not agree with the thrust of what these individuals told Job, we have to be very careful about quoting their words as God's word. They are God's word in the context of the book of Job as a whole, not when removed totally from their context. On the other hand, even Satan sometimes says things that are true, such as when he accepts that Jesus is the Son of God in Matt. 4:6. In the case of Job 5:13, Eliphaz's words were true.

7. For example, Seneca, *De Beneficiis* 7.3.2–7.4.3, quoted in Hays, *First Corinthians*, 60–61.

6

THE PRINCIPLE IN PRACTICE:
DON'T BE ARROGANT

1 Corinthians 4:1–21

In the final chapter of this first section of the letter, Paul gets down to business. The Corinthians have been using differences between their two most recent "pastors" to vie for superiority in the church. In particular, a group of believers whom Apollos had brought to Christ were claiming to be wiser than the earlier group that converted under Paul's ministry. They questioned Paul's wisdom, authority, and motives, while touting themselves and Apollos as truly wise.

Paul begins his conclusion to this first section of 1 Corinthians by once more putting into perspective the roles he and Apollos play in God's plan. The words Paul uses for **servants** and **those entrusted** (4:1) were used of roles subordinate to higher positions or masters. Like the image of field workers in 3:9, Paul places himself and Apollos as subordinates to the Lord. Aligning oneself with them was ridiculous—the Corinthians should be aligning themselves with the master.

Although this conclusion seems obvious, it is all too easy today to place our loyalties, even our faith, in human leaders we admire. It is not unheard of for a minister to

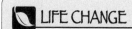

LIFE CHANGE

Our faith should stand on Christ the solid rock, not on the wisdom or charisma of an earthly person.

leave his or her church and to have people pit the wondrous wisdom of a former pastor against the new. They may even keep in contact with the old pastor, asking advice about the way the new pastor wants to do things.

More serious is when people connect their faith so closely with a particular minister or leader that they stop going to church when that pastor leaves. Some people's faith is so intertwined with the minister who led them to Christ that a moral failure on his or her part destroys their faith. Our faith should stand on Christ the solid rock, not on the wisdom or charisma of an earthly person. Those whom God calls to lead must always remember they are only servants, not the kings.

The language of mystery Paul uses here—**those entrusted with the secret things**—would probably have reminded the Corinthians of the "mystery religions" of their day, particularly the religion practiced in Eleusis just a little northeast of Corinth. These religious cults were a mixture of a pagan religion and a secret society. In fact, these mystery religions kept their secrets so well that we do not know much today about what they believed or did in them. Paul certainly did not endorse such mystery cults. But the language of mystery may have reminded the Corinthians that he and Apollos were not philosophers. They were the servants of a God whose ways were beyond human understanding. They were servants of the greatest mystery of all: redemption through the cross of Jesus.

In 4:2, since Paul is talking primarily about himself and Apollos (see 4:6), it is hard not to see comments like these as tactful warnings to Apollos in how he teaches. Certainly it fits well with Paul's statement in the previous chapter that "each one should be careful how he builds" the church (3:10). This **trust**, this matter in which they must be found faithful, is the way they serve and minister the mystery of Christ.

Paul now addresses those who have attacked him. He expresses his lack of concern in their or a court's judgment. The word rendered **court** (4:3) here is the word for day: "It is the least of my concerns that I am judged ... by a human day." Paul implicitly contrasts the "Day of the Lord," the day of God's judgment on the world, with a "day in court." Paul had mentioned the Day of the Lord earlier in 3:13. It is only this Day that Paul concerned with, not the passing opinions of his fellow human beings. Even he himself is not the final judge of himself—only God is.

Paul makes the important observation that our guilt or innocence before God is not strictly a matter of how we feel about what we have done (4:4). Paul does not actually use the word *conscience* here, but he hints at an important truth about our consciences. A conscience can be overactive and make you feel guilty for things about which you should not feel guilty. Yet a conscience can also be under-active or seared to where you do not feel guilty for things about which you should. The goal is to do only the things you are truly convinced are right (Rom. 14:5, 23).[1] But Paul also makes it clear that you can be wrongly convinced: "Blessed is the man who does not condemn himself by what he approves" (Rom. 14:22).

Judge nothing before the appointed time (4:5) is a hard statement for us to live out, and Paul does not mean it absolutely. Indeed, we will find Paul pronouncing judgment on an immoral man in the very next chapter: "I have already passed judgment on the one who did this" (5:3). He also indicates in chapter 6 that it is appropriate for the church to judge in disputes between Christians (6:2–3).

In the case of the sexually immoral man in 1 Corinthians 5, there was no doubt about what he was doing, nor was there any doubt about the immoral nature of his actions. Although we cannot know for certain, I have a hunch Paul thought the legal dispute between certain Corinthians was frivolous as well. In other words, he had no problem with church leadership passing judgment on matters such as these. Paul clearly believed that there was a time to pass judgment on the immoral *actions* of others, particularly other believers. But God was the one who would ultimately pass judgment on human **motives**.

The problem is that people tend to disagree about which moral issues are debatable and which are non-negotiable. We know that the judgment these new Christians at Corinth were passing on Paul was inappropriate and based on their own shallow human mindedness.

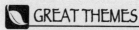

GREAT THEMES

ACTIONS VS. MOTIVES

Paul clearly believed that there was a time to pass judgment on the immoral *actions* of others, particularly other believers. But God is the one who ultimately passes judgment on hidden human *motives*.

Paul puts them in their place—it is not their place to judge him. God is the ultimate judge of all, not a human court. The balance is hard to keep. On the one hand, God has given His church authority on earth to "bind" and "loose" the will of heaven (Matt. 18:18), even to forgive and not forgive sins! (John 20:23). But we must balance the authority that God has given the church with the important principle Paul gives in this verse. Different times and different groups have a tendency to err either in their quickness to judge or their over-tolerance of sin. In general, it is best to err on the side of compassion than on the side of judgment, for this is the attitude God and Christ have modeled for us.

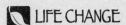

LIFE CHANGE

COMPASSION VS. JUDGMENT

In general it is best to err on the side of compassion than on the side of judgment, for this is the attitude God and Christ have modeled for us.

Some scholars believe that the particular word Paul uses for **applied** (4:6) means that Paul has only been comparing himself and Apollos in order to tactfully speak about the divisions at Corinth, that he and Apollos were not really in conflict.[2]

The statement, **"Do not go beyond what is written"** does not come from the Old Testament or any known Jewish writing. It is not absolutely certain that it was even a proverb or saying in the first place. However, the New Testament generally uses the phrase "what is written" in reference to the Old Testament. It is thus reasonable to think that Paul is warning them to stick to the truth Paul has presented in several of the verses he has quoted for them. In particular, he used both Job 5:13 and Ps. 94:11 in the previous chapter to argue against boasting of wisdom.

If they follow Paul's advice, they will not boast because Apollos or Paul baptized them. **For who makes you different from anyone else?** (4:7). Gordon Fee has suggested that this question amounts to the English, "Who in the world do you think you are, anyway?"[3] **What do you have that you did not receive? And if you did receive it, why do you boast as though you did not?** (4:7). Paul reiterates that God's grace is the ultimate source of everything about which we might want to boast. As Eph. 2:8–9 put it, "it is by grace you have been saved . . . not by works so that no one can boast."

Paul now takes off the gloves in 1 Cor. 4:8–13. He holds a mirror up to the Corinthians so they can see how absurd their boasting has been, and he uses a not so subtle sarcasm in the process. **Already you have all**

you want! (4:8). The boastful Corinthians were acting like the kingdom of God had already arrived in full, and they were ruling the earth already. They had already arrived. They were so spiritual and so wise!

But Paul did not feel the same exuberance about his current situation. How ridiculous of them to think they were ruling while he and other Christian ministers suffered for Christ! **How I wish that**

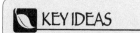

KEY IDEAS

NOT YET RULERS

The boastful Corinthians were acting like the kingdom of God had already arrived in full, and they were ruling.

you really had become kings so that we might be kings with you! (4:8). In other words, the idea that they were already on top in every spiritual way while Paul was still out suffering for Christ was really absurd.

The image Paul invokes in 4:9 is that of captives the Roman armies brought after their conquests around the world. Roman generals would inevitably bring prisoners back to parade around the capitol as a statement of Rome's power. Paul speaks of how powerless and defeated God allows even His apostles to be in the world, sport both to men and angels. We should remember that there are fallen angels as well as good ones. Paul mentions that Christians will judge such angels later on in 6:3. He may have these angels in mind when he mentions some of those before whom he has been paraded in the world as he suffered for Christ.

Meanwhile, the Corinthians were oblivious to the sacrifices of God's true ambassadors. **We are fools for Christ, but you are so wise in Christ!** (4:10). Paul's sarcasm is obvious—they are truly the fools for thinking themselves wise when they know so little of God's workings and plan.

To this hour we go hungry and thirsty, we are in rags . . . brutally treated . . . homeless (4:11). What have they suffered for Christ? How has their life demonstrated their commitment to the king? **We work hard with our own hands** (4:12). Some of the Corinthians may have been ashamed that Paul was so low on the social totem pole. Perhaps Apollos had followed the more usual practice of traveling teachers and accepted the patronage and support of some in the congregation. Paul himself did not accept such patronage from the churches he was at, probably because he did not want any "strings attached" to his ministry at a particular location;

he did not want any encumbrance to the gospel (9:12). He wanted the freedom to admonish without being bound to the obligations that came from receiving support from someone (2 Cor. 11:7–9).

The comments Paul makes in 4:12–13 sound suspiciously like what Jesus said in the Sermon on the Mount: "Do not resist an evil person. If someone strikes you on the right cheek, turn to him the other also" (Matt. 5:39). While the Corinthians were "already" kings, Paul was **up to that moment . . . the scum of the earth** (4:13).

After Paul has scathingly scolded the Corinthians for their idle boasts, he becomes more tender and pastoral in 4:14–17. He writes **to warn** them as his **dear children** (4:14). With regard to the issue of their favoritism toward leaders Paul was willing to give them some slack—he is steering them in the right direction, not shaming them. But later in the letter he will write to shame them over taking each other to secular court (6:5).

After placing himself and Apollos under God's lordship as fellow "field hands" working in the field, Paul now invokes one sense in which they should give him a higher place of honor than any other worker. **Even though you have ten thousand guardians in Christ . . . I became your father** (4:15). Paul may not have any more ultimate value than Apollos, but he deserves a special place in the Corinthians' hearts, since he founded the church.

Paul goes further with his role as father. **I urge you to imitate me** (4:16), just as a son might try to be like his father or, perhaps more poignantly, as a father might expect his son to obey him. **For this reason I am sending to you Timothy** (4:17). Paul does not consider himself to be of greater worth than Apollos, but he is the apostolic authority over the church at Corinth. Timothy will help them follow his example.

Paul ends these four chapters with a stern parental word. **Some of you have become arrogant, as if I were not coming to you. But I will come to you very soon, if the Lord is willing, and then I will find out now only how these arrogant people are talking, but what power they have** (4:18–19). This is the most intense language Paul has used up to this point and the clearest indication of how strong the "revolt" against him is in the church. "Talk is cheap," Paul in effect says. But he knows that these individuals do not have the power of the Spirit to support their claims of wisdom.

Paul is now fully in parental mode. He has no desire to "give them a spanking" when he comes. He would much rather come **with a gentle spirit** (4:21) and have a time of great communion with them. He ends this long unit (1:18–4:21) with an implicit reminder of where it began. Paul's mention of the **power** of **the kingdom of God** (4:20) reminds the Corinthians that the powerful cross of Christ (1:24) turns words of human wisdom into foolishness (2:1).

ENDNOTES

1. Paul did not have in mind the modern neurotic who is so introspective he or she doubts everything. God has only the most tender compassion for these distraught souls who often can only experience God's love and grace through the love we mirror from God to them as their fellow Christians.

2. For example, D. R. Hall, "A Disguise for the Wise ÌÂÙ·Û̈ËÌ·ÙÈÛÎÌ» in 1 Corinthians 4.6,? *New Testament Studies* 40 (1994): 143?49.

3. *The First Epistle to the Corinthians* (Grand Rapids: Eerdmans, 1987), 171.

RUMORS OF BODY PROBLEMS:
A MAN WITH HIS STEP-MOTHER
1 Corinthians 5

1. LOCATING THIS SECTION OF THE LETTER

At first glance 1 Corinthians 5–6 seem to cover unrelated topics of concern to the Corinthian church. But on closer look, all these issues relate to the integrity of the Corinthian body and the protection of its boundaries from corrupting outside influences. First Corinthians 5 deals with the spiritual corruption that sexual immorality brings to the church, a topic to which Paul returns in a different way in 6:12–20.

Meanwhile, the first half of 1 Corinthians 6 deals with the absurdity of taking issues of justice to a worldly forum. Not only will the church judge the world—thus the irony of letting the world judge the

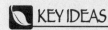 KEY IDEAS

The issues of 1 Corinthians 5 and 6 relate to the integrity of the Corinthian church and the protection of its boundaries from corrupting outside influences.

church—but this course of action once again opens up the church to the corrupting influence of the world. Paul continues to criticize Corinthian claims to wisdom and reiterates God's intolerance of unrighteousness as well as His gracious cleansing for sins. The next three chapters of this commentary deal with this part of 1 Corinthians.

2. A MAN WITH HIS STEP-MOTHER (1 CORINTHIANS 5)

First Corinthians 5 deals with an instance of sexual immorality in the church at Corinth. These verses clearly tell us that while Christians are not "under the law," God still has moral expectations of us. In other words, whatever changes in the law Christ's coming might have brought, God's expectations for sex were not part of them. Paul clearly believed that God's commands to stay away from sexual immorality were part of "Christ's law" (1 Cor. 9:21) and remained in force for the Christian.

A man has his father's wife (5:1). Apparently Paul had already written the Corinthians a letter that alluded to the sexual problems in their church (5:9), so news about sexual immorality was no surprise to Paul. What really shocked him was how atrocious this type of sexual immorality was. It was a kind of sexual relationship that even pagans found unacceptable: a man was apparently having sexual relations with his step-mother.

We do not know many details about the situation. The word *has* is a euphemism for sexual relations, so we know that the man was having sexual relations with the woman. The fact that Paul says **father's wife**, rather than "mother," probably means that the woman was not his mother. In other words, it was not incest. It is also hard to imagine that the man's father was still alive. Given that wives were often

 KEY IDEAS

CEREMONIAL VS. MORAL LAW

The question of what Old Testament laws God still wants Christians to keep and which He no longer requires can be a difficult one. In the centuries after the New Testament, some Christians came to make a distinction between the "moral" part of the Old Testament law and the "ceremonial" parts. While neither Paul nor any ancient Jew would have recognized this distinction, Paul pushes us in this direction when he distinguishes in 1 Corinthians 9:21 between the Jewish law and the "law of Christ." This law of Christ must include, above all, the love of our neighbors and enemies (for example, Matt. 5:43–48, 22:34–40; Rom. 13:8–10; Gal. 5:14; James 2:8; 1 John 4:7–8). As we have just seen, Paul similarly saw the sexual commands of the Old Testament as part of the new covenant, as well as commands relating to idolatry (compare 1 Cor. 10:21; 2 Cor. 6:16). Yet circumcision was not retained as a command (for example, Gal. 5:2–6), nor were any of the food laws (compare Mark 7:19).

much younger than their husbands in that day, it is possible that the father had died and the son had taken a liking to his father's wife, who was perhaps his age or even younger.

Leviticus 18:8 says, "Do not have sexual relations with your father's wife; that would dishonor your father."[1] In general, Leviticus 18 tells us what Paul means when he refers to sexual immorality (*porneia*, translated in the KJV as "fornication"). Paul did not seem to think that Christ's coming had changed any of these prohibitions, whether homosexual relations, incest, or bestiality.

If sleeping with your step-mother was obviously wrong to Paul, he was even more puzzled by the Corinthian reaction to it: **And you are proud!** (5:2). Apparently the Corinthians were not only tolerating this man's behavior, they took pride in it in some way. At first glance it is difficult to imagine how a Christian could actually be proud of such a thing in the church. On the whole, the best explanation is that they saw this behavior as a "glorious" example of the fact that Christians are no longer "under law but under grace" (Rom. 6:14). Perhaps Paul had emphasized to the Corinthians that we become right with God on the basis of faith rather than by keeping the law. Perhaps he had brought to his preaching his own struggle with other Christians who insisted that Gentiles be circumcised and keep the Jewish law.[2]

But we must always be careful about what message we preach to which audience or what advice we give to which fellow Christian. This is a problem that many pastors unconsciously face. Some were raised in legalistic circles with a heavy emphasis on "do's and don'ts." These individuals have a tendency to emphasize freedom in Christ. Others may have been raised in a context where "anything goes" and may emphasize absolute rights and wrongs.

In short, you might not want to give Galatians to the Corinthians! We must be careful not to do therapy with our congregations, using them to process our past struggles with parents or people from our childhood. When we are presenting God's Word to someone, we should share with the one in front of us, not with those behind us in our past.

Perhaps something of this sort had happened with the Corinthians. With his struggles against Judaizers in his mind (Jewish Christians who insisted Gentile converts become Jews and be circumcised), Paul proclaimed freedom in Christ to the Corinthians and that we are not under the law. But some applied this principle to the wrong context. They used their freedom to indulge their sinful natures (Gal. 5:13).

Paul was appalled. **I have already passed judgment on the one who did this, just as if I were present** (5:3). Paul's response is all the more startling given what he has said in the previous chapter about judging nothing before the appointed time (4:5). We might offer a couple observations.

The first is that sexual issues were not disputable ones for Paul. This matter under discussion was not ambiguous to him in the slightest. Sexual immorality of this sort was not only an abomination in God's sight; it was a corrupting influence on the church. It is the nature of our situation that there will always be "disputable issues" in every time and place. We have to be particularly careful to suspend our judgment of others to some degree on such disputable issues and let God sort out those who disagree with us.

But on many issues the church stands convinced and firm. It is the never-ending task of the church to let God work in us to "will and to act according to his good purpose" (Phil. 2:13), helping us to know when to impose church discipline and when to let God deal with it. This tight rope between not judging and exercising discipline in the church is a difficult one, and we should probably err on the side of compassion and tolerance rather than on the side of justice.

A second point of great importance is that Paul held an apostolic authority greater than anyone alive today. God invested incredible authority in the disciples and arguably the church. Matt. 18:15–20 tells us that God has granted the church authority to discipline those who sin against their brothers and sisters. John 20:23 even gives authority to the disciples to decide whose sins will be forgiven. But it is not the task of one individual church member to pass judgment on others.[3] As far as judgment is necessary, such authority pertains more to the church's leaders and to the church as a whole. It was thus inappropriate for the Corinthian church to pass judgment on Paul—they were in no position to do so.

The original language is somewhat ambiguous about where to put the phrase **in the name of our Lord Jesus** (5:4). It would be easy grammatically to connect it to the previous verse: "I have already judged the one who has done this thing in the name of the Lord Jesus." In other words, these words may confirm that this man was actually thinking himself spiritual because he was not under the law.

These verses are yet another favorite of those who argue for the "once saved, always saved" or "eternal security" position. In their interpretation, this man is thrust out of the church for his sin, but he will ultimately be saved because his spirit is eternally secure. The words the NIV renders as **so that the sinful nature may be destroyed** (5:5) can also be translated as "for the destruction of the flesh." Some thus see physical death as the punishment Paul has in mind, still allowing the spirit to be saved after death. But this interpretation is highly dubious and out of sync with what Paul says elsewhere.

We notice first in these verses the incredible authority God has given even an individual church. It is possible for the church to convene not just a meeting on earth, but a spiritual meeting that is taking place in the context of heaven itself. Look at who is gathered in this assembly. The power of the Lord Jesus is present and Paul's spirit as well. The Corinthian church itself was the body of Christ, the temple in which the Holy Spirit dwelt. This is a truly sacred assembly!

The idea of handing someone over to Satan for the destruction of his flesh is shocking to us. Paul has two purposes in mind: (1) to protect the church and (2) to redeem the man. In our context today it would be easy to use these verses as justification for vindictiveness. So many of us just love to cast out the sinner! The church must be extremely careful when it is exercising authority of this magnitude. We cannot even consider such action without the strongest examination of our own motives for wanting to do so.

We will find more than one interpretation of what Paul means by turning over this person to Satan for the destruction of his flesh (NIV: **sinful nature**). The NIV is

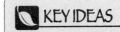

KEY IDEAS

CHURCH DISCIPLINE

Paul's command to kick the sexually immoral man out of the church served two purposes: (1) to protect the health of the church and (2) to bring the man to redemption.

probably correct that Paul has at least partially in view the destruction of the part of this man leading him into sin, his **sinful nature**. But the contrast between flesh and spirit in these verses may in this case imply that the man's physical flesh was part of the equation as well. After all, his sin involved both his fleshly body and the sinful sexual appetites that were a part of it.

Delivering this man to Satan is in effect the consequence of casting this man out of the church. As we will see in 1 Cor. 7:14, holiness can be contagious. There is a spiritual protection that is part of being in the church. The person in the church is insulated to some degree from the power of Satan at work in the world. We in the church dwell in a spiritual "force field" from the power of sin and of Satan. As Rom. 8:9 says, "You, however, are controlled not by the sinful nature but by the Spirit, if the Spirit of God lives in you."

To be cast out of the church is thus to be fed to the lions. It is to go from the protection of God's Spirit and return to the power of sin over you. The defeat of Romans 7 is sure to follow, like a piece of meat thrown into the hungry lion's cage. The situation in Corinth was not like today where you can simply start attending the church across the street. The church at Corinth was small and its boundaries well defined. A person cast out of its fellowship is effectively out of the church. This person is once again alone in the world without God.

The NIV does not express as clearly as it might that the final statement of verse 5 gives us one of the main purposes for such expulsion: **in order that the spirit might be saved on the day of the Lord**. By day of the Lord Paul is once again thinking of the day when Christ will return to earth with judgment for sinners and salvation from wrath for Christians. Paul hopes that this man can be part of that salvation and that he will come running back in desperation to the salvation that is in the church.

We cannot know whether this tactic worked. As we will see, much of 2 Corinthians is devoted to the resolution of such a problem in the church. After 1 Corinthians, Paul had written a harsh letter to Corinth that largely dealt with a particular sinner in the church (2 Cor. 7:8–13). Paul was delighted that this individual had repented after the church had disciplined him (2 Cor. 2:5–11). As such Paul now welcomed the person back and urged the Corinthians to forgive and comfort him. We cannot know for certain if this man was the same person that Paul speaks about in 1 Corinthians 5, but it is at least possible.

Paul was not only concerned with driving this man to repentance; he was also concerned with the spiritual health of the congregation at Corinth as well. While holiness is contagious, sin is infectious. That is why he told them to **get rid of the old yeast** (5:6–7). This danger was especially pertinent for a church like Corinth, which may only have had forty or fifty people.

One of the debates that has surfaced from time to time is the question of whether the church should be a "hospital for sinners" or a "haven for saints." Both have been true at different times and places. When a church is small and undergoing persecution, you will often find that it becomes an island in a sea of troubles. The books of the New Testament written under such circumstances often use the imagery of Christians as foreigners and strangers on the earth, citizens of heaven in a foreign country.

However, our mega-churches today scarcely look much like any of the churches Paul founded in the first century. Our small groups and prayer meetings are much more on the scale of his house churches. We should probably consider this aspect of our situation when applying this chapter to today. We must prayerfully consider whether Paul's goals would be accomplished today by the same disciplinary actions. Would the negative influence of an individual sinner play out the same way in a service of a thousand, which at times we treat more like the entry-way into the church as much as the church itself?

Verses 7 and 8, as the one right before them, use the story of the Passover to make a point. When Israel was in Egypt and God was about to deliver them, God instructed them to place the blood of a lamb on the doorpost of their houses. When the destroyer came around that night (Exod. 12:23), he "passed over" the houses with blood on their doorposts.

Christ is **our Passover lamb**, the Lamb of God, whose blood ensures that God will pass over our sins so that we can escape the judgment. But Paul reminds the Corinthians that the Israelites ate **bread without yeast** the night they ate the first Passover. He likens this bread to a church without the "yeast" of wickedness in it. With this sexually immoral man in their presence, the church at Corinth could not legitimately celebrate the feast. They needed to purify their lump.

Again, we must be very careful how we apply these principles. Some Christians have the "yeast of divisiveness" in their hearts, ironically as many at the church of Corinth did. These Christians often point out the sins of others and are all too ready to expel and divide. No doubt many a group has used Scriptures like this one as an excuse to split off from a denomination or church. Paul would likely be horrified that his words were used this way. He might more likely deliver the divisive group over to Satan to keep the church from the infectiousness of this leaven.

Paul now clarifies a comment he had made in a letter he had previously sent the Corinthians. The fact that Paul wrote other letters that God did not preserve reminds us that the ones that He preserved and brought to the New Testament were the ones whose content He wanted us to hear. It is not the fact that Paul is an apostle that gives his words authority; it is the fact that God has placed His authority on them.

I have written you in my letter not to associate with sexually immoral people—not at all meaning the people of this world who are immoral, or the greedy and swindlers, or idolaters. In that case you would have to leave this world (5:9–10). Paul's comment here reminds me of the Christian proverb, "We are in the world, but not of the world." From time to time Christians do try to get away from the world, to "come out from among them and be separate" (2 Cor. 6:17). Christian groups have sometimes formed communities far away from society. I do not object to those who feel led to separate in this way.

But most of us, including the Corinthians, do not really have the luxury of getting away physically from the immoral. Besides, how will we win these individuals for Christ if we are off in the desert? Both Paul and Jesus placed themselves right in the middle of sinners in the hope

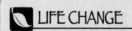

LIFE CHANGE

MAKE AN IMPACT

It is not time for us to leave the world yet. We should find avenues to have a positive impact on it.

that others would find redemption. It is neither possible nor redemptive for all of us to remove ourselves from contact with those outside the church.

Here is a helpful reminder for those of us who work and live almost entirely within Christian walls. The time is not right for us to leave the world. We should find avenues to have a positive impact on it.

Paul now clarifies what he meant when he told them not to associate with sexually immoral people. **You must not associate with anyone who calls himself a brother but is sexually immoral or greedy, an idolater or a slanderer, a drunkard or a swindler** (5:11). This verse reminds us of something Paul writes in 2 Thess. 3:14–15: "If anyone does not obey our instruction in this letter, take special note of him. Do not associate with him, in order that he may feel ashamed. Yet do not regard him as an enemy, but warn him as a brother."

Paul's intentions for this comment are similar to the reasons for expelling the sexually immoral brother: (1) to keep the community pure and (2) to redeem the sinner. We must be very prayerful and careful in how we apply this injunction not to eat with an immoral Christian brother or sister. There are two very significant differences between Paul's cultural context and ours that must make us consider whether this action would have the same meaning today that it had in Paul's day.

Eating together generally does not have the same connotations in our world that it did in Paul's. In the secular world of Paul's day you only ate with people of your same social status or people you wanted others to think you were like. In the Jewish world, you became impure if you ate with someone else that was impure. Perhaps we can begin to get some sense of the way they thought about uncleanness if we think of germs. Doctors tell us we would get far fewer colds if we washed our hands regularly after touching things like door knobs. Even if we have not touched anything, we sometimes wash our hands today just because we have been in certain "unclean" places—even if our mind tells us we do not need to. This "feel" of uncleanness is similar to how Jews experienced the concept with regard to impurity and holiness.

These are some of the reasons Jews did not eat with non-Jews (Acts 10:28) and why Peter and Paul argued at Antioch about whether Jewish and Gentile Christians could eat together (Gal. 2:11–14). These were also some of the reasons it was so scandalous for Jesus to eat with tax collectors and other notoriously immoral people (Matt. 9:10–13)—he was infecting himself and perceived to give approval to the way they stole money from the people. For Paul, eating and associating with immoral Christians was silent acceptance of their immorality.

Refusal to eat with them was also a shaming technique. Here we find a second difference between Paul's world and American culture. His was an honor-shame culture while we focus much more on individual guilt. In our culture, we value being "true to yourself" and "sticking to your guns" when you feel strongly about something. We "agree to disagree." We think of the conscience as a "little voice inside" that tells us whether we are living up to our principles. In contrast, the ancient world "honored" those who kept the values of the group and "shamed" those who deviated from them. You might be surprised at how much imagery in the Bible functions in this way. Paul says he is "not ashamed of the gospel" (Rom. 1:16), and Hebrews says Jesus went to the cross "scorning its shame" (Heb. 12:2). Similarly, the verses we mentioned from 2 Thessalonians give us actions meant to make the sinning brother or sister feel shame for his or her immoral behavior.

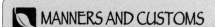

MANNERS AND CUSTOMS
HONOR-SHAME CULTURE

This is a culture oriented around the approval or disapproval of your group rather than around being true to yourself as an individual. Many of today's oriental countries place much importance on honor and shame.

Paul advised such actions because they stood a fair chance of bringing the sinning brother to repentance. In our world it is not clear that it would have such an effect. We would likely come across as vindictive or "holier than thou."

The principles behind Paul's instructions remain as true as ever: (1) we cannot silently allow sin to continue in the church and (2) we should do everything we can to bring the fallen Christian to repentance. The specific ways we go about these may not be the same as Paul's, but the principles and goals remain the same.

Paul concludes his discussion of the sexually immoral man with some words that lead naturally into his next topic. In his non-democratic world run by secular power, Paul saw the justice of the world as something beyond his control or interest (5:12). However, the issue was different within the church: **Are you not to judge those inside? God will judge**

those outside (5:12–13). We have already discussed this tension between not judging one another as individuals and carrying out discipline as a church. Both are appropriate in different situations.

The conclusion was as Paul had already said: **"Expel the wicked man from among you"** (5:13). Paul here alludes to a theme that plays itself out throughout the middle section of Deuteronomy.[4] Sin in the camp has a corrupting influence on the whole church.[5] Perhaps while the church today has rightly emphasized God's gracious forgiveness, it has also forgotten equally valid truths like the contagiousness of sin that is not brought to light and expelled from its presence.

Paul presents a very stark contrast between justice in the church and justice in the world in these verses. Paul seems to say that what happens in the world is not our business as Christians, it is God's business, not ours. Yet many, if not most, American Christians consider various political positions and viewpoints to be part and parcel of a Christian point of view. We have sanctified things like the Revolutionary War or the Union position in the Civil War. Perhaps some or all of these viewpoints are correct, but we will want to explore in the next section whether this "separation of church and state" is the only valid way for the church to relate to the world.

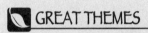

GREAT THEMES

CHURCH DISCIPLINE

The principles of church discipline remain the same—the purity of the body and the reclamation of the sinner. But the ways we go about attaining these goals may differ from those of Paul.

ENDNOTES

1. See also Deut. 27:20 and Lev. 20:11.

2. We know from passages like Rom. 3:8 and Acts 21:21 that people thought Paul taught against living morally and against keeping the Jewish law.

3. The well known passage in Matthew 18 about confrontation is directed at the specific person wronged by someone else, not to just anyone (18:15–17). James 5:19–20 and 1 John 5:16–17 are about the reclamation and redemption of a sinner rather than the judgment of one.

4. See Deut. 17:7, 19:19, 21:21, 22:21, 24, 24:7.

5. See Joshua 7 for the story of Achan and how his sin in the midst of Israel led to defeat in battle.

8

RUMORS OF BODY PROBLEMS:
TAKING EACH OTHER TO COURT

1 Corinthians 6:1–11

Paul will return to sexual immorality and the infectious danger it posed to the Corinthian community in a moment (in 6:12).[1] In the middle of these discussions relating to sexual immorality, 1 Cor. 6:1–11 deals with another situation at Corinth that threatened to "infect" the church. Some members of the church were taking other members to court. Paul believed that by Christians taking fellow believers before pagan authorities, the Corinthians were not only showing that they were spiritually defeated, but they were shaming Christ before the world. They were disgracing the church in front of pagans and submitting to an authority that came from the realm where Satan held control.

If any of you has a dispute with another, dare he take it before the ungodly for judgment instead of before the saints? (6:1). First Corinthians 6 reinforces our sense that Paul believes the church has the authority to make decisions about the personal lives of those within it. Other than him, Paul's churches did not have centralized authorities who might make such authoritarian decisions. It is not clear that they had something like a "senior pastor." Rather, Paul's churches seem to have a group of "elders" and "overseers" who together served as an authority in the church (Phil. 1:1). Paul clearly felt that God's authority extended to personal matters like marriage (1 Cor. 7:36), but the early Christians largely continued to make decisions like these on their own, just as they had before they came to Christ.

However, Paul believed those who took other Christians to court were giving the world authority over Christ. Remember that the church is the place of the Spirit, the place where we are sanctified and protected from the power of sin and Satan. In contrast, the world is the place to which Paul had just expelled the sexually immoral man, delivering him over to Satan. It was a place where sin holds power over the flesh. The world's values and standards of judgment were not those of God!

Paul now reminds them of the authority God will grant to Christians. **The saints will judge the world . . . we will judge angels** (6:2–3). We can be thankful to the Corinthians for their problem, for these verses give us some missing pieces in Paul's teaching on the end times. Clearly Paul believed that we would participate in the judgment of the world along with Christ, assisting Christ in some way to administrate the outpouring of God's wrath on the earth.

So often when we read 1 Thess. 4:17, we picture ourselves rising from the earth to meet Jesus and then going off to be with him in heaven forever: "we who are still alive and are left will be caught up together with them in the clouds to meet the Lord in the air. And so we will be with the Lord forever." Of course Paul does not say *where* we will be with the Lord. Apparently at some point after this "rapture" we will return to the earth to judge the world and angels.[2] Jesus mentions in Matthew that the disciples will "sit on twelve thrones, judging the twelve tribes of Israel" (Matt. 19:29). We thus have good reason to think that God has some work for us to do on earth immediately after the resurrection.[3]

Is it possible that there is nobody among you wise enough to judge a dispute between believers? (6: 5). While Paul did not want to shame the Corinthians for the way they were thinking themselves superior to him, he felt much more strongly about what they were doing to each other. His wording in these verses is very sarcastic. They were claiming to be truly wise and denigrating his knowledge and intellect. Meanwhile, they had no one "wise" enough in the church to settle trivial matters.

Paul sarcastically suggests that even the individuals in the church **of little account** (6:4) could judge these matters. By this comment Paul may refer to the actual leaders of the church, individuals who supported Paul but whom the Apollos group demeaned. We realize that Paul's comments about taking each other to court were not made in a vacuum. He knows the specifics and the attitudes involved in this situation and considers them inappropriate. This is an important element to consider when we apply these verses to today. Just as Paul says not to judge in 4:5 and then judges in 5:3, we must always remember that Paul is not just giving us theory and theology in 1 Corinthians. He is addressing specific situations.

One brother goes to law against another (6:6). It is unlikely that a wealthy member of the church would take a poor person in the church to court. What hope would there be of gaining anything? Similarly, the Roman legal system was not a place where the poor could take the rich to court. It is therefore likely that this is a squabble among the more materially empowered members of the community.

It is not at all clear that justice would have been the outcome of such trials. Indeed, Paul's prolonged appearances before the governor Felix in Acts were in effect solicitations for bribes (Acts 24:26). In Paul's appearance before a proconsul at Corinth, the proconsul dismissed the issue as irrelevant to him (Acts 18:12–17). I suppose if someone had offered Gallio money, he might have shown more interest. Justice was clearly not necessarily to be expected in the Corinthian court.

In short, the whole matter was a farce to Paul. **The very fact that you have lawsuits among you means you have been completely defeated already** (6:7). The incident of taking one another to court was yet another proof that the church was full of a carnal, divisive spirit. This was the same factional spirit they showed when they ranked each other on the basis of who had baptized them (1:13–17, 3:1–9). Paul tells the Corinthians that it would be better to suffer wrong and be cheated than to take their brothers and sisters in Christ to court. As previously noted, these were probably wealthy individuals who had no real need, taking the others to court over their honor, teaching the others a lesson, and making a point.

Is there ever a situation where a Christian can legitimately take another Christian to court? Thankfully most of us will never have to face this issue. If we do, Paul makes it clear that an "I'm going to get mine" attitude is not one Christ supports. Our attitude should rather embody the values Paul mentions when he says, **Why not rather be cheated?** (6:7). You could easily argue that sin is almost always involved somewhere when a Christian takes another Christian to court.

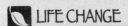

LIFE CHANGE

DON'T TELL IT TO THE JUDGE

Sin is almost always involved somewhere when a Christian takes another Christian to court. Christians should never take others to court without a serious examination of their motives and the consultation of other Christians with spiritual discernment.

Yet it is equally clear that Paul is addressing a specific situation with specific individuals in mind. As with his comments on judging, Paul knows that the specific action they are taking is inappropriate and un-Christlike. In a democratic society whose justice system in part reflects Judeo-Christian values, Paul might in some cases consider it appropriate to settle matters in the public forum. Clearly many American Christians draw much less of a line between the church and the state than Paul did, as we often vote for laws that we think promote Christian values. In other words, we often consider the things of Caesar to be matters of interest to us today. As always, the application of Scripture to today is a matter for intense prayer and consultation of the body of Christ.

Do you not know that the wicked will not inherit the kingdom of God? (6:9). Here is a clear indication that Paul does not have an "eternal security" view of individual salvation. He is talking to people in the church, people who have been "sanctified in Christ Jesus" (1:2). He is warning them that their wicked attitudes and behavior endanger their eventual participation in the kingdom of God.

Nor does Paul hold the Lutheran view that we are "at the same time sinner and righteous if we are always repenting."[4] Paul consistently expects blameless moral behavior from his churches (Phil. 2:15; Col. 1:28). If a wicked lifestyle arises or persists after you have come to Christ, you are in danger of missing the kingdom.

Sexually immoral ... idolaters ... adulterers ... male prostitutes ... homosexual offenders ... thieves ... the greedy ... drunkards ... slanderers ... swindlers (6:9–10). The emphasis of this list may imply that the trivial case in some way related to the sexual immorality of the church, although we cannot know for certain. This verse nevertheless helps connect the flow of the entire section (chaps. 5–6) with its emphasis on sexual sins.

A question we might ask is whether one incidence of drunkenness makes a person a drunkard. On an issue like adultery, the impact of just one act of adultery has such incredible consequences that we would probably think of a person as an adulterer after a single instance of adultery. But my sense is that Paul has *types* of people in mind here rather than a person who commits a sinful act *one time*. This observation does not lesson the sinfulness of adultery, greed, or slander. Paul tells us that as Christians we are not to let sin reign in our mortal bodies (Rom. 6:12). Our quest here is rather to hone in precisely on what Paul is saying in this passage.

What we know about ancient Mediterranean personality pushes us to think that they saw people as "types" of people. A homosexual offender was thus the type of person who regularly sleeps with those of the same gender. An adulterer was a person who was repeatedly sleeping with other people's wives. A drunkard was someone who was always getting drunk. In other words, it does not seem likely that Paul is thinking so much about a person who does something *one time* in these verses, but about people whose behavior is consistently a certain way. If I slander someone one time, I must repent and ask God's forgiveness for my sin, as well as the forgiveness of the other person I have slandered. But I do not become a slanderer in the way Paul means here unless I have an unrepentant attitude toward the slander I have done and continue to slander. Paul is thus not making a "one sin you're out" point. His point is rather that these kinds of behaviors are inconsistent with the kingdom of God, and a person who persists in them cannot be a part of it.

An item of particular interest to our modern context is Paul's mention of "male prostitutes" and "homosexual offenders." The second word in particular (*arsenokoitēs*) does not appear in any known Greek literature prior to Paul, giving us uncertainty about its precise meaning. But the best suggestion, in my opinion, is that it grew out of the Greek translation of Lev. 18:22: "Do not lie with a man [*arsēn*] as one lies with a woman [literally, a woman's bed, *koitē*]; that is detestable." In Paul's day, a "homosexual offender" is someone who practices homosexual acts on another. He would probably be married and have children as well. The practice was apparently somewhat common in some ancient Greek circles, particularly between older men and adolescent boys.

Accordingly, the word translated "male prostitutes" [literally, "soft ones"] probably refers to the passive partners who participate in such acts, possibly for pay. Paul thus considers both types of participation in homosexual activity a wicked practice, just as the man who was sleeping with his father's wife or those apparently visiting prostitutes. As we mentioned in our discussion of 1 Corinthians 5, Paul considered all the sexual prohibitions of the Old Testament to remain in force for the Christian.

Paul probably conceptualized this issue a little differently from the way some do today. For example, Paul was thinking of someone who practiced homosexuality in these verses. The concept of a homosexual *orientation*, a propensity that might or might not express itself in action, would probably be foreign to Paul. A homosexual to Paul was someone who *participated* in homosexual actions. If we expand the discussion to include Jesus' comments in Matt. 5:27–30, we can include as immoral someone who lusts after someone else of the same sex, just as it is inappropriate for someone to lust after someone of the opposite sex.

Another important question is whether God will always take away homosexual desires when such a person comes to Christ. Certainly God always gives us the strength to overcome the specific temptations to *actions*, but may not always take away the *orientation,* just as He doesn't take away sexual desire from a heterosexual or always remove the propensity for addictive behavior from the one tempted with drunkenness.

These are issues I think the church is only beginning to pray through, issues we may face increasingly in the days to come. Homosexuals who come to Christ or rededicate their lives to Christ often do not find welcome in our churches. We often lack faith that God can really give them victory over sinful desires. Some view their sin with such disgust that they can hardly bring themselves to love them. These are areas where we must trust in God's power to give us victory over sin, as well as them.

And that is what some of you were. But you were washed, you were sanctified, you were justified in the name of the Lord Jesus Christ and by the Spirit of our God (6:11). Here we get a glimpse into the make-up of the Corinthian church. Paul does not tell us which of the sins he has mentioned were those of some of the Corinthians, but apparently some practiced one or another of them. Given Paul's emphasis on sexual immorality, this area seems the most likely prior sin he has in mind. Indeed, since Paul goes on in the latter half of the chapter to address the matter of visiting prostitutes, Paul's "past tense" statement here is probably a not-so-subtle reminder for the Corinthians to get back in line on some of these issues.

Paul does not give us a strict order of salvation in this verse: washing, sanctification, justification. The context makes it clear that he is talking about various aspects of what happens when a person first comes to Christ. Washing reminds us of the external act of baptism and, more importantly, the internal cleansing of our sins. When they came to Christ, the individuals who had practiced these "unclean" lifestyles were cleansed of the sin of their actions.

Sanctification in this context (initial) is somewhat synonymous to cleansing, but also evokes the image of the Holy Spirit coming within us (2 Thess. 2:13). In addition, it implies that we become God's "property"; we become identified as "holy" to God. Finally, justification is a legal term and has to do with our legal innocence before God, made possible by the sacrificial death of Christ. We will now be found "not guilty" on the Day of Judgment and will be saved from God's wrath.

ENDNOTES

1. First Corinthians 5–6 thus have somewhat of an A-B-A pattern, a pattern where an author briefly interrupts a topic with a related subject and then returns to the original topic. Thus 5:1–13 and 6:12–20 deal with the issue of sexual immorality as a threat to the community from the outside. In the middle of this discussion, 6:1–11 deal with the threat that comes from taking matters of the church to a worldly forum.

2. The word *rapture* is a word many Christians today use in reference to the "seizing" of Christians from the earth mentioned in 1 Thessalonians 4. Strictly speaking the Bible does not use the word in reference to this event.

3. The question of how to integrate Revelation's teaching with Paul is a difficult one. Paul gives us no sense that the resurrection of which he speaks is only

of those martyred for Christ (1 Thess. 4:16: Rev. 20:4–5). Of course he does not say it is not, so one way to fit these two together is to see Paul's resurrection as a resurrection only of the martyred. However, another option is to see much of Revelation as symbolic at these points. For example, if Paul's resurrection only refers to the martyred, then John himself will not be raised until after the millennium, since he is the only disciple not to die for his faith!

4. Martin Luther's, *Lectures on Galatians*.

9

RUMORS OF BODY PROBLEMS:
VISITING PROSTITUTES
1 Corinthians 6:12–20

It is not immediately obvious to us how the various themes of these verses relate to one another. On the one hand, they seem to anticipate a number of the topics Paul will take up in the second half of the letter (1 Cor. 7–16). Such topics include the appropriate context for sexual relationships (1 Cor. 7), food sacrificed to idols (1 Cor. 8–10), the body of Christ (1 Cor. 12), and the truth of the resurrection (1 Cor. 15). In this sense these verses serve as a good transition to the second half of the letter.

On the other hand, we can interpret all these comments in a way that relates them to sexual immorality in the Corinthian church. In particular, some of the men in the church were apparently taking advantage of the city's prostitutes. We should remember that prostitution was both legal and acceptable in ancient Mediterranean culture. Although it is not clear if Corinth had temple prostitutes at this time, temples of the ancient world did sometimes have such "services" available—particularly the temples of fertility goddesses.

We should also keep in mind that Mediterranean society did not consider it adultery for a man to sleep with a prostitute. Adultery was commonly defined as the shaming of a man by sleeping with his wife.[1] Secular society only considered sleeping with another woman adultery if she was married to someone else. In other words, Mediterranean society placed great restrictions on a female, but almost none on a male. As we mentioned in our discussion of 1 Cor. 6:9, it was apparently even acceptable in many circles for men to have sexual relationships with boys.[2]

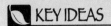 **KEY IDEAS**

Sexual immorality was one of the main problems Paul and other early Christian missionaries addressed regularly with Gentile converts to Christianity.

Sexual immorality was thus one of the main problems Paul and other early Christian leaders had to address regularly with Gentile converts to Christianity. They would need to teach such individuals that visiting prostitutes was inappropriate for a Christian. So many of the sexual values we consider obvious would not have come up on the "radar screen" of new Gentile converts, even if they were the common values of the Jews of the day. We notice that Paul's tone is less aggressive in this section than it was with regard to the man sleeping with his step-mother. Thus Paul does not command the church to expel the individuals he is addressing in 6:12–20.

The trigger for the section seems to be the verses that just precede it. In them Paul has stepped back from the topic of lawsuits at Corinth and generalized about the fact that the unrighteous will not inherit the kingdom of God (6:9). In the process of recounting some of the most obvious unrighteous acts, he has mentioned several varieties of sexual immorality, including homosexual practice, adultery, and sexual immorality in general.

In this context 6:12 begins to counter the sense of some at Corinth that there were no restrictions on the way a Christian man used his body: **"Everything is permissible for me"** (6:12). The NIV has rightly put this statement in quotations, meaning that Paul is citing a Corinthian slogan at this point. The fact that the same words appear verbatim twice here and then again in 10:23 gives us good reason to think that Paul was either citing a clause from the Corinthian letter they wrote him (7:1) or referring to a known slogan of some in the community.

One of the things that makes the train of thought in this section so difficult to follow is that Paul seems to be quoting a number of things the Corinthians have been saying to excuse their behavior, Corinthian slogans. But unfortunately, ancient Greek does not have quotation marks, so it is sometimes difficult for us to know when Paul is quoting them and exactly where the quotations end. Here is yet another reminder that we are reading someone else's mail, an inspired conversation between Paul and the ancient Corinthians. They would have known immediately who said what. Unfortunately, we have to do our best to figure it out.

When discussing 1 Corinthians 5 we brainstormed about where the Corinthians might have gotten the idea that there were no moral restrictions on a Christian. We wondered if some of them had twisted Paul's teaching that the Christian is "not under the law" (1 Cor. 9:20) to mean that Christians had complete liberty. But clearly Paul did have definite moral expectations for a Christian and, as we saw in chapter 5, he especially did not accept sexual immorality in the church.

We see for the first time in this part of chapter 6 a strategy we will see many more times before the letter is done. Rather than flat-out contradict the Corinthians, Paul starts where they are and gently leads them toward healthier courses of action. We might be surprised that he does not just say, "No, you're wrong. Everything is *not* permissible to you." Instead, he accepts their claim and then qualifies it.

Not everything is beneficial (6:12). Paul accepts in theory that everything is permissible for them. We are reminded of Augustine's famous teaching, "Love God and do what you want."[3] The idea is that if you truly love God you will not want to do bad things or things that displease Him.

Paul's responses are clever. If the Corinthians were priding themselves for their wisdom and boasting in Apollos for his secular training, Paul responds with a couple answers from contemporary rhetoric and philosophy. "Not everything is beneficial," he tells them (6:12). This answer comes straight from the handbooks on how to make persuasive speeches. One of the techniques was to show the audience that your course of action is beneficial, while the opposite course is harmful.

I will not be mastered by anything (6:12). This comment reminds us of two essays by a contemporary of Paul, Philo of Alexandria: "Every Bad Person Is a Slave" and "Every Good Person Is Free." Paul uses a little Stoic philosophy on them: the person who lacks virtue is not truly free. Here we see that Paul knows secular wisdom; he just does not take pride in it like the Corinthians.

"Food for the stomach and the stomach for food" (6:13). The NIV is probably correct to consider this statement as a Corinthian slogan. At first it is not clear how it relates to sexual immorality, reminding us of how much we do not know about this conversation. It is also not immediately clear whether the entire statement should be in quotes. Some scholars cannot see Paul saying that God will destroy the stomach, since they think it implies a negative view of the body. These scholars would extend the quote to the end of the sentence.

On the whole, we favor the following interpretation. These Corinthians were comparing the body's need for sex to the stomach's need for food. Their slogan was something like our sentiment, "You've got to eat." In their case, they were saying that men need to fulfill their sexual urges because that is what the male body was made for.

Again, some see the comment **God will destroy them both** as part of the Corinthian slogan. The thought of the Corinthians would thus be, "God is going to destroy our bodies anyway, so what does it matter what I do with it." While the Corinthians may have thought this way, I suspect the NIV has identified the quote correctly. Paul points out that food and the stomach are both aspects of this age, not the next.[4] These "needs" are not as important as the Corinthian men are making them out to be. One cannot live without food, but can live quite well without intercourse.

Yet even if the current form of our bodies will pass away, God needs to be Lord of them. God is Lord of our bodies, not just our spirits. **The body is not meant for sexual immorality, but for the Lord, and the Lord for the body** (6:13). Paul did not see our bodies and spirits as unrelated. Some of the Corinthians may have thought that their bodies had nothing to do with their spirituality, but Paul did not agree. God has claims to our bodies, just as to our spirits.

He will raise us (6:14). When we discuss 1 Corinthians 15 we will see that some of the Corinthians did not believe in the resurrection of their bodies. The idea that we get our bodies back after death would have been ludicrous to many ancients. They may have believed in the immortality of their souls, but they saw no future for their bodies.

Paul here foreshadows his later discussion by noting that God is concerned with our bodies. Not only does our body belong to the Lord now, but God has a claim on the body of the Christian in the future as well. When Christ returns, the dead in Christ will rise and our bodies will become transformed.

Do you not know that your bodies are members of Christ himself? (6:15). Paul now gets to the issue at hand: the sexual immorality of some in the church who are visiting prostitutes. He starts with a theme he will develop in chapter 12. We all as Christians make up together the body of Christ. We are each a part of his body. Since our bodies are also the Lord's, our bodies are also part of the body of Christ.

Shall I then take the members of Christ and unite them with a prostitute? Never! (6:15). Paul is very graphic here and gives us a distasteful picture. The person who "unites" his "parts" with a prostitute is uniting the members of Christ with her. The absurdity of such an action is immediately obvious. "God forbid!" Paul says in the strongest terms. What are you thinking?

We can say the same thing today. We can wonder if the amount of sexual immorality in the church today would decrease if the tempted would "take Christ with them" into such situations. If the Christians tempted to commit adultery were aware that they were taking Christ into that bedroom, would they make a hasty retreat? This principle might change a great many outcomes, not just in terms of our sexual behavior, but in all the areas of our life.

"The two will become one flesh" (6:16). Paul here reminds the Corinthians of the bond that results from the sexual act. It is a bond that God intended for marriage, as Paul's mention of Gen. 2:24 indicates. It is not an activity that one simply "does" and then walks away. It is not a casual activity for fun or sport. It is meant to be an act that creates a bond that is never "put asunder." Under the influence of TV, movies, and contemporary American culture, some Christians today are tempted to think too lightly of sex. To such people, Paul's words remind us of how seriously the Bible treats every sexual union.

On the other hand, other Christians run the risk of over-reading passages like these. The Corinthians needed to learn that having sex with a prostitute was uniting with someone *like* you unite with someone in marriage. Some today have gone further and argued that sex *equals* marriage in God's eyes and thus that you are forever married to the first person with whom you have sex. This is a potentially dangerous idea that neither Jesus nor Paul taught.

It is true that if everyone acted according to God's ideal, everyone would be married to the first person with whom he or she had sex. But because of sin, sex sometimes takes place outside of a marriage relationship. In such cases, both Jesus and Paul did teach that you have become "one flesh" with the other person. But they did not teach that you must then marry the person with whom you sinned. Some Christians believe that teenagers who fall into pre-marital sex *must* marry because they are "already married" in God's eyes. I have even heard some Christians advocate that individuals who are divorced and remarried should divorce the people they are currently with and return to their original spouses. The idea is that in God's eyes they are still married to the first spouse anyway.

These are very dangerous interpretations indeed with potentially devastating consequences. The Bible never says that becoming "one flesh" *is* marriage. Becoming one flesh *is meant for* marriage, but it is not the same as marriage. Paul's teaching with regard to the prostitute makes the point. Paul never says that a man who has had sex with a prostitute should track that prostitute down and marry her. I suspect the very thought would have horrified him. None of the biblical authors discuss the act of sex in such mechanistic terms. Indeed, the very concept of "first sex-act equals marriage" runs into logistical difficulties if one of the partners is not a virgin. Even if visiting the prostitute was the first sex act for the Corinthian man, it certainly would not have been hers. Would Paul then argue that all these individuals must remain celibate? He does not, because this line of thinking is foreign to what he was thinking.

We notice also that the Old Testament actually prohibited a man from remarrying his first wife after she had married someone else, even calling it an "abomination" to the LORD (Deut. 24:4).[5] A polygamous man presumably became "one flesh" with each of his wives, entailing the same level of unity between him and each of them. Thus Jacob became "one flesh" with Leah, Rachel, Zilpah, and Bilhah. We begin to see how foreign the legalistic perspective we are addressing is from that of Jesus, Paul, and particularly the Old Testament.

Paul points out the significance of the sex act to the Corinthians—it is as serious as marriage. But he did not teach that the act *created* a marriage or had the same consequences as marriage. As Christians we believe that there is forgiveness for sin—even for sexual sin. Paul has nothing to say about the future relationship of these individuals with the prostitute. They have sinned; they must stop. If two teenagers are having sex before marriage, they should stop. Perhaps one day they will marry each other. But sound wisdom, not to mention the statistics on teenage marriages, should make us think long and hard before pressuring these children to commit to a life-long relationship. If two Christians are divorced and remarried, they should start over from where they are. Whatever sin is in their past is just as forgiven as any other. They should move on in the Lord.

But he who unites himself with the Lord is one with him in spirit (6:17). Paul reminds the Corinthians that they take Christ's spirit with them wherever they go and whatever they do. As deep as the physical connection is with someone with whom you are "one flesh," the connection is even deeper with Christ. It is spiritual. In the end, our whole person belongs to the Lord: "The body is... for the Lord" (6:13) and we are "one with him in spirit" (6:17).

Flee from sexual immorality (6:18). Here Paul begins a fitting end to his discussion of prostitutes and indeed an appropriate end to the entire section (chapters 5 and 6). This general statement is what the Corinthians should draw from the entire discussion: sexual immorality and Christianity do not mix. **All other sins a man commits are outside his body, but he who sins sexually sins against his own body** (6:18). The first part of this sentence has generated endless discussion, since the word *other* is not in the Greek. Some scholars have thus suggested that we are dealing once again with a Corinthian slogan: "Sin does not have anything to do with the body." Paul would then counter that sexual sins are indeed sins against your body.

This interpretation makes sense, although Paul has not left us any clues that he was quoting the Corinthians here. Perhaps we should thus do our best to interpret the verse as it stands, taking it very loosely: most sins do not harm one's body in the way that sexual sins do. But whatever the precise meaning, Paul was not thinking about physical harm here, things like sexually-transmitted diseases and such. Rather, he had spiritual harm in view.

Paul has already warned the Corinthians that sexual sin has a corrupting effect on the church, the body of Christ. This is the kind of yeast that works its way through the whole lump (5:6). When Paul says that sexual sin is sin against one's own body, he is thus using the word *body* in two ways at the same time: (1) the physical body of the person visiting the prostitute and (2) the body of Christ, the church.

Do you not know that your body is a temple of the Holy Spirit, who is in you, whom you have received from God? (6:19). This statement is striking in that the word *body* is singular, but the word *your* is plural. Earlier in the letter Paul has told the Corinthians as a whole that "you yourselves are God's temple" (3:16). Now he says that "your [plural] body is a temple of the Holy Spirit." Paul may thus give a double meaning to his words. The person who sins sexually sins against his body—both his individual body and the body of Christ.

LIFE CHANGE

The person who sins sexually sins both against his or her own physical body, but also against the body of Christ. This fact doubles our need to be careful in this area of our lives.

Christians have often used this verse to argue against things like smoking and drinking. Certainly we should be good stewards of the bodies God has given us, just as we should be good stewards of the environment He has provided for us. But the meaning of this verse is as much or more about the body of Christ as it is about my individual body, and the harm in view is much more spiritual than physical. It refers more to Christians together, the "temple of the Lord," than to me as an individual Christian.

Yet the Holy Spirit does live in our individual bodies, as He inhabits the church as a whole. For Paul, the Holy Spirit was the most essential element in being a Christian: "if anyone does not have the Spirit of Christ, he does not belong to Christ" (Rom. 8:9). The Holy Spirit is God's guarantee to us of what is to come, a foretaste of glory divine (2 Cor. 5:5). He is God's seal of ownership on the Christian (Eph. 1:13). **You are not your own; you were bought with a price** (1 Cor. 6:19–20). Paul reminds the Corinthians once again who they now are. God has paid for them by offering the blood of Christ to purchase their redemption. As Christians they are not the "free agents" they would like to think they are.

Therefore, honor God with your body (6:20). The logical conclusion is that we should honor God with our bodies. Ultimately they are not ours; they are His. Some Corinthians may have thought that it was only their minds and spirits that mattered to God. This is not the case. While we are free, we are also "slaves of Jesus Christ." Paul will make it clear later in the letter that while he is not under the law, "I am not free from God's law but am under Christ's law" (9:21).[6]

Endnotes

1. B. J. Malina and R. L. Rohrbaugh, *Social-Science Commentary on the Synoptic Gospels* (Minneapolis: Fortress, 1992), 53.

2. So C. H. Talbert, *Reading Corinthians: A Literary and Theological Commentary on 1 and 2 Corinthians* (Crossroad, 1989), 32.

3. *Confessions.*

4. What Paul actually says is "but God will destroy both this [belly] and these [foods]" (6:13). Paul does teach that our resurrection body will be in continuity with our earthly, physical body. But our resurrection body will be a spiritual body, not a fleshly one with a stomach or intestines.

5. Likely due to the immense shame such a remarriage would have brought at that time.

6. He will not make the same mistake with the Romans, if indeed the Corinthians were twisting Paul's own teaching. There he will ask, "Do we, then, nullify the law by this faith? Not at all! Rather we uphold the law" (Rom. 3:31).

10

SHOULD CHRISTIANS HAVE SEX?

1 Corinthians 7:1–24

1. LOCATING THIS PART OF THE LETTER

Now for the matters you wrote about (7:1a). These words in Greek, which begin with the phrase "Now concerning," appear several times in the second half of 1 Corinthians.[1] In most, if not all of these cases Paul is responding to a letter sent to him from the Corinthians. While we do not have this letter, it is not too difficult to figure out what they were asking. The second half of 1 Corinthians thus runs from 7:1 to 16:18 and largely gives us Paul's responses to the questions of the Corinthian church.

2. SHOULD CHRISTIANS HAVE SEX? (7:1–24)

HUSBANDS AND WIVES (7:1–7)

Although the NIV translates the first issue as **it is good for a man not to marry** (7:1b), this translation is somewhat misleading.[2] A more word-for-word rendering is "it is good for a man not to touch a woman" (NASB, KJV). In other words, some of the Corinthians were asking Paul whether Christians should be intimate.

Previous generations of Christians would no doubt find this question more appropriate than most of us do. Most of us rightly reject the idea that sex is a "necessary evil," intended merely for procreation. We have come to affirm that sex is a gift from God to be enjoyed in the context of the husband-wife relationship. We believe that God delights in our pleasure, as long as it is exercised within appropriate boundaries and contexts.

But many Christians throughout the centuries have not thought this way. The view that someone who can abstain from sex is more holy than others no doubt played a role in the process by which the medieval church increasingly pushed for priests to be celibate. The early Christian Origen (200s) actually emasculated himself on the basis of Matt. 19:10–12, and Augustine (400s) associated sex with the original sin of Adam and Eve in the Garden of Eden.

It thus requires some work for us to understand exactly what Paul was saying in these verses. We should keep several things in mind.

First, we should remember from 1 Corinthians 5 and 6 that some of the Corinthian Christians were sexually promiscuous. Remember the man who was sleeping with his step-mother (5:1) and those who were visiting prostitutes (6:16–20). Unfortunately, it is often human nature to over-react to situations like these and go to the other extreme. Some Corinthians may have reacted or at least pretended to react this way. They apparently wondered whether it was not only wrong to have immoral sex, but perhaps better not to have sex at all.

We do not have enough information on these over-reactors to know exactly who they were or what they were thinking. Were they women in the congregation using Christianity as an excuse to leave their husbands? (7:10–11). Were they men who thought that since there would be no sex in heaven (Matt. 22:30), we should start working toward that goal here on earth? We do not know enough to answer these questions definitively.

A second thing we should keep in mind as we read this chapter is that Paul rightly lived with the expectation that the "time was short" before Christ's return (7:29). God asks this of all of us, to live in the expectation that Christ could return any day. But we have every reason to believe that this expectation was even stronger for Paul than it is for us.

The two thousand years that have passed since Christ's ascension have often led Christians to think more about going to heaven when they die than about the possibility that Jesus could return any day. But Paul gives us ample reason in his early writings to believe he initially expected

Christ to return sooner rather than later, perhaps even within his own lifetime. We will return to this point as we work through chapter 7.

In the light of these factors, Paul's argument in this chapter is pragmatic: **each man should have his own wife, and each woman her own husband** (7:2). The logic here is very straightforward: celibacy is a nice goal, but because of sexual temptation, have sex with your spouse. The word "have" here probably means "have sex."[3]

Paul's tactful way of addressing this issue is similar to his tactics later in the letter. He starts by partially agreeing with the Corinthian position, affirming the Corinthians. Then he goes on to qualify their position and modify it, carefully leading them to the attitude they should have on the issue in question. He will use the same technique later with regard to meat sacrificed to idols and with regard to tongues, starting with the Corinthian position and nudging them in a more beneficial direction. Here we have some great lessons in Christian tactfulness: we often have more success when we woo and commend than when we confront militantly. Paul knew how to do both.

It is worth pointing out that Paul presumes monogamy in 7:2, although it is not the point of the verse. We will search hard in the Old Testament for a prohibition of polygamy. Indeed, the Bible says nothing negative about Jacob having two wives and two concubines or about David's several wives.[4] But by the time of Christ monogamy had become the standard Jewish practice.

As Christians we believe that this was God bringing His people toward the ideal: marriage as a relationship between one man and one woman. Monogamy reflects the equal value of women and men in God's eyes. In contrast polygamy tends to deflate the value of each wife while inflating the value of the husband.

Paul continues his train of thought in 7:3: **The husband should fulfill his marital duty to his wife, and likewise the wife to her husband.** We remember that Paul's point is to avoid sexual immorality. Marriage is spiritually beneficial at least in part because it provides an appropriate channel for our sexual impulses and reduces our temptation to express these desires in inappropriate directions. It only makes sense, then, that husbands and wives should have sex regularly to minimize the temptation to go looking for sex elsewhere.

KEY IDEAS

Marriage is spiritually beneficial at least in part because it provides an appropriate channel for our sexual impulses and reduces our temptation to express these desires in inappropriate directions.

Paul follows with the fact that the bodies of husband and wife belong to each other, not just to themselves (7:4). The second part of this statement is remarkable in the light of the culture of Paul's day. Paul amazingly says that the husband's body belongs to his wife! This statement must have been shocking to many, that a wife would have this authority over her husband's body. If God held the ancient Corinthians responsible for this degree of equality in that context, we can only imagine the standard He must want of us in a culture that *wants* to afford men and women equal status.

First Corinthians 7:5 reinforces this line of thinking: **Do not deprive each other except by consent and for a time**. Christian husbands and wives should not withhold sex from each other except by agreement for a spiritual purpose like prayer, and even then only for a short time. To do otherwise would give Satan a powerful tool with which to tempt them. But even this allowance for temporary abstinence is a **concession** on Paul's part; it is not a command (7:6).

I wish that all men and women **were as I am** (7:7). Paul here at least touts celibacy as a theoretical ideal. It is true that he is emphasizing his agreement with some of the Corinthians so that he can lead them toward a more balanced view. That is, Paul was not moving the Corinthians toward *marital* celibacy in his argument, but away from it. Paul does not push anyone to remain single in this chapter.

But we should at least acknowledge what Paul claims to be his ideal position: celibacy. He does not think most Christians have this gift from God: **one has this gift, another has that** (7:7). He himself had the gift. Keep in mind that Paul likely wrote in the expectation that Christ would soon return (7:29), an expectation that definitely put mundane things like marriage into perspective. Paul's burden to evangelize the lost was all-consuming for him. Marriage would have slowed down his ministry.

Most of us are not in danger of over-emphasizing Paul's ideal preference. Marriage is clearly the ideal among Protestant Christians today. We resonate with 1 Tim. 4:3's indictment of those who would forbid marriage and Heb. 13:4's pronouncement that marriage is honorable. Indeed, Protestant churches often look negatively toward pastoral candidates who are single. Perhaps it is worth a reminder from time to time of how differently we look at this subject than Paul did.

The question of whether Paul himself had been married earlier in his life is an intriguing one. Most rabbis were married, and one apparently had to be married to be on the leading Jewish council, the Sanhedrin. Paul certainly aspired to become a rabbi (Acts 22:3), and Acts 26:10 says Paul "cast his vote" against the early Christians. But Acts probably meant only that Paul agreed with the decisions of the Sanhedrin, not that he was actually a voting member.[5] We thus do not have enough information to know for certain whether Paul had been married earlier. It would not be surprising if he had been, but it is also possible he had not.

If Paul had been married, he was no longer by the time he wrote the Corinthians. He considers himself among the unmarried in 7:8: "to the unmarried... as I am." Among those who think he had once been married, some think his wife had died previously. Some argue that Paul had widowers in view when he talked about the unmarried in 7:8. If so, Paul included himself among them. Others think that Paul's wife may have left him when he came to Christ. These interpreters see great significance when Paul talks about an unbelieving spouse departing (1 Cor. 7:15). But we just do not have enough information to conclude definitively.

GETTING AND STAYING MARRIED (7:8–16)

The first seven verses of 1 Corinthians 7 have addressed the issue of sex within the context of marriage. But after Paul has broached the issue of marital status in 7:7, he now slides toward the question of marriage itself. **Now to the unmarried and the widows I say: It is good for them to stay unmarried, as I am** (7:8). Some have suggested that Paul had widowers in mind when he spoke of the unmarried in this verse, especially since he goes on to discuss virgins later in the chapter (7:25). It may very well be the case that Paul was primarily thinking of men who had been married previously. But on the whole it is safer to see a general reference to all unmarried men here, regardless of how they came to be unmarried.

Paul's advice to the unmarried is to stay unmarried if possible, anticipating his comments later in the chapter about remaining in whatever state you find yourself (7:17–24). But with temptation in mind again, he advises such individuals to marry **if they cannot control themselves** (7:9). Paul is again eminently practical: **it is better to marry than to burn with passion**. The words "with passion" are not in the original Greek, but the NIV probably captures Paul's sense correctly. The ideal may be celibacy, but marriage is better than sexual immorality.

Since Paul advocates marriage in this verse over burning with passion, 7:8–9 are the clearest indication in the New Testament that single men should remain celibate until marriage. Verses elsewhere that forbid what the King James Version translates as "fornication" are references to sexual immorality in general rather than specifically to sex before marriage. While the issue never directly comes up elsewhere, 1 Cor. 7:8–9 make it clear that Paul did not consider pre-marital sex appropriate for a Christian.

First Corinthians 7:10–16 then turns to married couples. Paul has told us that the unmarried need not marry. He now teaches that the married should not separate. If Paul still has his discussion of marital relations in view at all, we can wonder whether some at Corinth wanted to use the idea of celibacy as an excuse to divorce. Indeed, it is possible that Paul now gets to what is really behind the Corinthian question: the desire of some to use Christianity as an excuse to leave their spouses. Perhaps Paul now cuts to the chase, leaving behind the "smokescreen" of the Corinthian question about marital relations.

Some scholars have noted Paul's unusual attention to wives in 1 Corinthians 7.[6] He more typically addresses men in general in a way that assumes women as well, but does not specifically mention them. But Paul carefully mentions what is required of both wives and husbands in this chapter, especially wives. It is particularly noteworthy that his summary to the whole chapter in 7:39–40 returns to the question of wives leaving their husbands.

This emphasis leads us to wonder whether some of the Corinthian women, perhaps those also addressed in 11:3–16 and 14:34–35, were trying to use Christianity as an excuse to leave their husbands. Obviously this suggestion is only an educated guess. Realizing how much we do *not* know about the context of Paul's words is humbling. It cautions us not to apply these words to today blindly but always with God's loving and merciful character in view.

Paul begins his discussion of divorce at Corinth by invoking the teaching of Jesus: **A wife must not separate from her husband. But if she does, she must remain unmarried or else be reconciled to her husband. And a husband must not divorce his wife** (7:10–11). Scholars debate whether Paul is referring to a spiritual message he received from the risen Christ or to the teaching of Jesus while he was on earth. On the whole, Paul probably has in mind the teaching recorded in Mark 10:9–12. Here Jesus says not to "separate" what God has joined, and that "[a]nyone who divorces his wife and marries another woman commits adultery against her. And if she divorces her husband and marries another man, she commits adultery."[7]

Once again, it is interesting that Paul focuses so much on the wife in his presentation of Jesus' teaching, for Jesus himself did not. This focus reinforces our sense that Paul is addressing specific concerns at Corinth. Whatever specific situation he may have in mind, he gives two general instructions to the Corinthians: (1) Christians should not divorce and (2) if a woman does separate from her husband, she should not remarry.[8]

Paul goes on to give instructions Jesus did not give while on earth. If a Christian's spouse is not a believer, this is no excuse for divorce (7:12–13). **But if the unbeliever leaves, let him do so** (7:15). The principle Paul mentions is crucial here: God has called us to live in peace. It is an important reminder of the spirit behind these instructions on divorce and remarriage.

When Paul says that the believing spouse is **not bound**, he uses the same term he uses later in the chapter for being married (7:27). In other words, Paul is telling the Corinthians not to fight an unbelieving spouse who wishes to divorce him or her. Later in the chapter he will allow remarriage for at least divorced Christian men (7:28). The fact that Paul can modify and reapply the general principles of marital relationship to different contexts reminds us that Jesus and Paul's teaching on divorce was never intended to oppress or enslave—it was meant to protect and empower.

Paul now interestingly says that an unbelieving spouse is **sanctified** by a believing one (7:14). Paul does not mean that the unbeliever will "go to heaven," for he goes on to ask **How do you know, wife, whether you will save your husband? Or, how do you know, husband, whether you will save your wife?** (7:16). In other words, the unbelieving spouse will not escape God's wrath on the Day of Judgment simply because he or she is married to a Christian.

> ### ◧ LIFE CHANGE
>
> The fact that Paul can modify and reapply the general principles of marital relationship to different contexts reminds us that Jesus and Paul's teaching on divorce was never intended to oppress or enslave—it was meant to protect and empower. We violate the spirit of Jesus and Paul when we look at the Bible's teaching on divorce as rigid rules rather than as examples of God's love and protection.

On the other hand, this sanctification is more than just a matter of psychological influence—it is a spiritual influence that both draws and protects spouse and children. The unbeliever and the children of this marriage are affected by the Spirit inside the believing spouse. Their placement within the power of this sacred force gives them greater insulation from the power of sin than other unbelievers and in the end does make it more likely that they will come to God.

Some have used the last part of 7:14 as an argument in favor of infant baptism: **Otherwise your children would be unclean, but as it is, they are holy**. The verse implies that the child of a Christian is more "in" than "out," even though he or she has not yet made Christianity his or her own. Indeed, few of us believe that such children would go to hell if they died, for we believe in God's prevenient grace that keeps them safe until age at which a child becomes aware enough to know the difference between right and wrong, as well as to recognize his or her need for Christ.[9] The "holiness" pictured in this passage does not ultimately save your children, but it implies a strong spiritual influence on them for Christ.

PAUL'S BOTTOM LINE: STAY AS YOU ARE (7:17–24)

First Corinthians 7:17–24 back up from the particular instructions Paul has been making and lay down a more general principle for the Corinthians. Perhaps Paul now gets at the real motivation behind their questions on sex and marriage. Perhaps the Corinthians were trying to use

WHAT OTHERS SAY

"PREVENTING" GRACE

"Salvation begins with what is usually termed (and very properly) *preventing grace*; the first wish to please God, the first dawn of light concerning his will, and the first slight transient conviction of having sinned against him." John Wesley, "On Working Out Our Own Salvation"

their newly found Christianity in one way or another as a means by which they might change or improve their status at Corinth. Paul did not advocate wives leaving their husbands, even if their husbands were unbelievers. In 1 Corinthians 11 we will find him curbing the actions of some Corinthian women whose "freedom" was shaming their husbands in the community.

Paul's instructions are straightforward: **each one should retain the place in life that the Lord assigned him and to which God has called him** (7:17). Are you a circumcised Jew who accepted Christ? Don't stop being a Jew. Are you an uncircumcised Gentile? Don't get circumcised. We should neither over- nor under-emphasize Paul's language of calling here. Paul could say that God had assigned us a certain lot in life without meaning we should abandon all hope of improvement.

Were you a slave when you found Christ? Don't worry about it. Sure, if you have an opportunity to be freed, go ahead. But it really is not too important. As we see later in the chapter, Paul views all these social roles from the perspective of eternity and Christ's approaching return. As he says later in the passage, **the time is short. From now on those who have wives should live as if they have none** (7:29). From the perspective of eternity it will not be too long before these things will not matter any more. Live with your priorities focused on eternity rather than on passing earthly things.

Before moving on we should mention one more interesting comment Paul makes in this paragraph: **Circumcision is nothing and uncircumcision**

is nothing (7:19). But **keeping God's commands** did matter to Paul. We have another good reminder here that the old "faith versus works" debate relates more to *our* way of thinking about things than how Paul thought about things. Faith and works were not opposing principles for Paul: they went hand in hand.True, he did teach that no one could merit God's favor because of how well they kept these commands. But most Jews thought this way too. What is more significant is that Paul did not include circumcision as one of God's commands. Rather, Paul considered the command to love our neighbor as the essence of God's requirements (Rom. 13:8–10; Gal. 5:14). Galatians 5:6 captures Paul's sense here well: "in Christ Jesus neither circumcision nor uncircumcision has any value. The only thing that counts is faith expressing itself through love."

ENDNOTES

1. 1 Corinthians 7:1, 25; 8:1; 12:1; and 16:1.

2. Accordingly, the TNIV (an updated translation of the NIV) now translates it "It is good for a man not to have sexual relations with a woman."

3. Paul later tells the unmarried to remain unmarried (7:8), so he is not likely arguing for singles to marry in 7:2. In 7:2 he is arguing for sex within marriage.

4. The commandment of Deut. 21:15–17 presumes the legitimacy of polygamy.

5. The best evidence we have indicates a person would need to be at least forty to be a voting member of the Sanhedrin (Babylonian Talmud, *Sotah* 22b). But if Paul was this old in the early A.D. 30s, he would be in his sixties when he was conducting his main missionary journeys. Such an advanced age seems somewhat unlikely for the Paul of Corinthians, although he does call himself an old man (probably at least in his 50s) in Phlm. 8, traditionally written almost ten years after 1 Corinthians.

6. For example, R. A. Horsley, *1 Corinthians* (Nashville: Abingdon, 1998), 95.

7. There is some question about this translation. It is not clear that people at this time had any concept of committing adultery against a woman. Compare B. J. Malina and R. L. Rohrbaugh, *Social-Science Commentary on the Synoptic Gospels* (Minneapolis: Fortress, 1992), 53.

8. Many scholars suggest that the second statement—"But if she does, she must remain unmarried or else be reconciled to her husband"—is a parenthetical comment of Paul's, since we have no record of Jesus making a statement of this sort.

9. Not to mention a covenant of responsibility for the church to raise the child in the "training and instruction of the Lord" (Eph. 6:4).

11

SHOULD VIRGINS GET MARRIED?

1 Corinthians 7:25-38

It is not clear whether Paul now discusses a new Corinthian question or whether he is simply covering more issues related to sex and marital status. Since both the questions we find in 1 Corinthians 7 deal with sexuality, I have numbered them Questions 1A and 1B. In 7:25 Paul proceeds to the matter of virgins, a word that specifically refers to virgin women (*parthenos*). He does not claim to have a clear message from the Lord on the subject, but he believes his thinking is faithful because of **the Lord's mercy** (7:25). As he will say later in the chapter, his thinking is guided by the Spirit (7:40).

Paul begins by repeating and shedding further light on what he has said in the previous paragraph: **Because of the present crisis, I think that it is good for you to remain as you are** (7:26). Interpretations of this crisis vary from those who see it as a reference to some local or passing problem, such as a famine, to those who see it in relation to the approaching return of Christ. We will return to this question in a moment.

Paul now gives somewhat of a summary of his instructions up to this point: **Do not seek to be released. . . . Do not seek a wife. But if you should marry** (7:27–28, NASB). We notice that Paul does not prefer remarriage after divorce in this passage, *but he allows it*. Such comments do not contradict his earlier instructions that a divorced woman should remain unmarried, for 7:28 is directed at a divorced man.

These observations could lead us to a double standard if we do not pay careful attention to the context. At first glance it appears that Paul prohibits a divorced woman to remarry (7:11) while allowing a divorced man to do so (7:28). The best way of reconciling the two statements is probably to see Paul's comments on the remarriage of a woman as heavily directed at Corinthian women who wanted to divorce their husbands without any appropriate basis.[1] In other words, the prohibition of remarriage earlier in the chapter related to women who left their husbands for inappropriate reasons. Another possibility is that cultural factors made it more inappropriate at that time for a divorced woman to remarry than for a divorced man.

Paul now gives the Corinthians a fuller justification for his instructions to remain in whatever status they had when they became a Christian (7:29–30). Paul is almost certainly thinking of the return of Christ, the day of salvation and judgment. This fact makes it unlikely that the "present crisis" of 7:26 is some local problem like a famine. The second coming of Christ puts things like marriage and widowhood into an eternal perspective: they are truly passing situations.

Are you rejoicing at your marriage? It will not be long before we will no longer marry. Are you mourning at the passing of a spouse? It will not be long before widowhood is no more. Paul does not mean to minimize grieving or celebration, only to put them into an eternal perspective.

A more precise translation of the statement that the **time is short** would be "the time has been shortened." Some scholars have emphasized this point to deny that Paul thought the Lord would return within his own lifetime.[2] They do not believe Paul was saying Christ would return shortly but that the time before the end was shorter than it used to be (Rom. 13:11). These scholars help us keep Paul's teaching in its proper perspective. Paul is indeed talking more about keeping an eternal perspective on the things of this world than he is about the fact that Christ will soon return—the main point is more the attitude than the timing. For the remainder of the time, we should think of **those who use the things of the world**, as if they cannot use them to their full extent.[3] **For this world in its present form is passing away** (7:30–31).

This eternal perspective would be true even if Paul had initially thought Christ would return within his own lifetime. He never makes such a claim directly, but he seems to imply that he thinks it at many points. For example, although Paul was at Thessalonica for over a month, he never seems to have told them what happens to Christians when they die (1 Thess. 4:13). Since Christians today regularly evangelize by talking about where you go when you die, we find it puzzling that Paul would not have amply covered this question when he was there. The best explanation is that his preaching must have focused on Christ's immanent return. As such, the issue of Christians who die before Christ's return must not have come up in a significant way.

Paul relates his teaching on marriage to the "present crisis." We should remember how much persecution and difficulty he experienced in his ministry from the very first. We see this fact particularly in Paul's account of his hardships in 2 Cor. 11:23–29. In Paul's day the life of a Christian was one of trial—not the ideal context in which to marry and raise children. We have already heard him shame the Corinthians for acting like they "ruled" in God's kingdom while he was still being led around like a captive (1 Cor. 4:8–9). Acts 14:22 captures Paul's perspective well: "We must go through many hardships to enter the kingdom of God."

Paul continues: **An unmarried man is concerned about the Lord's affairs . . . a married man is concerned about the affairs of this world** (7:32–33). Paul goes on to say similar things about women. The concerns of married individuals divide their attention, hindering to some degree their ability to serve the Lord as extensively as a single person. Certainly Paul is not prohibiting marriage: **I am saying this for your own good, not to restrict you, but that you may live in a right way in undivided devotion to the Lord** (7:35). But it would be hard to deny that celibacy was preferable because of the way it freed a person to be single-minded in their devotion to the Lord.

Paul is being very pragmatic here. He does not say that an unmarried Christian is a *better* or *holier* Christian than a married one. Even more importantly, Paul implies that a married person *should* be devoted to the concerns of his or her spouse. Some of the most influential Christian men of the past, including John Wesley, have neglected their wives in the name of ministry. Paul leaves no room for such a thing—it is not a sign of godliness. Paul *assumes* that a Christian husband or wife *will* attend to pleasing his or her spouse.

We can translate 1 Cor. 7:36–39 in two quite different ways: (1) in terms of a man thinking about marrying a virgin to whom he is engaged

---

GREAT THEMES

Paul assumes that a Christian husband or wife will attend to the needs of his or her spouse—even ministry does not take precedence.

---

or (2) in terms of a father thinking about letting his virgin daughter get married. The NIV prints the first possibility in the main text, but also provides the second rendering in a note. While most ancient commentators preferred the second option, most modern interpreters have opted for the first.

In the first way of translating the paragraph, Paul is addressing a man who **thinks he is acting improperly** toward his virgin. In this interpretation, scholars often take the improper behavior to have a sexual edge to it: perhaps he is not able to control his passions toward her.[4] Paul tells this man that he is not sinning if he marries the virgin to whom he is engaged (7:36). On the other hand, Paul considers it even better if he can control himself, if he has **settled the matter in his own mind. . . . So then, he who marries the virgin does right, but he who does not marry her does even better** (7:37–38).

This passage is striking to us in the way that it leaves the desires of the virgin herself out of consideration, although the man in question does consider the fact that **she is getting along in years** (7:36). The man seems to be doing all the deciding. It is, however, another clear indication that Paul did not consider pre-marital sex appropriate behavior. Earlier, we saw this idea in relation to an unmarried man (7:8–9). Our current passage presumes that an unmarried woman should also be a virgin when she marries.

The passage would take on even stronger cultural dimensions if translated a second way. "If any man thinks he is acting unbecomingly toward his virgin *daughter*," he does not sin if he lets her marry (7:36, NASB). On the other hand, if he is resolved "to keep his own virgin," he also does well (7:37, NASB). I personally wonder at the idea of "keeping a virgin." It seems to fit better with a father debating whether to give his daughter in marriage than to someone thinking of marrying. Similarly, the New American Standard Bible provides a slightly more likely translation of 7:38: "So then both he who gives his own virgin [daughter] in marriage does well, and he who does not give her in marriage will do better."[5] The case is very close linguistically. Even if I suspect that the balance leans slightly toward the father-daughter option, it is hard to resist the husband-wife interpretation. After all, it is the position favored overwhelmingly by modern scholars.

Paul wrote these words in a world where marriages were frequently arranged and fathers often decided whom their daughters would marry. I have known Christians who have argued against dating and in favor of churches arranging marriages on the basis of texts like these. Indeed, some of the churches overseas in my own denomination have at times followed this practice. To a great degree, we ultimately have to trust the Spirit to lead Christians in other cultures to discern God's will for them in their own cultural context. But the fact that the idea of arranged marriages is so foreign to most Christians in the Western world makes us wonder whether these particular words of Paul were more for their time and context than for ours. After all, the principle that in Christ there is neither male nor female pushes us toward giving our daughters more voice in their earthly destiny than Paul's world did.

First Corinthians 7:39–40 really conclude the entire chapter. But for convenience we will discuss them here. In a way, they fit with Paul's discussion of virgins in 7:25–28—the second half of the chapter seems to focus on unmarried women. Other commentators see Paul as finishing up his discussion of marital status and remarriage by a quick comment on widows.[6] Yet in many ways these verses seem to provide a somewhat general statement that wraps up the entire chapter's theme.

Perhaps the way Paul chose to close the chapter hints at what the most prominent marital issues were for the Corinthians. **A woman is bound to her husband as long as he lives** (7:39). We can probably infer that some Corinthian women wanted to divorce, and some Corinthian widows were contemplating remarriage.

Of great significance is the fact that Paul insists Christian women remarry "in the Lord": Christians should marry Christians (2 Cor. 6:14). But Paul thinks it even better if they remain in the unmarried state they find themselves. **In my judgment, she is happier if she stays as she is** (7:40).

First Corinthians 7 is one of those chapters in the Bible that reminds us so clearly that we are listening in on God's words to the Corinthians through Paul in this passage. Recognizing this fact leads us to two important considerations as we prayerfully appropriate these words in the church today.

First, we recognize how significantly the nuances of a passage like this one can change as we learn more about its original situation. Since we will never know this situation fully, we must always be somewhat tentative in the way we appropriate it.

Secondly, doing exactly what they did is often *not* doing what they did—what certain actions meant in their world is often *not* what they would mean in our world. Like Paul, we need the Spirit of God in us to help us "rightly divide" the word of truth, so that we apply the spirit of the written word authentically to the world today.

ENDNOTES

1. It is not clear that that portion of Paul's statement in 7:11 came from a saying of the earthly Jesus.

2. So Witherington, *Jesus, Paul, and the End of the World* (Downers Grove, IL: InterVarsity, 1992), 28.

3. This phrase is notoriously difficult to translate. I have tried to preserve the sense in my translation.

4. For example, C. Blomberg, *1 Corinthians* (Grand Rapids: Zondervan, 1994), 153. I do not find this interpretation convincing for two reasons: (1) the man "thinks" he is behaving improperly—if his shame was sexual, he would know; and (2) the improper behavior relates to the marrying age of the virgin, not to sexual behavior.

5. The Greek word Paul uses here usually means to "give in marriage" rather than to "marry."

6. For example, A. C. Thiselton, *The First Epistle to the Corinthians* (Grand Rapids: Eerdmans, 2000), 603.

12

WHAT ABOUT IDOL MEAT:
EAT WITH
OTHERS IN MIND

1 Corinthians 8:1–13

1. LOCATING THIS PART OF THE LETTER

The second topic about which the Corinthians asked Paul related to things sacrificed to a pagan god: **Now about food sacrificed to idols** (8:1). Paul will address this issue either directly or indirectly for the next three chapters of 1 Corinthians (8:1–11:1). Accordingly, we will devote the next three chapters of the commentary to this part of the letter.

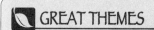 GREAT THEMES

DISPUTABLE MATTERS

The issue of meat sacrificed to idols gives us an example of how to work through disputable matters, issues about which Christians disagree.

On the surface, this is an issue that seems far removed from us. Most of us have never come into contact with the temple of another god or had the opportunity to eat food that has been offered to a demon. Nevertheless, this issue gives us an example to follow of how to work through "disputable matters," issues about which Christians disagree.

First of all, Paul primarily has in mind meat that has been sacrificed to idols. To get a good sense of what was going on, we need to keep in mind that meat was the luxury of the rich in Paul's day. Like the issue of taking one another to court, the question of meat sacrificed to idols was another example of those with means causing problems for those of lesser status and means.

Much of the meat that was available in the marketplace would have come from local temples (10:25). When an animal was sacrificed, only a small part of it was devoted to the god. Some of it was consumed by the priests of the temple and by those who brought the animal. Offering a sacrifice could become something like going out to eat for a family. But especially after a feast, much of the meat from these sacrifices would make its way to the nearby market.

This situation created a matter of conscience. Those with a particularly sensitive conscience could not know whether the meat they were buying at market had come from a nearby temple. Apparently, some Jews effectively became vegetarians for this reason (Rom. 14:2). Most of the ancients were almost vegetarians for the sole reason that they could not afford meat in the first place.

2. EAT WITH OTHERS IN MIND (8:1–13)

The consciences of some in the Corinthian church were not bothered at all by eating such meat. Most scholars agree that 1 Cor. 8:1 gives us another one of their slogans: **"We all possess knowledge"** (8:1).[1] Just as they claimed to be wiser than Paul and others in the church (3:18), they also claimed to have knowledge that others in the church did not have.

We will find out what that knowledge was in a few verses (8:4). In the meantime, Paul puts the value of knowledge into perspective: **Knowledge puffs up, but love builds up** (8:1). We will see this same theme later in chapter 13 when Paul says that even the person who has all knowledge is nothing if he or she does not also have love to go along with it (13:2).

Clearly boasting in knowledge and wisdom was a besetting sin of this church. The proud in the church also were self-centered and built themselves up to the detriment of others. We will see them using tongues as well to build themselves up while contributing nothing to the church as a whole (14:4).

Those who think they know a lot probably do not know much at all. You may have heard the saying, "the more you know, the less you know."

In other words, the more knowledge you acquire, the more you realize how much more there is to learn—and the more uncertain our knowledge really is.

What is important is not how much you know, but Who you know. The way the NIV reads, the person who loves is truly known by God. This statement would point to the fact that our knowledge is nothing compared to that of God. It would perhaps also point to the importance of a special relationship with God over our desire for personal knowledge.

So then, about eating food sacrificed to idols: We know that "an idol is nothing in the world" and that "there is no God but one" (8:4).[2] The clauses I have put in quotes were probably things the Corinthians said in their letter to him. Their argument probably went something like this: We only worship one God. An idol is not really a god. Therefore, why should we worry about eating meat that has been sacrificed to one?

It is possible that we are hearing the teaching of Apollos on this point. We can suspect that some Jews did not worry about pagan temples because they thought that "nobody was home" there. This "enlightened" position thought nothing of the pagan cults and viewed those who worshipped at them as ignorant for giving their worship to something made of stone or wood (Isa. 44:9–20). Other Jews and Christians saw demons and evil forces at work in the meat and therefore forbade eating it in the strongest terms (Acts 15:20, 29; Rev. 2:14, 20).

Indeed, it is interesting that Paul does not invoke the conclusion of James at the Council of Jerusalem in Acts 15 which concluded that one of the few requirements of Gentiles Christians was not to eat meat sacrificed to idols (Acts 15:20, 29). Perhaps Paul did not agree with this conclusion as an absolute. Perhaps he saw "laying down the law" as the wrong tactic to convince the Corinthians, or maybe he did not want to appear to be under the authority of Jerusalem. For whatever reason, Paul takes a tactic that in the end may have been more effective. He starts with where his audience is and moves them to where they need to be.

The idea that "there is no God but one" comes directly from the cornerstone of Jewish faith, the Shema of Deut. 6:4: "Hear O Israel: The Lord our God, the Lord is one." We call this belief monotheism, the belief in one God. The Corinthians argued, if there is only one God, then why should I worry about what I do at these pagan temples or with meat that has been sacrificed there?

An ancient city was filled with countless pagan temples to countless gods. Paul acknowledges this fact: **there are so-called gods** (8:5). Acts tells us that the presence of so many idols had seriously grieved Paul in the short time when he was in Athens (Acts 17:16). Despite this plethora of idols, Paul affirmed with the Corinthians that **for us there is but one God, the Father . . . and there is but one Lord, Jesus Christ** (8:5–6).

To some extent Paul is dealing tactfully with the Corinthians here. Apollos or others may have dismissed the pagan temples, but to him they were inhabited by demons (10:20). He tactfully begins with where they are: idols are nothing. He will then lead them to where he is at: idols involve demons. While he did not think that these demonic origins made the meat demon possessed—otherwise he would have prohibited them completely—he clearly wanted to inculcate a healthy distance from them. When we get to chapter 10, we will talk more about what might have motivated some Corinthians to want to visit pagan temples.

First Corinthians 8:6 is one of the earliest "creed" type statements in the New Testament. Notice the balance:

One God, the Father,
From whom all things and we for him,
One Lord, Jesus Christ
Through whom all things and we through him.[3]

What is so significant about this "creed" is the way it brings Christ into the heavenly administration of the creation. Many would say that Christ is here brought within divinity.[4] This verse is the first time on record that Christ is declared the agent of creation, the one through whom God made all things.

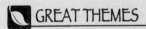 GREAT THEMES

1 Corinthians 8:6 gives us the first time in Scripture that Christ is declared God's agent in creation.

But whether this verse was originally understood in exactly this way or not, God used it among other verses to lead the church to these understandings. The first part declares God as the ultimate source of all things and the One for whom everything exists (Rev. 4:11). God thus determines what is truly valuable and good. If it is to His glory, it is good (Col. 3:17). If it does not glorify Him, it is not.

I suspect that the emphasis of the second part of the verse is on Christ as the one "through whom" God has brought salvation to us and indeed the whole world (Rom. 8:19–22). In other words, when it says that Jesus is the one "through whom [are] all things and we through him," it may emphasize that God has made possible the redemption of all things through Jesus. Nevertheless, the statement may also imply that Christ was somehow involved in the very creation of the world, that He was the agent of creation (John 1:3; Col. 1:16, Heb. 1:2). If so, Paul may be thinking of Jewish traditions that talked of how God made the world through His wisdom or through His Word (John 1:1).

We cannot help but wonder whether even at this early date Christians were already applying to Jesus Jewish traditions about God creating the world through His wisdom and His Word. Other parts of the New Testament clearly draw on these types of tradition.[5] Jesus thus becomes the full embodiment of God's wisdom for the world (Matt. 11:19). Like God's Word that speaks things into existence (Gen. 1:3) and that always does what it sets out to do (Isa. 55:11), Jesus is the full embodiment of God's will for the world. He is the one in whom "all things hold together" (Col. 1:17).

Paul grants the Corinthians the truth of their slogans. But that is not the end of the story, not for the Christian. It is not just about truth. It is about building up each other. **[N]ot everyone knows this** (8:7). Not everyone knows how impotent these idols are, **and since their conscience is weak, it is defiled** (8:7).

It is not immediately clear where these individuals would encounter such food. Were the Corinthians with "knowledge" actually taking others along with them to pagan temples to eat? It is possible, although we cannot be completely sure. Archaeology has revealed that some of these temples may actually have had rooms attached to them for dining.[6] Given what Paul will say in 8:10, it is more likely that members of the "knowing" group ate at some pagan temples.

Perhaps some of them occasionally served such meat during the fellowship meals Paul will mention in 11:20–34. How ironic it would be if some meat from a pagan temple was sometimes used for the Lord's Supper! In any case, Paul's comments are general—what if your freedom causes a brother or sister in Christ to stumble.

[F]ood does not bring us near to God (8:8). Paul's point is that this practice may be "allowed," but it does not actually benefit anyone. As Paul as said in 1 Cor. 6:12, all things may technically be lawful for me as a Christian since I am not under law, but that does not mean that I *should* do everything. Food will not make the knowing Corinthians any better, but it might actually harm the spiritual health of someone else. Therefore, why would they flaunt it or eat it in a way that tore down their brothers and sisters?

Paul now makes his point explicit. **Be careful, however, that the exercise of your freedom does not become a stumbling block to the weak** (8:9). Paul uses language that flatters the "knowing" party. He calls them "strong" of conscience because they are not bothered by eating meat that has been sacrificed to an idol. While he aligns himself in theory with their understanding, he clearly does so in order to move them to the opposite course of action. This is the same tactic we see him take repeatedly in this letter. He starts by affirming what he can in their position and then moves them in a more appropriate direction.

For [won't] **anyone with a weak conscience sees . . . be emboldened to eat what has been sacrificed to idols?** (8:10). The issue in this verse is someone who would eat at a pagan temple. Like the rooms archaeologists have found in the ruins of the Temple of Asclepius, any number of social functions might occur in such a place.

When we consider that a man like Erastus was involved in city politics (Rom. 16:23), the temptation to visit a pagan temple makes some sense. Anyone involved in politics or interested in climbing the corporate ladder knows that you almost have to "schmooze" to get anywhere. You have to attend public functions and events to circulate your personality. Clearly much of this type of activity would have taken place in conjunction with the city's religious events. Someone like Erastus would have been very drawn to participate in such activities at the temples.

Paul's vocabulary in these chapters is very interesting. Some of the words he uses appear nowhere else in all earlier Greek literature except in 1 Corinthians. Either Paul himself coined these terms or, more likely, they may have been words Greek speaking Jews used around the Mediterranean world. For example, the word "food sacrificed to idols" (*eidōlothuton*, 8:1) may be a word Jews made out of a Greek word that means "food sacrificed at a temple" (*hierothuton*, 10:28). It is a little like what some used to do when they called television, "hell-ovision." Paul "slams" such food by replacing the part of the word that meant "temple" (*hieron*) with the word for idol (*eidōlon*). The switch shows what such food really is—not sacred food but food offered to speechless marble, stone, and wood.

We can suggest the same with regard to Paul's reference to an "idol's temple" (*eidōleion*, 8:10). The names of many temples at Corinth would have ended in *–ion* like this word (for example, *Asklēpieion*, temple of Asclepius; *Apollōnion*; temple of Apollo). By calling these temples "eidoleions" instead of by their regular name, Paul not so subtly slammed them and pegged them for what they were—not temples to real gods but temples to non-existent idols.

So this weak brother, for whom Christ died, is destroyed by your knowledge. . . . [I]f what I eat causes my brother to fall into sin, I will never eat meat again, so that I will not cause him to fall (8:11–13). This is one of the most important statements in the New Testament on what to do when your conscience is okay with doing things that others do not feel free to do. Christians frequently disagree on issues of lifestyle and action. First Corinthians 8–10, along with Romans 14, provide us with the most important biblical passages on how to work through disputable matters.

Paul's instructions to the Corinthians do not call their freedom into question, nor does he deny their understanding. What he does is reorient their thinking from themselves to others. It is not about your rights, he tells them. It is also about others.

To be sure, there are dangers on every side of this question. On the one hand are those whose consciences are not active enough. These are individuals who feel free to do things that God does not accept. Paul will allude to such people in Rom. 14:22: "Blessed is the man who does not condemn himself by what he approves." In other words, it is possible to be convinced wrongly about what you are free to do. Paul may take a relativist position on some issues, but he does not take one on *all* issues.[7]

On the other hand, there are always those who disagree with us but whose consciences are not endangered by our freedom. For example, some Christians do not believe a person should wear wedding rings or any rings, for that matter.[8] Yet my wedding ring is no threat to their conscience. I put no stumbling block before them by wearing a ring around them. Clearly I should not have an offensive or unloving attitude in the exercise of my "freedom." But if my attitude is pure, then we can agree to have different understandings.[9]

Paul was dealing with a situation where an action that some felt free to do might have endangered the faith of another Christian. Finding an exact equivalent to Paul's situation is not easy. It might be something like if a converted Satanist were encouraged to participate in Halloween or see movies with elements of his previous life in it. The issue of Christians and alcohol might also have some similar connotations, even if it is little further removed. What if a Christian were to say their conscience did not bother them to have one glass of wine with their meal, and they promoted this idea to an ex-alcoholic?

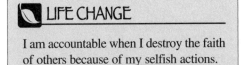

LIFE CHANGE

I am accountable when I destroy the faith of others because of my selfish actions.

Paul's bottom line is clear. None of us are in this Christian walk alone. The way I behave toward others, especially my fellow Christians, is the way I am behaving toward Christ. I am accountable when I destroy the faith of others because of my selfish actions. When I do it to them, I do it to Christ.

ENDNOTES

1. The quotation marks are not in the NIV.
2. I have added the quotation marks to the NIV text.
3. Author's translation.
4. Most famously, by L. W. Hurtado, *One God, One Lord: Early Christian*

Devotion and Ancient Jewish Monotheism (Philadelphia: Fortress, 1988) and now in *At the Origins of Christian Worship: The Context and Character of Earliest Christian Devotion* (Grand Rapids: Eerdmans, 1999).

5. Particularly in places like John 1:1–14; Col. 1:15–20; and the gospel of Matthew.

6. For example, the temple of Asclepius in Corinth.

7. Relativism is the position that holds rights and wrongs to be a matter of cultures or individuals. All of us have some issues on which we are relativist. More typically, we call these "convictions," areas in which we feel God requires something of us that he does not require of others.

8. Following their understanding of verses like 1 Tim. 2:9 and 1 Pet. 3:3.

9. Causing someone to stumble is very different from doing something about which they are personally offended.

WHAT ABOUT IDOL MEAT:
PAUL AS
AN EXAMPLE

1 Corinthians 9:1–27

This chapter divides into three basic parts. In the first, Paul makes it clear to the Corinthians that he has all the rights of an apostle like Peter or James, the Lord's brother (9:1–14). In the second part, he indicates to them why he has not availed himself of these rights, namely, to benefit the furtherance of the gospel (9:15–23). The final verses, 9:24–27, serve as a kind of conclusion to the chapter, where Paul reminds the Corinthians what the goal is and how to work toward it.

First Corinthians 9:1–14 reinforces our sense that some at Corinth either questioned or outright rejected Paul's authority. **Am I not free? Am I not an apostle? Have I not seen Jesus our Lord?** (9:1). When Paul calls himself free, he identifies himself with the Corinthians. They feel free to eat meat offered to idols (8:9). Paul also is free in conscience—he will tell them in a moment that he is not "under law" (9:20).

Paul also considers himself an apostle, someone sent with a commission from God. For Paul, this claim presupposed that he had seen the risen Christ after His crucifixion. Paul considered himself the last one Christ commissioned this way (15:8). This would not qualify him to be one of the Twelve, the original disciples. He did not fit the qualifications of a replacement for Judas because he had not followed Jesus from the time of John the Baptist and throughout his earthly ministry (Acts

1:21–22). But he was an apostle of the sort Barnabas apparently was, someone who had witnessed and received a commission from Christ after He rose from the dead.

The Corinthians themselves were proof that Paul was commissioned in this way: **For you are the seal of my apostleship in the Lord** (9:2). Paul tells them that to deny his authority and apostleship was tantamount to denying their own Christianity. These verses remind us of what he had said at the end of 1 Corinthians 4 about being their "father" in the Lord: "Even though you have ten thousand guardians in Christ, you do not have many fathers, for in Christ Jesus I became your father through the gospel" (4:15).

After this short introduction to the chapter, Paul now mounts a defense of his "rights" as an apostle. **Don't we have the right to food and drink . . . to take a believing wife along with us . . . ? Or is it only I and Barnabas who must work for a living?** (9:3–6).

This comment is a rare window into the private lives and the public ministries of the early Christians. For example, we learn that they also conducted itinerant ministries like Paul, somewhat like the district super-intendents, general superintendents, and bishops of our day. However, unlike today, they probably stayed in one place for longer periods of time before moving on. We learn that Peter, James the brother of Jesus, and the majority of the apostles were married and took their wives along with them as they ministered from place to place.[1]

We learn that most of them accepted the support of those to whom they ministered. Only Paul and Barnabas, for reasons we will soon see, did not accept such patronage from the churches where they were minis-tering. Paul's reference to food and drink thus relates to the mundane sup-port a person needs to live. While Paul and Barnabas worked so they could secure food and drink on their own, the other apostles accepted these things from the churches.

Paul then gives three examples from everyday life to make his point: One **[w]ho serves as a soldier . . .** [one] **[w]ho plants a vineyard . . .** [one] **[w]ho tends a flock** (9:7). In other words, Paul claims to have every right to the support of the Corinthians. We remind ourselves of the overall context of 1 Corinthians 9. He is telling the Corinthians that just because a person has freedom and "rights" does not always mean that a person should use or exploit those rights, especially if doing so has adverse effects on others. Paul insists that he has every right to the same privileges that other apostles—even Peter and James—have.

After three examples from everyday life, Paul supports his point from Scripture. **For it is written in the Law of Moses: "Do not muzzle an ox while it is treading out the grain."** (9:9). Paul here uses spiritual interpretation to show a deeper truth behind an Old Testament verse. The original meaning of Deut. 25:4 probably did have something to do with literal oxen. After all, God's eye is on the sparrow! (Matt. 10:29–31).

But Jesus and Paul model for us the fact that applying the Scripture is not just a matter of scientifically determining the original meaning. There are broader spiritual principles we can infer from its words. God inspires Paul here to see in this isolated comment the truth that it is appropriate for those served to provide for and honor those who serve them. We remember Paul's comment in 2 Thess. 3:10 to those who do not work, but want the benefits of the Christian community: "If a man will not work, he shall not eat."[2]

Deuteronomy 25:4 thus demonstrates Paul's right to the support of the Corinthians: **Yes, this was written for us** (9:10). In the next four verses Paul will reiterate his point with a number of other metaphors and examples. In verse 11 he uses the example of a plowman, who shares in the harvest.

In 1 Cor. 9:13–14 Paul uses the example of the priests in the temple being supported in their work. **In the same way, the Lord has commanded that those who preach the gospel should receive their living from the gospel.** We remember the saying of Jesus that "the worker is worth his keep" (Matt. 10:10).

The principle that Paul lays down is simple and hopefully one that does not need emphasis. We should materially support those through whom God ministers to us. Some churches hesitate to pay their ministers too much. After all, some think he or she only works one day a week. We certainly do find Scriptures that impugn Christian laziness (2 Thess. 3:6–15). But most pastors work far more than their congregations know. Many work constantly, are on call 24/7, and must live with the absence of any privacy or "space" to call their own. In the end, *all* Christian workers are worth their keep, and we dishonor God if we do not support them as materially as we would a worker in any other service.

Paul has now put himself in a position of strength. He has confirmed the indebtedness of the Corinthian congregation to him. Not only are they not his patrons—he is their patron. They owe him; he does not owe them! **And I am not writing this in the hope that you will do such things for me** (9:15).

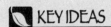

KEY IDEAS

Christian workers are worth their keep, and we dishonor God if we do not support them as materially as we would a worker in any other service.

One aspect of the ancient world that we need to keep in mind as we read these verses is the fact that it frequently operated on the basis of informal "patron-client" relationships. In such relationships, a "have" (patron) supported a "have-not" (client) materially. The have-not did not earn or merit such "grace." The patron or "have" did it for other reasons, such as the prestige of being noble or various other favors a have-not might render. In return, the have-not, the "client," returned whatever honor or service was appropriate.

In some parts of the Roman Empire, the newly rich would compete for status by accruing as many clients as they could.[3] Such clients might be expected to come to the patron's house once a day and do whatever menial tasks the patron required. In return they would get at least one meal that day along with the possibility of future help. The entanglements of patron-client relationships provide us with a good explanation for why Paul on principle did not receive material support from the churches where he was ministering. He would take support from churches elsewhere, such as the support he received from the Philippian church while he was at Thessalonica (Phil. 4:15–16). But he refused support from the cities where he currently served.

So Paul and Barnabas both worked while they ministered so that they could be free to preach the truth without worrying about such power struggles.

On an earthly plane, Paul might boast of this status. **Yet when I preach the gospel, I cannot boast, for I am compelled to preach**

(9:16). Here is another subtle reminder that their boasting attitude is wrong. Paul uses himself as an example of someone who might boast on a human level, but could not boast ultimately in the light of God's grace. He did not conduct his mission work because he liked it or because he found it rewarding. He did it because God had called him "from birth" to the task, particularly to the task of preaching to the Gentiles (Gal. 1:15–16).

Some have used Paul's own feelings to argue that you should not to go into ministry unless God will not let you do anything else. We should be careful not to make absolute statements, but there is probably some truth to this sentiment. Would Paul have survived the intense persecution and opposition he faced, "conflicts on the outside, fears within" (2 Cor. 7:5), if he had not had within him the absolute confidence that God had called him to this task and mission? Ministry can become a war zone; mission work too. A sense of an unwavering call—"woe to me if I do not preach the gospel"—is of inestimable value in tough times.

What then is my reward? Just this: that in preaching the gospel I may offer it free of charge, and so not make use of my rights in preaching it (9:18). Unlike the way the Corinthians were treating their fellow Christians, Paul did not abuse

 **LIFE CHANGE**

Ministry can become a war zone. An unwavering sense of God's call is of inestimable value in tough times. We can extend this principle to every Christian—knowing you are in the center of God's will is an awesome defense against the assaults of discouragement.

his "rights" as an apostle. His focus was not on himself but on the furtherance of the gospel. In contrast, the Corinthians were only looking out "for number one."

Though I am free and belong to no man, I make myself a slave to everyone, to win as many as possible (9:19). The contrast Paul makes here between himself and the Corinthians could hardly be greater. They think of themselves as kings (1 Cor. 4:8); he operates as a slave. His goal is to bring as many people to faith as possible. He is willing to surrender his rights for the betterment of God's people and the salvation of the lost.

The next two verses are of great value in understanding Paul's ethics and theology of mission. **To the Jews I became like a Jew, to win the Jews. To those under the law I became like one under the law (though I myself am not under the law), so as to win those under the law** (9:20). Interpreters have sometimes portrayed Paul as devaluing the Jewish law. On the contrary, we know from Romans that he actually valued it and affirmed it as holy and good (Rom. 7:12). But he clearly believed that it was powerless to make a person acceptable with God (Rom. 3:20), and its greatest function was in showing us our need for Christ (Gal. 3:24). A person in Christ is no longer judged by the standards of the Jewish law but on the basis of our relationship with Christ. We are no longer "under the law."

Yet we have no reason to think that Paul simply threw his keeping of the Jewish law out the window. My sense is that he probably continued to keep the Jewish law except when it came into conflict with higher Christian principles. Thus Paul probably continued to observe the Jewish Sabbath except when it came into conflict with his Christian values.[4]

Similarly, he probably observed the food and purity laws except when it came into conflict with his Christian values, and we know that they occasionally did. At Antioch, Peter and Barnabas separated from Gentile Christians, no doubt, because of purity laws (Gal. 2:11–14). Paul opposed their actions vigorously. He never argues that they have misunderstood the Law. His argument is rather that they are hypocrites for expecting the Gentiles to follow rules that they themselves do not keep (Gal. 2:14).

On the other hand, Acts tells us that Paul circumcised Timothy, likely so he could help with the Jewish side of Paul's ministry (Acts 16:3).[5] Acts 21 strongly implies that Paul still kept the law to a significant degree (21:20–26). While Paul vigorously affirmed that he was not under the Jewish law, he did not exploit such freedom at the expense of the gospel. Paul seems to have respected the Jewish law even though he did not feel obligated to some elements of it.

Christians often will find themselves in disagreement on various issues with other Christians. Paul makes it clear what our attitude should be in such circumstances. There is a place for standing up for the truth of the gospel. Paul models this kind of protest when he stood up before the church at Antioch and opposed Peter. But standing up for our own rights is not such a situation. If it does not hurt you and it helps others, why not become a "Jew to the Jews"? Why not become **weak** to the weak, so you can win and preserve the weak?

Correspondingly, **to those not having the law I became like one not having the law . . . so as to win those not having the law** (9:21). Here we see the reason why Paul could abandon purity laws when the unity of the church was in question. Here is the basis for the false accusations that Paul taught Jews not to keep the laws of Moses (Acts 21:21) and that we should sin so that grace would come (Rom. 3:8). Perhaps this teaching had caused problems with the Corinthians. Perhaps they had also concluded wrongly that a Christian could do any and everything. Perhaps the man sleeping with his stepmother had drawn this conclusion.

But Paul makes it clear that he is under "Christ's law" and still under "God's law." Much of the Jewish law still fell in this category, including its teaching on sexual immorality and idolatry. Paul was no antinomian, someone who rejects all law and moral standards all together. He had as much to say against the moral libertarian as against the Pharisaic legalist. His mission principle was **"I have become all things to all men so that by all possible means I might save some"** (9:22).

First Corinthians 9:24–27 constitute the conclusion of the chapter. Paul slides neatly from how he conducts himself to a general statement of how he and the Corinthians can both make it to the end. **Run in such a way as to get the prize** (9:24). Paul did not mean to say that only one person or one Corinthian would make it to the end. But he makes it clear that the Christian "race" is not something to run in a half-hearted manner. It is a race we should run "all out" with all our heart. Many of us do not run so seriously or vigorously. While "winning isn't everything," we should run the Christian race as if it is—not because we are in competition with other Christians but to show God how important He is to us.

Everyone who competes in the games goes into strict training (9:25). Paul ran the race of this life this way. Wherever he was in the race at any point, his approach was "Forgetting what is behind and straining toward what is ahead, I press on toward the goal to win the prize for which God has called me heavenward in Christ Jesus" (Phil. 3:13–14). As he says here, **I do not run like a man running aimlessly; I do not fight like a man beating the air. No, I beat my body and make it my slave so that after I have preached to others, I myself will not be disqualified for the prize** (9:26–27).

It seems doubtful that Paul really thought his eternal salvation was in danger. His remarks were calculated far more to remind the Corinthians of their need than to express any fear on Paul's part. Nevertheless, this statement affirms the possibility that even someone whose faith was as remarkable as Paul's might not make it to the end. The prize that Paul has in mind is to be "saved" on the Day of Judgment (9:22).

The idea of disciplining our body is a very appropriate metaphor for Paul to use. After all, it is my flesh that is most susceptible to temptation. In Galatians and Romans, Paul speaks of our flesh as the part of us whose desires are diametrically opposed to the will of God (Gal. 5:17). As an athlete trains his or her body, Christians must rely on the Spirit to hold sway over their physical flesh so that they are not "in the flesh" spiritually. The Corinthians needed to subordinate those desires that conflicted with their "training." The situation at Corinth with regard to idols and meat sacrificed to idols was no exception.

ENDNOTES

1. Traditioins like the Roman Catholic and Orthodox churches do not interpret the word "sister" in this passage as a reference to a wife. Nevertheless, this interpretation seems the most likely.

2. We must be careful not to make this truth into an absolute such that it contradicts the equally valid principles Jesus laid down of caring for destitute and impoverished (Matt. 25:31–46). Both Jesus and Paul indicate that most of God's injunctions are universal but allow for exceptional circumstances (Luke 14:5).

3. For more details, see Malina and Rohrbaugh, *A Social-Science Commentary on the Synoptic Gospels*, 326–29.

4. Jesus got into trouble for letting his disciples violate the Sabbath in Mark 2:24. We would have preferred Jesus to say something like, "They aren't doing

anything unlawful." But that is not Jesus' reaction. His reply is that there is a time when more important values lead us to make exceptions to the Law.

5. We remember that Paul vigorously told the Galatians not to become circumcised (Gal. 5:2–4) and boasts to them in the fact that he did not circumcise Titus (Gal. 2:3). While it is possible that Paul came to this conclusion after he had circumcised Timothy (which would require that Galatians be written during or after Paul's second missionary journey), a more likely reason is that Timothy was half-Jewish. It would thus be a good of example of Paul becoming a Jew to the Jews so that he might win the Jews.

WHAT ABOUT IDOL MEAT:
BACK TO THE
SUBJECT OF IDOLATRY

1 Corinthians 10:1–11:1

1. THE DANGER OF IDOLATRY (10:1–13)

Paul now slowly returns to the topic of meat offered to idols and sexual immorality, first by addressing the danger of idolatry. Some scholars have noted tensions in the way Paul discusses meat offered to idols in 1 Corinthians 10 and the way he did in chapter 8. While he seems in theory to have no problem with it in chapter 8, he now adopts a more negative tone. The key is to realize that he is tactfully starting where they are and moving them in a more profitable direction. So, he begins this section appealing to Israel's history.

Like the Israelites in the desert, **our forefathers were . . . all baptized into Moses in the cloud and in the sea** (10:1–2). Paul is constructing somewhat of an allegory of the exodus story. He compares the Israelites passing through the Red Sea with a kind of baptism. The Corinthians have also been baptized, albeit in the name of Jesus Christ. They are in the fold, they have become the people of God just as the Israelites who passed through the Red Sea were.

Just as Christians partake of the Lord's Supper, eating the same spiritual food and drink that represents the body and blood of our Lord, the Israelites also **all ate the same spiritual food . . . they drank from the spiritual rock that accompanied them, and that rock was Christ**

(10:3–4). Given the clear reference to the Lord's Supper in 10:16–17, Paul clearly has what we call communion in mind. As we will see at the end of chapter 11, the Corinthians also had problems in the way they practiced the Lord's Supper, which at this point in church history was an actual meal.

Paul did not see the Lord's Supper as the blasé ritual so many see it as today. We have every reason to think that he believed it to be charged with power for the believer. It is *spiritual* food and drink that sustains the Christian. But perhaps some Corinthians were tempted to think it powerful all by itself. If some of us undervalue its importance, others overvalue it. Some Christians today think they will be accepted by God if they only participate regularly in the Eucharist, the Lord's Supper.

Paul makes it clear that neither baptism nor the Lord's Supper are enough. **Nevertheless, God was not pleased with most of them; their bodies were scattered over the desert** (10:5). As Heb. 3:17 confirms, it is possible to start out your spiritual journey, to be baptized, to participate in the sacraments of the church, and yet not make it to the end. Here was a subtle warning to the Corinthians to watch how they lived, as well as a reminder to us that it is not enough merely to participate in Christian life and church. We must live it.

Paul uses this opportunity to reinforce some of the teaching he has already given in the letter thus far. **Now these things occurred as examples to keep us from setting our hearts on evil things as they did** (10:6). Some Corinthians were guilty of this mind-set. **Do not be idolaters, as some of them were** (10:7). Here is a hint that Paul thought there was more to the Corinthian protests than just a taste for meat. Sitting down to eat and drink probably alludes to sitting down at a pagan temple, something Paul has already discouraged (8:10) and will now basically forbid (10:20–21). Israel ate such food while Moses was on Mt. Sinai, and they were soundly judged.[1]

We should not commit sexual immorality, as some of them did (10:8). Paul has also told them how inappropriate sexual immorality is for a Christian in chapters 5 and 6. The story to which Paul alludes seems particularly relevant to the Corinthians. Numbers 25:1–9 tells the story of how God sent a plague on Israel for their sexual immorality, which was associated with idolatry in that instance as well. If Paul had the context of this story in mind, then the prostitution he mentions in chapter 6 may very well have been associated with pagan temples.

These things happened . . . as warnings for us . . . be careful that you don't fall! (10:11–12). Paul's warning continues. If the Israelites were not exempt from God's judgment when they practiced idolatry and violated God's clear will, then the Corinthians certainly will not escape. The only appropriate course of action is to renounce idolatry and actions that are associated with it.

No temptation has seized you except what is common to man. . . . But when you are tempted, he will also provide a way out (10:13). This verse is extremely important, even if often overlooked by Christians today. Paul asserts not only that the Corinthians should be victorious over the temptation to commit idolatry, but that no temptation is ever insurmountable for the Christian.

Contrary to the sentiment of so many Christians today, Paul never asserts that a Christian will inevitably sin.[2] Rather, Paul affirms the power of God

LIFE CHANGE

Paul teaches that the power of God is strong enough to give you victory over any temptation that comes your way.

to give victory over any temptation that might come our way. He tells the Corinthians, and thus us, that no one will ever face a temptation that God cannot enable them to conquer.

Paul probably had very concrete circumstances in view in this context. For example, someone like Erastus might have felt pressure to participate in activities at a pagan temple, since he held prominent public office at one time. Paul assures the Corinthians that God always has an escape plan. Such an escape does not mean God will always keep us from suffering or pain. But God always makes it possible for us to do the right thing when we will submit ourselves to His will.

2. PAUL'S FINAL ANSWER (10:14–11:1)

Therefore . . . flee from idolatry (10:14). Paul now gets down to business. Much of what he has written in the last two chapters has laid the theological groundwork for his conclusion. He has affirmed in theory the freedom of those with a "strong" conscience. He has set forth and illustrated the principle that building up others is more important than getting our rights. He has also affirmed the importance of remaining true to God in our lives, particularly in the area of idolatry. Paul is not now contradicting the freedom he theoretically extended to the Corinthians in chapter 8. He is rather getting down to what their motivations are.

[T]he cup of thanksgiving . . . the bread that we break (10:16). Paul seems to target eating at pagan temples particularly in the next few verses. In 8:10 he has urged the Corinthians not to eat at such a temple because of the harmful effect it would have on others in the church. Now Paul will show that eating at such a temple does not even make sense for a Christian.

In the process of making this point, Paul leaves us with a statement that is so magisterial that many churches say it every time they celebrate the Lord's Supper. **Because there is one loaf, we, who are many, are one body, for we all partake of the one loaf** (10:17). Paul makes this comment to remind the Corinthians that eating a sacred meal implies the unity of all those partaking both with one another and with the divinity whom the meal honors and supplicates.

We will discuss the Lord's Supper in more detail at the end of 1 Corinthians 11, but Paul's words remind us of some important elements to communion that are unfortunately missing from so many of our churches. There is the danger that we will not meditate on Christ's sacrificial death on our behalf. The Lord's Supper is to remind us of Christ's sacrifice. His sacrifice is both the satisfaction of God's justice and the cleansing of our sins. Repentance and thankfulness are thus appropriate to the occasion. Indeed, the bulk of Christian tradition calls the Lord's Supper the "Eucharist," which means thanksgiving.

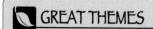 **GREAT THEMES**

The very word *communion* implies that it is an act that binds us with each other as well as with God.

But the element most missing from the celebration of the Lord's Supper in our circles is the absence of any sense of the unity it is supposed to represent. While the use of individual cups and wafers is understandably convenient and hygienic for serving a large congregation, it is a symptom of the hyper-individualism of our culture. The Lord's Supper was never meant to be an individual experience. The very word *communion* ironically implies that it is an act that binds us with each other as well as with God.

But ultimately it is the attitude of the person that matters, not the method. Paul indicts the Corinthian church because the Lord was not the Lord of His own supper. They were treating the Lord's own family with contempt at a dinner in his honor. We will rightly fulfill the purposes of the Lord's Supper today if we call to mind the purpose of Christ's death and the hope of His return, if we renew His place as Lord of our lives, and if we rightly discern His family as our own, as brothers and sisters partaking of His supper with us.

Do not those who eat the sacrifices participate in the altar? (10:18). In other words, those who made sacrifices in the Old Testament and then ate those sacrifices were participating in the worship of God and receiving spiritual benefit from the connection. **[B]ut the sacrifices of pagans are offered to demons** (10:20). The person at the pagan temple makes a harmful and defiling connection with the demon that inhabits that temple, and **[y]ou cannot drink the cup of the Lord and the cup of demons too** (10:21).

 WHAT OTHERS SAY

"One of these [means of obtaining help] is the Lord's Supper, which, of his infinite mercy, he hath given for this very end; that through this means we may be assisted to attain those blessings which he hath prepared for us; that we may obtain holiness on earth, and everlasting glory in heaven." John Wesley, "The Duty of Constant Communion"

Here is the conflict between the Corinthians and Paul. On the one hand, the Corinthians are saying that an "idol is nothing in the world" (8:4), and Paul agrees (10:19–20). But at the same time, there are spiritual forces involved in pagan temples, demonic forces. While Paul did not think that this demonic presence continued in the meat itself, the idea of eating *at an actual temple* went too far. It implied allegiance and acceptance of the demon of the temple. **Are we trying to arouse the Lord's jealousy? Are we stronger than he?** (10:22). These kinds of actions were just begging for the Lord to show them who the true God really was.

I grew up with regular reminders of the King James verse "avoid the very appearance of evil" (1 Thess. 5:22, KJV). While a better translation would be to avoid every *form* of evil, the sentiment that a Christian should not dabble with evil is clearly true. The appropriate attitude is not to try to get as close to evil as we are allowed to. The heart of a Christian should not desire evil in the first place.

A youth once asked me how far he could go physically with a girl friend before he would go to hell. But this was the wrong attitude all together. The heart of a Christian is not oriented around how much he or she can get away with. A Christian wants to please God and asks what course of action will most glorify Him. Apparently, some of the Corinthians wanted to get as close to idolatry as they could without sinning. Paul indicates that what they should really do is to flee from idolatry, to get as far away from it as they could.

Paul recaps his argument from chapter 8: **"Everything is permissible"—but not everything is beneficial . . . Nobody should seek his own good, but the good of others** (10:23–24). They may not be under the law, but the question is not what they *can* do. It is what will *glorify God* the most. The question is what will be most helpful, most constructive, and what will help the others in the church the most.

Paul has strongly implied that they should not eat at a pagan temple. Now he will cover the other circumstances in which they might encounter meat that had been sacrificed to an idol. **Eat anything sold in the meat market . . . for, "The earth is the Lord's, and everything in it."** (10:25–26). Paul did not see anything evil inhering in the meat because of its contact with a pagan god. The meat is God's, Paul says, so he saw no problem eating it. Just do not ask the seller of the meat where it came from.

Paul has similar comments to make in Romans: "I am fully convinced that no food is unclean in itself. But if anyone regards something as unclean, then for him it is unclean" (Rom. 14:14). It was not the meat itself that caused the problem but the context. We can wonder whether Paul's teaching here impacts what we might think about issues like whether a Christian can celebrate Halloween or whether objects that have been associated with witchcraft or Satanism have evil inside them. Many Christians have similarly opposed books and movies because some of the characters in the story are witches.

In some ways, these issues come closest to the one Paul was addressing at Corinth. I know I would not feel comfortable with a book of witchcraft or

Satanism in my house. I can certainly imagine someone who had come out of Satanism strongly resisting Halloween. On the other hand, I personally grew up without making any such associations with Halloween. I also know that most children would make no association between the characters of some books and true witchcraft any more than I did with the *Wizard of Oz.*

In short, this is a matter where the consciences of some Christians will be strong and others will be weak.

Paul now discusses another potential situation. **If some unbeliever invites you to a meal . . . eat whatever is put before you** (10:27). Just as at the meat market, Paul says not to ask where meat came from if you are eating with an unbeliever. The meat itself is not unclean; it is the Lord's.

But if anyone says to you, "This has been offered in sacrifice," **then do not eat it** (10:28). The situation Paul seems to picture is one in which you and another Christian are at a third person's house. The Christian with you tells you that the meat you are about to eat came from a pagan temple. For the sake of your brother's conscience, Paul says you should abstain from eating the meat.

However, even in this case you are not abstaining because of your relationship with God, but to protect the conscience of your brother, **[f]or** **why should my freedom be judged by another's conscience? If I take** **part in the meal with thankfulness, why am I denounced because of** **something I thank God for?** (10:29–30). Here is another reminder that there is genuine room for different understandings among Christians.

In several places the New Testament tells us that the entire Old Testament law is summed up in the command to love God and love our neighbor.[3] It is clear enough what it means to love our neighbor: to act and think in such a way that we have the true benefit of others in view. Sometimes it is more difficult to figure out concretely what it means to love God with all our heart. In this issue of meat offered to idols Paul gives us a fair guideline for what this principle looks like: **So whether you eat or drink or whatever you do, do it** **all for the glory of God** (10:31). In other words, to the best of your knowledge live and think in such a way that you are always doing and thinking what will honor Him the most. Colossians gives us a similar dictum: "whatever you do, whether in word or in deed, do it all in the name of the Lord Jesus, giving thanks to God the Father through him" (Col. 3:17).

What glorifies God is never to let our rights and freedoms in the Lord become something that will **cause anyone to stumble** (10:32). This principle was Paul's own, as he tried **to please everybody in every way. . . . Follow my example, as I follow the example of Christ** (10:33–11:1).

Christians have always struggled to distinguish between "non-negotiables" and issues on which God allows for some variation among Christians. The extremes are not usually the issues that Christians rankle over. Few would argue that a Christian can sometimes murder, nor do many worry about keeping the Jewish Sabbath on Saturday. But a host of questions live in the middle ground, particularly on ground that no New Testament author could possibly have imagined. First Corinthians 8–10 give us some guidelines, and Romans 14 helps even more.

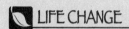

LIFE CHANGE

Being a Christian is not about getting your rights or exercising your freedom. It is about glorying God and building up others.

First, act from faith and conviction (Rom. 14:5, 23), not from an attitude that is selfish or evil. God knows when you are making an argument because you want an excuse to sin. Second, be careful. It is possible to be convinced wrongly that what you are arguing for is okay when in fact it is not (Rom. 14:22). Thirdly, if you are convinced you are free to do something that other Christians question, act in such a way that builds up the body of Christ and does not hurt the conscience of anyone else. Being a Christian is not about getting your rights or exercising your freedom. It is about glorifying God and building up others.

ENDNOTES

1. Exodus 32.

2. We read Rom. 7:7–24 wrongly if we take it as a statement of some ongoing struggle of Paul with his flesh. Romans 7:5–6 make it clear that Paul is expanding on the situation of someone controlled by the sinful nature in those verses. As Rom. 7:6 indicates, Paul would not place himself in that category.

3. For example, Matt. 22:37–40; Rom. 13:8–10; James 2:8.

15

CHRISTIAN TRADITIONS AND WORSHIP:
NO LONGER MALE AND FEMALE

1 Corinthians 11:2–16

1. LOCATING THIS PART OF THE LETTER

It is not clear whether 1 Corinthians 11 addresses a Corinthian question. Paul may simply be returning to things he has heard about in the church. On the other hand, the way 11:2 is worded may indicate that the Corinthians had boasted at this point in their letter about how well they were keeping certain Christian traditions. If so, they may have been surprised to find out that Paul did not approve.[1]

Paul has just finished the preceding section by telling them to imitate him (8:1–11:1). He begins the next thought with praise for the way they already remember him: **remembering me in everything and for holding to the teachings** (11:2). The word "teachings" here refers to "traditions" Paul taught them.

These traditions were beliefs and practices that were common to "the churches of God" (11:16) and probably his churches in particular. Here we find an element of Paul that is often underappreciated: his appeals to common Christian belief and practice. First Corinthians 11 seems to deal with two such traditions. It is not exactly clear what the first tradition was, but Paul's response deals with head coverings in worship. The second tradition Paul discusses is the practice of the Lord's Supper (11:17–34). We will find a few more traditions of this sort before the letter is through.

2. TRADITION 1: THERE IS NO LONGER "MALE AND FEMALE" (11:3–16)

The way Paul begins his discussion of head coverings leads us to believe that, once again, the Corinthians are living out Paul's teaching in inappropriate ways. As usual, Paul begins by affirming them: he praises them for holding fast to the traditions he delivered to them (11:2). But apparently they were appropriating those traditions in a way that was divisive and causing disruption to the community.

One interesting suggestion is that some Corinthians were using the Christian principle "no longer male and female" in inappropriate ways. Scholars have long suggested that Paul's churches may have pronounced something like Gal. 3:28 at a person's baptism: "There is no longer Jew or Greek, there is no longer slave or free, there is no longer male and female; for you are all one in Christ Jesus" (NRSV). It is in the context of baptism that Paul cites this verse in Galatians (Gal. 3:27), and Colossians also presents this concept in the context of "putting on" the new person (Col. 3:11) when coming to Christ.

But apparently the Corinthians were trying to enact these heavenly principles on earth in a way that was inappropriate for their context. In 1 Corinthians 7 we have already seen Paul advising them to "retain the place in life that the Lord assigned" (1 Cor. 7:17). He tells slaves not to worry about the fact that they are slaves (7:21). Similarly, he commands Christian women to stay with their husbands whether they are Christian or not (7:10–11, 13). We found echoes of Gal. 3:28 in our exposition of that passage as well.

We can now make a fuller suggestion that certain women at Corinth were trying to exploit the spiritual principle of their equality in ways that led to disruption in the Corinthian church.[2] Perhaps some were trying to twist this principle to get out from "under the thumb" of their husbands, whether in regard to marriage or the appropriate head covering in the presence of other men. These kinds of suggestions are all speculative since we just do not have enough information to know for certain one way or another.

The idea that there are proper and improper ways to cover your head in worship has largely become a foreign idea in American Christianity.

152

We can still see traces of it in the tradition that a man should take his hat off indoors, as well as in the practice of women wearing bonnets and hats to church. While a number of Christian groups do attempt to keep the literal practice of these verses today, the vast majority of Christians immediately recognize a strong cultural element in the passage. This dimension is borne out by the fact that commentators have found it so hard to agree on exactly what these verses mean—a tell tale sign that the dynamics of this passage have a great deal to do with the culture of ancient Corinth.

Now I want you to realize that the head of every man is Christ, and the head of the woman is man, and the head of Christ is God (11:3). Paul here provides a general statement, the implications of which he will unfold in the verses that follow. The word the NIV translates as "now" can also mean "but," which may actually render Paul's train of thought more accurately: "I praise you for keeping the traditions, *but* you should keep in mind that…"

Before we go further we should observe that Paul is talking about husbands and wives in this passage, not about men and women in general. Paul does not say that every man is the head of every woman, only that the husband is the head of his wife. We come to this conclusion for several reasons. For example, the specific Greek words Paul uses (*anēr-gynē*) normally imply a husband-wife situation, a fact undisputed in the head-ship passages in the "household codes" of Ephesians and Colossians (Col. 3:18–19; Eph. 5:22–33). The husband-wife relationship also seems to fit best the dynamics of the argument that follows.

Headship in this passage implies both authority and point of origin. Some have tried to argue that headship only implied originally that something was the source of another thing, particularly a source of nourishment. Those who argue this way sometimes claim that the ancients did not know the function of the brain in the head and thus did not necessarily think of the head as exerting leadership or direction over the body.

On the one hand, the sense of a "head" as a point of origin is indeed one nuance of headship, as is the idea of the human head as the source of the body's nourishment. Notice in 1 Cor. 11:12 Paul's mention that the "woman came from man," making the man her "head" as a point of origin. Even more noteworthy in this vein is Col. 2:19, which speaks of

Christ as the head of the church, "from whom the whole body, supported and held together by its ligaments and sinews, grows as God causes it to grow." The head clearly nourishes the body in this verse.

But ultimately headship also implied authority for Paul, and the ancients did sometimes think of the head as the "ruler" of the body. For example, the ancient philosopher Plato taught hundreds of years before Christ that the relationship between a ruler and his or her people should be like that of the head to the rest of the body. When Paul said that the husband was the head of the wife here, he implied at least some degree of authority.

But we should not immediately jump to conclusions on how to apply this concept for several significant reasons. The first is the Corinthian context Paul is addressing. The uniqueness of the topic in these verses makes it clear that Paul is addressing a problem in Corinthian worship. While Paul does address the proper head covering for husbands in this passage (or rather lack thereof), the overall thrust of the passage seems more directed at wives.[3] In other words, there were likely women at Corinth who were shaming their husbands in worship because their heads were not properly covered.

It is not a desire to rationalize, but our eager longing to be faithful to the Scriptures that leads us to consider carefully the way in which the Corinthian situation might have impacted the way God inspired Paul to make this argument. We know from Paul's style throughout 1 Corinthians that he was very tactful in the way he dealt with problem issues. He often said things in ways that were effective in leading the Corinthians to the right conclusion—but which he scarcely would have put the same way if he were writing out of the blue. Paul's use of the headship concept here was calculated to lead a particular group of women to the right attitude and behavior. But it is not clear he would have emphasized the same point under different circumstances.

A second consideration is the significant difference between the first century context in general and our context. Again, we do not take this difference into consideration because we want to "get out of" doing what God requires. The differences between ancient and modern culture are vast at times, and to ignore them always pushes us in the direction of the

Pharisee and the Judaizer. Blindly doing exactly what the early Christians did is *not* doing what they did at all if the significance of the actions turns out to be significantly different in our world.

In the ancient world, there was nothing specifically or uniquely Christian about saying that a husband was the head of his wife. The Greek philosopher Aristotle wrote centuries before Christ that "the head of the household rules over both wife and children, and rules over both as free members of the household. . . . His rule over his wife is like that of a statesman over fellow citizens. . . . The male is naturally fitter to command than the female, except where there is a departure from nature."[4] When Paul urged these women to recognize their place in relation to their husbands, he was telling them to conform to the values of the non-Christian world, not to some new and heavenly principle. (Slavery was another value of the non-Christian world, rather than a universal, godly principle.)

We can also map American Christianity's heightened emphasis on male headship to the increased power women have had in American culture since World War II. We can see the same influence after World War II even on the Wesleyan tradition, which actually played an important role in the beginnings of the women's rights movement.[5] Our forebears believed they were working out the truth of the

 MANNERS AND CUSTOMS

In Paul's world, there was nothing uniquely Christian about saying that a husband was the head of his wife. It was when Paul stressed the equal sonship or value of women that he was being uniquely Christian.

gospel by opposing slavery as an institution and working for women to be able to vote. These men and women were extremely conservative by any contemporary standard. But they believed they were furthering the gospel by working toward these goals.

But the empowerment of women since the 1940s, along with the rise of secular feminism, has brought with it a backlash in some conservative Christian circles. The ordination of women has steadily declined since the fifties in groups that had traditionally ordained them. We have increasingly seen an emphasis in our circles on male headship passages—an emphasis that Paul would not likely place if he were writing to our current culture. Ironically, many Christians are moving away from what seems to be God's ideal while broader culture is moving closer to it. The idea that God equally considers both male and female His children is increasingly almost more a principle of the world than of the church!

A final point of interest in 1 Cor. 11:3 is the way in which Paul subordinates Christ to God. We have already discussed this aspect of Paul's Christology in 3:21–23 and will see it again in 15:28. Passages like these became strong bones of contention in the debates over the Trinity in the 300s, for the Trinity implies that Christ is equal to God. Those who argued against the Trinity used verses like these to emphasize the distinction between God the Father and Christ. Of course Paul was completely unaware of questions like these. God worked out these things for us in the church long after the New Testament was finished—another indication that God's Word is a living Word rather than a dead letter (Heb. 4:12).

Paul plays on a double meaning for the word *head* in 11:4–5. The one meaning is the literal head: that which is either covered or uncovered. But Paul has just defined the head of a man as Christ and the head of a wife as her husband. The sense of these verses is thus that the man who prays or prophesies with his head covered dishonors Christ, his "head." Similarly, a woman who prays or prophesies with her head uncovered dishonors her husband, her "head."

The first question we have is, "What is the 'covering' in this passage?" Not too long ago many in the Wesleyan tradition took this passage to be about women having long hair as a covering. A woman with short hair in the 1960s and 70s in such circles was sometimes stigmatized, labeled as a "liberal," or even thought to have "backslid." Many Mennonite women wear "prayer bonnets" in order to keep this passage.

These groups typify for us two of the main interpretations of these verses: (1) the idea that this passage was primarily about women having long versus short hair, and (2) the idea that this passage was primarily about a literal covering or veil, the general consensus of the ancient church.[6] A third view commands an increasing number of scholarly support as well: (3) the idea that this passage is about hair styles, particularly whether the hair is bound up and wrapped or allowed to hang loose.[7]

It is worth reminding ourselves that the connotations of the passage would have been immediately obvious to the Corinthians. Here we have yet another reminder that these words were not written originally to us and that we are reading a letter God inspired in the first place to someone else. From our current perspective, even with all our knowledge of Greek grammar and ancient culture, we must concede that the choice between these potential interpretations is difficult to make. Each interpretation makes good sense of some part of the passage.

We favor the interpretation most favored by the early church, namely, that Paul was primarily speaking of an actual covering on a woman's head. The phrase Paul uses for the man here, literally "having down the head," appears in the Greek version of Esther 6:12. In this passage, it seems to be an external covering, as it also seems to be in other non-Christian sources.[8] Thus the covering Paul had in view for a man was most likely an external covering of some sort rather than short hair.

The phrase Paul uses with regard to the woman, "with uncovered head," is a little more ambiguous, but probably refers to an actual covering and not simply long hair. The Greek version of Num. 5:18 uses this word in reference to an adulteress whose "uncovered" hair flows long, whose hair is not covered or bound at the top of her head. But even more revealing are the words of a contemporary Jew named Philo who uses exactly the same phrase as Paul. He clearly has a veil in mind, an external covering.[9] These examples from other Jewish writings push us toward seeing the covering in 1 Corinthians 11 as an actual covering on the head rather than simply long hair.

Notice that the main context Paul is addressing is that of worship. It is when a man or woman is *praying or prophesying* that the issue of head covering comes most into view. The setting for such prayer and prophecy was clearly the worship of the community—prophecy is not something you do in private. Paul is dealing with the practices of the "churches of God" here (11:16), not the personal devotions of the community's members. Since you could hardly change your hair length on your way to worship, Paul must either have some sort of removable covering or a hair style in view. The second interpretation (long vs. short hair) does not fit this kind of situation very well.

Several other features of ancient Mediterranean culture provide us with possible backgrounds for Paul's comments. For example, Corinth was a Roman colony whose citizens largely looked toward Rome for their cultural identity. Is the background for this passage the fact that Roman men and women typically wore a veil when offering sacrifices? On the whole it seems doubtful. It is possible that some Corinthian men thought they should cover their heads when praying or prophesying because of the Roman model. If so, this fact would explain Paul's claim that men should not cover their heads when praying. But this Roman practice does not begin to address the problem with women and veiling— the Roman model would actually have pushed them *toward* veiling their heads in worship!

We find conflicting values with regard to the veiling of women in Mediterranean culture at the time. On the one hand, the Roman influence seemed to allow for women to go around in public without a veil. Both the pictures of women on coins and in portraits at Corinth typically depict them with uncovered heads.[10] This factor alone might go some way toward explaining Paul's comments here. The secular culture of Corinth may have allowed women—especially women of status—to go unveiled.

On the other hand, we find several pertinent comments from Greek-speaking Jews of the day that may be helpful. We have already mentioned Philo, an extremely wealthy Jew from Alexandria. He wrote that an "innocent" woman regularly wore a head covering as a symbol of modesty.[11] Similarly, a Jewish novel about Joseph from this period (*Joseph and Aseneth*) has Joseph's future wife remove her veil when she converts to Judaism. She removes it because her virginity is restored when she converts. In other words, the veil symbolized a chaste, married woman, while a virgin did not cover her head.

 KEY IDEAS

The Corinthian women were shaming their husbands by unveiling their hair, which in that culture had sexual connotations, in front of the other men in the church as well as in front of God and angels.

We feel that these comments from the Jewish writings of the period provide us important background for understanding the dynamics of this passage in 1 Corinthians. Some of the Corinthian wives in the church were not using veils in worship, perhaps affirming their equality with men before God. However, in so doing they brought shame on their husbands and were dressing like "available" women. They acted this way in house churches where they were in close quarters with men who were not their own husbands. When we consider that a woman's hair was considered highly sensual in that culture, we have a volatile and shameful mix.

The third century church father Tertullian, writing in the early 200s, gives us some sense of what such a veil might have looked like. In his treatise *On the Veiling of Virgins*, Tertullian argues that a veil should cover a woman's hair down to her shoulders, but not her face.[12] The purpose was to cover the hair, which a number of ancient Greek physicians apparently thought was a sexual organ actually involved in the reproductive process.[13] While we find these Greek views of reproduction rather foreign to us today, they no doubt reflected the sensual connotations a woman's hair had in Greek culture.

In 11:5–6 Paul uses an "honor-shame" argument that appeals to the cultural values of the Mediterranean world. He compares the shame of an uncovered woman to that of a woman whose hair has been shaved off— **a disgrace**. Since you would not want this shame, he argues, women should cover their head. Note that Paul's ultimate point is not that short hair was a shame for women and long hair a shame for men. Rather, these are values he assumes and shares with the culture at large. He draws on them to make his point regarding the veiling of women.

A man ought not to cover his head, since he is the image and glory of God (11:7). Again, it is difficult for us today to follow Paul's line of thought here. His comments seem to assume things that were "common sense" to him but that are extremely unclear to us. On the whole, the thought seems to be that since a man "reflects" God's glory, the mirror should be uncovered so the glory shows. In contrast, Paul tells us elsewhere that Moses covered his face so that the Israelites would not see the glory of the old covenant fade away (2 Cor. 3:13). True glory is something that should be seen and displayed.

The Old Testament indicates that both men *and women* were created in the image of God. Genesis 1:27 clearly indicates that God made all humans in His image. Accordingly, we should notice that Paul does *not* go on to say that woman is the image of man in the next verse. Woman is also the image of God.

Similarly, the early Christians likely understood Ps. 8:4–5 to mean that God will eventually crown both men *and women* with glory and honor (Heb. 2:6–7, 10), the glory that we all fall short of when we sin (Rom. 3:23). We must take Paul's distinction in 1 Cor. 11:7–8 as a very narrow one aimed primarily at Corinthian problems. Other New Testament passages with a more eternal perspective do not use these concepts in these ways.

Thus as we just mentioned, Paul omits mention of the "image" when he turns to the woman/wife, who **is the glory of man. For man did not come from woman, but woman from man** (11:8). Here is an argument from the order and purpose of the creation of Eve, who was also wife to Adam.[14] Adam came first; the woman came from him. The purpose of her creation was to help him, rather than the other way around.

This argument from "birth order," as well as the stereotyping of all later men and women on the basis of Adam and Eve, had great force in Paul's day. It is more difficult for us to understand, since we tend to identify ourselves as unique individuals. We would not think that our relationships are somehow limited by those of our grandparents or great grandparents. A modern Western individualist thinks, "What does the relationship between Adam and Eve have to do with how my wife and I, two unique individuals, relate to each other?"

In heaven there will be no marriage and thus no subordination of wife to husband (Mark 12:25). In Christ, there is no longer male and female (Gal. 3:28). These are the eternal principles all right. But the Corinthian situation led Paul to reassert earthly priorities, a situation in which wives were using these principles to disrespect their husbands and were tempting other men in the process. We can see this fact in the way Paul draws back from this sense of hierarchy in the next few verses (11:11–12).

Paul thus reasserts that a wife is the glory of her husband. She should cover her head to show that she belongs to him, that she is "attached." A woman with her head uncovered is saying that she is available. She is disrespecting her husband, treating him as if he did not exist. The connotations were a little like if a wife today would take her wedding ring off, put on a sexy dress, and go somewhere where singles hang out to find dates.

For this reason, and because of the angels, the woman ought to have a sign of authority on her head (11:10). Scholars have found this verse incredibly difficult to understand, particularly the significance of the angels here. Our first question is the question of authority. What does Paul mean when he implies that the woman whose head is covered during prayer or prophecy has authority?

We can probably distinguish two ways in which this head covering provided the Corinthian woman with the authority to pray and prophesy. The first is in relation to the Christian community of which these women were a part. For a woman to pray or prophesy in this context was for her to play an unusual role of prominence. It automatically created social tension and awkwardness. It created awkwardness with regard to her husband in that his honor as a husband might be questioned. It created awkwardness with the other men because of the attention it drew toward her. It created tension with the wives of the other men for the same reasons. In this setting, the head covering brought stability to a socially tense situation. It said, "I am a respectable woman in proper relationship to my husband and to the other men in the church." It showed that her physical head was under the authority of her familial "head," her husband.

The second way in which it brought stability was in terms of the angels. The precise connotations of Paul's words are notoriously difficult, but a few points seem clear enough. The first is that praying and prophesying involve interaction with the spiritual realm, the realm that angels inhabit. A woman was thus interacting with the world of angels when she did these spiritual things.

Second, we should remember that the Jews thought of angels as far more male than anything else. For example, we will not find any angels in the Bible with female names. Indeed, ancient Jews and Christians interpreted Gen. 6:2 as angels having intercourse with human women.[15] A woman praying or prophesying was thus not only in the presence of the males in the church, but also in the presence of male-like angels.

The head covering thus confirmed a woman's modesty around men and angels. We will find the same dynamic later on in 11:13 when Paul mentions the fact that a woman is praying in the presence of God as well. God has no sexual organs and so is not literally male. Nevertheless, the language of revelation refers to Him in masculine terms most of the time. Some of the same basic dynamics thus apply. How comfortable would we be to pray naked to God? Show some decency, we might say, put on some clothes before you pray. So Paul suggests a woman should cover her head before she prays. It was the modest and decent thing to do.

First Corinthians 11:11–12 are a good indication that Paul has only invoked issues of hierarchy to address the situation in Corinthian worship. He feels compelled to balance the picture out with the value of women in the Christian equation. The head covering was necessary given the social implications of going without one. But ultimately, male and female are equal spiritual beings.

We have already mentioned verse 13 above. Paul invokes the "common sense" of the Corinthians. This common sense involved (1) the fact that an uncovered woman was considered immodest in the presence of other men, and (2) the fact that God is at least putatively male. Paul asks them, doesn't this situation feel wrong to you?

These next few "common sense" questions are a kind of climax to the section. The fact that these climactic questions address the covering of women confirms that the role of women in Corinthian worship was the underlying problem. Perhaps some men also needed to stop veiling their heads, but they do not seem his main concern.

Does not the very nature of things teach you that if a man has long hair, it is a disgrace to him, but that if a woman has long hair, it is her glory? (11:14–15). These verses play well into other interpretations of this passage, such as the idea that Paul has long hair or a particular hairstyle in view for women. But since these interpretations do not fit as well with the train of thought thus far, it seems more likely that Paul is now generalizing in the same way he did in 11:5–6.

A woman without a head covering in public is like a woman with shorn hair—she is acting disgracefully. But a man would not wear a veil any more than he would have long flowing hair like a woman. These things are common sense, things that nature teaches without us even having to think about them, Paul argues. A woman's hair is her glory—it is something very honorable about a woman. Why would a woman present it in a way that brings disgrace?

For long hair is given to her as a covering (11:15). This verse provides the strongest support for the view that Paul was really talking about hair length or hair style in this passage. In particular, the phrase "as a covering" can easily be translated as "instead of a covering," where Paul's point would become that a woman should have long hair and then she will not need a covering.

However, in light of the passage as a whole, Paul's point seems to be the direction of God's work in relation to a woman's head. See, he says, God has already covered her head with long hair. The principle is thus that God wants a woman's head to be covered. Therefore, she should be sure to cover her head when she is praying to God—it is what He expects of her.

If anyone wants to be contentious about this, we have no other practice—nor do the churches of God (11:16). The way this final comment is worded is somewhat ambiguous. Does Paul mean that we have no practice other than the covering of women's heads or that Christians do not practice contention? It seems impossible to form an absolute conclusion given this brief statement.

However, since the idea of contentiousness stands closest grammatically to Paul's mention of "such a practice," it seems slightly more likely. In other words, it is not the Christian way to be divisive

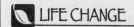 LIFE CHANGE

It is not the Christian way to be divisive over issues. It is the Christian way to have the kind of servant attitude that works to the glory of God and the service of the church.

over things like these. Christians are not people who fight to get their way or who exercise their rights "in the face" of others. The churches of God do not believe in behaving this way, so neither should the Corinthians. On this interpretation, Paul's comment goes right along with what he has already told them about meat offered to idols and the other divisions in the community.

ENDNOTES

1. See the excellent suggestions of R. B. Hays for what they might have written to Paul, in *First Corinthians* (Louisville: John Knox, 1997), 182–83.

2. This position is most fully worked out by A. C. Wire, *The Corinthian Women Prophets: A Reconstruction through Paul's Rhetoric* (Minneapolis: Fortress, 1990). A great deal of her book seems problematic, but there may be some merit to some of her basic claims.

3. Although some scholars have argued that the passage is more about men than about women (for example A. C. Thiselton, J. Murphy-O'Connor) or equally about men and women (B. Witherington).

4. *Politics*, 1.1259a–b.

5. This movement was born in a Wesleyan Methodist Church in Seneca Falls, New York.

6. Thus the church father Tertullian (early 200s) wrote a treatise "On the Veiling of Virgins."

7. Thus R. A. Horsley, *1 Corinthians* (Nashville: Abingdon, 1998), 153–54.

8. For example, G. D. Fee (*The First Epistle of Paul to the Corinthians* [Grand Rapids: Eerdmans, 1987], 506–7) mentions Plutarch's *Moralia* 200F, where it also refers to an external covering.

9. *On the Special Laws* 3.56.

10. Although usually with their hair bound up on their heads.

11. *On the Special Laws* 3.56.

12. Chap. 17.

13. For example, Hippocrates, *Nat. puer.* 20; Aristotle, *Generation of Animals* 739a.37–739b.20. See the challenging article by T. W. Martin, "Paul's Argument from Nature for the Veil in 1 Cor. 11:13–15: A Testicle Instead of a Head Covering, *Journal of Biblical Literature* 123 (2004): 75–84.

14. We find the same argument from the order of creation in 1 Tim. 2:13.

15. Jews: 1 Enoch 6; Christians: Tertullian, *On the Veiling of Virgins*. Tertullian thought Paul gave this instruction so fallen angels would not be tempted to repeat the sins of Genesis 6.

CHRISTIAN TRADITIONS AND WORSHIP:
THE LORD'S SUPPER
1 Corinthians 11:17-34

have no praise for you (11:17). We remember that Paul began this chapter by praising the Corinthians for holding to the traditions he passed on to them (11:2). In contrast, he begins this topic with no praise for how they are keeping the traditions of the Lord's Supper. The way they are behaving when they come together is atrocious: **your meetings do more harm than good** (11:17). The heart of the problem is once again divisions in the community.

Paul once again raises the issue of disunity in the congregation in 11:18. He has already discussed this issue in the first four chapters with regard to their favoritism toward various leaders. Now he will show them that their behavior during the Lord's Supper is a perfect illustration of this same problem.

The fact that the entire community could apparently **come together** into the same house, probably Gaius's house (Rom. 16:23), implies that the size of the church at Corinth was relatively small, perhaps forty to fifty people. At this point in the letter it is puzzling that Paul would have any doubts about disunity—**to some extent I believe it**. He knew they were divided! We wonder if this part of the letter was drafted in the very early stages of its writing before Paul had fuller information. On the other hand, perhaps Paul was using understatement.[1]

No doubt there have to be differences among you to show which of you have God's approval (11:19). This comment is somewhat enigmatic. Paul's sense seems to be that in a place like Corinth—where some people were thinking and behaving inappropriately—there needed to be some differentiation between those who were appropriate and those who were inappropriate. The tensions they were having were necessary because some of them did not have the right attitudes and actions, and this fact needed to come out into the open.

We should be careful how we apply a verse like this one. Churches split all too easily on the pretense of standing up for what people think is right. We must remember that Paul's bottom line in 1 Corinthians is unity, not division. We should also remember that we do not have the apostle Paul around to make God's will clear to us. This verse does not give carte blanche to those who love to create controversy over "the truth."

When you come together, it is not the Lord's Supper you eat (11:20). We see a few differences in this passage between the early church's celebration of the Lord's Supper and the way we take communion today. For example, while many Protestants only occasionally celebrate the Lord's Supper, the early church apparently ate it regularly, perhaps even every Sunday. We know they came together "on the Lord's Day," Sunday (1 Cor. 16:2).

A second difference is that it was a full meal rather than a small, isolated ceremony in the middle of a worship service. Matthew, Mark, and Luke all tell us that Jesus' final meal with His disciples, the "Last Supper," was a Passover meal. So the early Christians celebrated the "Lord's Supper" as a meal as well. The closest we come to eating a meal like this is the pitch-in dinners some churches have when a whole church eats together. The Lord's Supper was like a "potluck dinner" that the early Christians had regularly in remembrance of Christ's death, except it is not clear that they brought food with them.

The Corinthian church met in homes, and much of the food may have been provided by the host. The ancient world was a "patron-client" world. Such a world operated to a large extent on the basis of informal relationships between the "haves" and the "have-nots." One could gain prestige and status in part by your patronage of the less fortunate, and you could "show off" your wealth by entertaining important guests. Some of these dynamics may have been at work at Corinth during the Lord's Supper.

The host of the house where the Christians met may have provided the best of the food at his or her own expense. It is also possible that others brought some food as well. The Corinthians probably were spread out through the house for reasons of space and, unfortunately, because they were letting human considerations of status interfere with their celebration, only those with status seemed to get food. Another suggestion is that some Christians may have had to arrive later than others (11:33), particularly slaves and those who had to work. By the time they arrived, whatever common food the host might have provided was gone.

We know that there were individuals in the community wealthy enough to provide such food. If Gaius could fit forty to fifty people in his house, he must have had some wealth. Erastus could not have contributed pavement or been the director of public works at Corinth if he did not have status and wealth (Rom. 16:23).[2] Crispus (Acts 18:8) and Sosthenes (Acts 18:17) could not have been synagogue rulers if these individuals did not command significant resources.

Given the social conventions of the day, this was a conflict just waiting to happen. The rules of society would have pushed the host to have the most important members of the church eat together in the dining room. In some settings, each seat in the dining room held a different status, perhaps even an individualized menu. The closer you were to the host, the more important you were deemed.[3]

We can wonder whether this setting was also one in which the issue of meat sacrificed to idols had become an issue as well (1 Cor. 8, 10). Some Jews apparently had become vegetarians to avoid any possibility of eating such "tainted" meat (Rom. 14:2). It may have been of great concern to some Jewish Christians what the Christian host was serving during the meal.

The NIV obscures an important contrast Paul makes at this point. Paul has just said that it was not the *Lord's* supper they were eating when they came together. Instead, he says, "each takes *his own* supper."[4] What the NIV translates as **each of you goes ahead without waiting for anybody else** (11:21) was meant to show that they were not eating the *Lord's* supper at all by what they were doing. They were just having another meal *for themselves*. By drawing lines of status between the members of the church, their meal had nothing to do with the Lord, before whom we all stand equally.

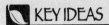

KEY IDEAS

By drawing lines of status between the members of the church, their meal had nothing to do with the Lord, before whom we all stand equally.

The issue at Corinth was not about etiquette or waiting for everyone to get to the table before starting to eat. Nor was it about the need to wait for a blessing or prayer before eating. It was about some gluttonously eating and drinking without concern for what anyone else but themselves might eat, and that at the Lord's Supper. Certain individuals were ironically feasting gluttonously while others went hungry in a meal that signified the oneness of the body of Christ (11:21). As Paul has already written in 10:16–17, "Is not the cup of thanksgiving for which we give thanks a participation in the blood of Christ? And is not the bread that we break a participation in the body of Christ? Because there is one loaf, we, who are many, are one body, for we all partake of the one loaf."

Paul was deeply disturbed. **Don't you have homes to eat and drink in . . . Shall I praise you for this? Certainly not!** (11:22). It is amazing that Christians—then and *now*—so often continue to operate so blindly on the basis of worldly values.

Paul reminds the Corinthians of the origins of the Lord's Supper and thus of its true meaning. This passage is the earliest record of these words and an important window into the final days of Jesus.[5] **I received from the Lord what I also passed on to you** (11:23). While some have taken this comment to mean Paul received this instruction by way of spiritual revelation, he probably is passing on early Christian tradition. He is using the same basic language he will use again in 15:3 and that he used earlier in this chapter itself (11:2).

Paul's words in this chapter are very significant indeed, for we have good reason to believe that he is passing on the essence of what Jesus was thinking the night He was arrested.[6] **The Lord Jesus, on the night he was betrayed . . .said, "This is my body, which is for you; do this in remembrance of me"** (11:23–24). These words clearly imply that Jesus saw His impending death coming, and that He knew it would have atoning value for His disciples.

Paul's version of these words is the earliest one, and Luke follows it fairly closely (Luke 22:17–20).[7] Like Luke, Paul preserves the context of these words at a supper, for the words over the cup do not take place until later, **after supper** (11:25) was finished. The mention of a new covenant in His blood makes it clear that Jesus was thinking of His coming death as a sacrifice for sins.

Neither Jesus nor Paul set down precisely how often they expected believers to have the Lord's Supper. Paul seems to expect such a meal to take place "when you come together" (11:20), which might mean every "first day of the week" (16:2). Acts 2:42 indicates that the earliest community broke bread together very frequently—probably even more than once a week. While such meals may not have had a rigorously sacramental character, each meal probably evoked the image of Jesus' death for the early Christians—at least Paul thought they should.

Paul now returns to the issue at hand: the shameful way the Corinthians were "remembering" Christ's death. **Therefore, whoever eats the bread or drinks the cup of the Lord in an unworthy manner will be guilty of sinning against the body and blood of the Lord** (11:27). Paul is not debating issues like whether the bread literally becomes the body of Jesus—those issues will arise much, much later in Christian history. Paul was thinking of the divisive and selfish practices of the Corinthians. The unworthy manner of the Corinthians' supper was its complete lack of love.

A man ought to examine himself before he eats of the bread and drinks of the cup (11:28). Some Christians find this verse torturous—some even avoid taking communion so they will not take it unworthily and be condemned. But Paul was not setting in motion some introspective festival in which you scour the recesses of your mind so you can ask forgiveness of every unconfessed sin. On the contrary, such incredible introspection ironically pushes the focus back on you as an individual rather than on the body of Christ around you. Paul refers to those who corrupt the body of Christ by the selfish and unchristian manner in which they eat together (Jude 12). In contrast, when we are fully aware of our dependence on Christ's death for the forgiveness of our sins, then we realize that we all stand equally before God's grace. It is deeply lamentable that some

Christians misunderstand this verse to mean that only those who are perfectly righteous can partake of the Lord's Supper!

That is why many among you are weak and sick, and a number of you have fallen asleep (11:30). This aspect of biblical teaching is one that we hear very little about today, but it is the clear claim of Scripture that spiritual sin can result in physical sickness, even death (James 5:15). To be sure, Paul does not teach that *all* sickness results from our sins. Indeed, the Gospel of John makes it clear that not every malady results from sin (John 9:3). Nevertheless, Paul clearly believed that *some* sickness and death resulted from sins such as that of the Corinthian church during the Lord's Supper.

Such judgment was easily avoided (11:31–32). Although it is difficult to tell by the NIV's translation, the first word for "judged" in verse 31 is the same word translated "recognizing" in verse 29. Paul is thus saying that if we recognized (*diakrino*) the nature of the body of Christ and thus recognized (*diakrino*) ourselves, we would not be judged (*krino*) by the Lord in the way these sick individuals have been. You can see from the Greek words Paul used that he was making a play on words.

Two considerations are important when applying such a verse. The first is that Paul is speaking in the plural here. In other words, his focus is on the church as a whole more than on particular individuals. If they as the church were aware of themselves as the body of Christ, then God would not have to discipline them to get them back in line.

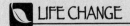

LIFE CHANGE

Communion is much more than a good time to hit the "reset" button on our personal walk with God, although it is certainly that. But we do even better to think of it as a time to hit the reset button of the whole congregation in its walk with God too, a time for us to remember where we are going together and that we are to bear each other's burdens along the way.

Secondly, we should primarily see the longsuffering of God in such a statement. God is not eager to let us go even if we sin (2 Pet. 3:9) . For some period of time He gently and sometimes not so gently nudges us to where we need to be. As Heb. 12:6 says quoting Prov. 3:12, "the Lord disciplines those he loves." God is not some overzealous police officer who is just waiting to catch us messing up. Jesus is a defense attorney who wants to see us acquitted (1 John 2:1).

First Corinthians 11:33–34 sum up Paul's instructions on this issue for the Corinthians. **So then . . . wait for each other**. Paul here was not discouraging them from eating the Lord's Supper at all when they came together. But he was trying to eliminate the causes of the gluttony and hunger that was taking place. If they were so hungry that they were bound to eat up all the food and drink up all the wine, then they should eat before they came so it would not happen at the Lord's table. Perhaps factors like these pushed the Lord's Supper in the direction of a smaller, more sacramental sub-service within the gatherings of the early churches.

ENDNOTES

1. C. Blomberg suggests that the divisions in Paul's mind here are divisions along the lines of rich/poor rather than rivaling Apollos/Paul parties (*1 Corinthians* [Grand Rapids: Zondervan, 1994], 228). Yet it seems likely that these two groups overlapped significantly and that the Apollos group had significant economic resources.

2. See the Introduction, "Corinth: The Destination."

3. Interestingly, some have suggested that in the seating of the Last Supper in John, Judas was seated next to Jesus in a seat of great honor (John 13:26). The Beloved Disciple was similarly next to Jesus (John 13:23). Peter, who is seated much further away, has to motion to the Beloved Disciple to ask Jesus a question (John 13:24). See A. A. Bell, Jr., *Exploring the New Testament World: An Illustrated Guide to the World of Jesus and the First Christians* (Nashville: Thomas Nelson, 1998), 202–4.

4. My translation.

5. The gospels were probably written some fifteen (Mark) to forty years later (John).

6. As we will mention in our discussion of 1 Corinthians 15, some of the Corinthians probably favored Peter over Paul and would have loved to catch him in a lie. In other words, it would have been suicide to Paul's authority to make up a story like this one. This factor gives us strong reason to believe that Paul is passing on genuine early Christian tradition here and elsewhere.

7. Matthew 26:26–29 and Mark 14:22–25 have formalized the words a little.

17

WHAT ABOUT SPIRITUAL GIFTS:
SPIRITUAL GIFTS IN THE CHURCH

1 Corinthians 12:1–31

1. LOCATING THIS PART OF THE LETTER

First Corinthians 11 dealt with two issues relating to Corinthian worship: head coverings and the Lord's Supper. With 1 Corinthians 12 Paul resumes answering the questions the Corinthians had sent him in their letter. The next question apparently dealt with the exercise of spiritual gifts in the church. We have already seen in 1 Corinthians 2 that the problem Corinthians probably thought that they were "spiritual" in contrast to other Christians in the church (2:15, 3:1). Apparently one way in which that arrogance showed up was in their exercise of spiritual gifts in worship. First Corinthians 12 through 14 give us Paul's treatment of this issue.

2. SPIRITUAL GIFTS IN THE CHURCH (12:1–31)

First Corinthians 12:1 begins with the same phrasing we saw in 7:1, 25, and 8:1, most likely meaning that Paul is once again addressing an issue from their letter to him. While we know that Paul is about to discuss spiritual gifts, it may be significant that he does not actually use the word *gifts* in this verse. It might actually capture Paul's nuance better to translate the verse "Now about spiritual things." Such a translation probably would imply a good deal of irony on Paul's part, for the

Corinthians did not think of themselves as ignorant of spiritual things!

Paul lays the fundamental criteria for how to discern spiritual activity that is of God from spiritual activity that is not. No doubt the Corinthians were well acquainted with pagan expressions of spirituality from the time before they came to Christ (12:2). It is possible that some of the Corinthian use of prophecy and tongues-speaking mirrored the pagan practice of their environment. As he did with the issue of pagan temples in 1 Corinthians 8–10, Paul quickly distinguishes Christian expressions of spirituality from pagan ones.

It seems unlikely that any Christians at Corinth had actually suggested that **Jesus be cursed** (12:3), although scholars have advanced many a hypothesis on the basis of this strange comment. Paul would certainly have given much more attention to the topic if that were the case.[1]

The confession that Jesus is Lord must be more than mere words for us. The stakes of such confession were considerably higher in Paul's context, and we must assume that Paul means a true, heart-felt confession. We remember that the confession of Jesus as Lord entailed an affirmation of the resurrection (Rom. 10:9; Phil. 2:9–11).

First Corinthians 12:4–11 presents the idea that while there are a number of different spiritual dispensations to individuals, they all come from **the same Spirit** and they all work for the common good (12:4–6). As we said before, the Corinthian letter may have only asked Paul about spiritual *things* (12:1). Paul now adds the word *gifts* to the equation—highlighting the fact that God is the source of any spiritual dimension to which the Corinthians might make claim.

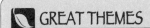 GREAT THEMES

grace (*charis*): "unmerited favor," God's propensity to give to us despite the fact that we do not merit His gifts

gift (*charisma*): that which God gives because of His grace

The Greek word for gift (*charisma*) is related to the word for grace (*charis*). The gifts to which Paul refers are thus instances of God's grace. Paul is thus emphasizing the same things he emphasized in 1 Corinthians 1–4. No one can boast of their spirituality or greatness. True wisdom and spiritual power comes from God. What this fact means is that we should be very careful about making some simple equation between spiritual gifts and natural abilities. Paul's emphasis is on God as their source and origin, not on something built into us.

Another interesting aspect of this comment is the way Paul mentions all three persons of the Trinity. Although Paul was far from making a statement on the Trinity—that would take almost another three hundred years—Paul mentions the Spirit, the Lord Jesus, and God (the Father). The Spirit represents God in the world, Jesus is the King/Lord of the universe, and God is the ultimate source of everything.

There is one Spirit behind all spiritual gifts, but the Spirit "gifts" different individuals in different ways. **Now to each one the manifestation of the Spirit is given for the common good** (12:7). If Paul's previous comment reminded the Corinthians that they could not take pride in their gifts because they all come from God, this one reminds them that the gifts, in the end, are not for them. The gifts of God are meant for building up the whole church (14:4) rather than for personal benefit.

Paul gives us no indication that the list of spiritual gifts that follows is anything like an absolute list. It is fairly common these days to take spiritual gift tests meant to assess one's spiritual giftedness. Such tools are useful if they do not become self-fulfilling prophecies that we use to box God in. But Paul's lists are generally relevant to the specific audience he

GIFTS IN ROMANS, 1 CORINTHIANS, AND EPHESIANS

Romans 12	1 Corinthians 12	Ephesians 4
1. prophecy	1. apostles	1. apostles
2. ministry	2. prophets	2. prophets
3. teaching	3. teachers	3. evangelists
4. exhortation	4. workers of miracles	4. pastor-teachers
5. giving	5. healing	
6. leadership	6. helpers	
7. compassion	7. leaders	
	8. tongues	
	9. interpretation of tongues	

is addressing. His list of gifts in Rom. 12:3–8 differs significantly from his list in 1 Corinthians because the ways in which God had poured out His grace on them was different. The list in 1 Corinthians was thus relevant to the concerns of the Corinthian community.

To one there is given through the Spirit the message of wisdom, to another the message of knowledge (12:8). We remember that these terms, *wisdom* and *knowledge* were two things to which some of the Corinthians laid claim. Some claimed to be wise in a human way that Paul rejected (3:18). Some claimed to have knowledge that they used to the detriment of other Christians (8:1–2). Paul here acknowledges that wisdom and knowledge are gifts of God, but they are gifts from the same Spirit-ual source. No human can take credit for true wisdom and knowledge.

Paul continues: **to another faith . . . to another gifts of healing . . . to another miraculous powers** (12:9–10). We do not have much evidence that any Corinthians were claiming superiority by way of these gifts. But these were things of which Paul might boast if he wanted to boast. He presumes that there is spiritual power behind his ministry and at one point feels compelled to tell about his spiritual status (1 Cor. 4:19–20; 2 Cor. 12:1–10).

Paul ends this list of various spiritual gifts with the ones that seem to have been most at issue at Corinth, those that stood in the background of the question they had asked Paul. It is some of these on which Paul will focus when he gets down to specifics in 1 Corinthians 14: **to another prophecy, to another distinguishing between spirits, to another speaking in different kinds of tongues, and to still another the interpretation of tongues** (12:10). As he has done so often in 1 Corinthians thus far, he only mentions these here to sow the seed. He will take the issue up again in full force in due time.

First Corinthians 12:12–26 uses the human body as an illustration of how the individual members of a church should relate to one another. **The body is a unit. . . . For we were all baptized by one Spirit into one body** (12:12–13). This is the general principle that Paul will flesh out in verses 14–26. He emphasizes the unity of the church because of the one Spirit that inhabits it.

As we have seen earlier in 1 Cor. 3:16, Paul thought of God's Spirit dwelling in the body of Christ as a whole more than of God's Spirit inside me as an individual. After all, a spirit lives in a body, and the body here is that of Christ. This simple shift in our thinking helps us realize that we are most likely to hear God's Spirit on any subject when we are talking and listening to as much of the body of Christ as possible. While Paul was speaking mainly of the Corinthian church, clearly he would have agreed that the body of Christ is ultimately made of up all Christians in all times and places, what we might call the "communion of saints."

Sometimes in the Wesleyan tradition we have so emphasized the work of God's Spirit in entire sanctification that we have lost sight of Paul and much of the New Testament's own emphasis on the Spirit as the main indication that one has become a Christian. Paul associates baptism with receiving the Spirit in 12:13.[2] He is not speaking of a second or further work of God in this instance, but to the common ground of all Christians.[3]

The paragraph 12:14–20 begins and ends with the same point: **the body is not made up of one part but of many** (12:14). It would thus be ridiculous for the foot to say, **"Because I am not a hand, I do not belong to the body"** (12:15). Paul notes that **it would not for that reason cease to be part of the body** (12:15). The same is true if the ear were to think it was not part of the body because it is not a hand (12:16).

In these instances, Paul interestingly does not speak of the part that thinks itself superior but of one that thinks itself inferior. Perhaps even more common than individuals thinking they are more important than they should are the numberless individuals in the church who do *not* think they are important at all. Paul provides them with strong encouragement here by affirming that no part of the body is insignificant. God's grace and the giftedness that comes from the Spirit apply to all His people, not just a few who stand out. **God has arranged the parts in the body, every one of them, just as he wanted them to be** (12:17–18). God's policy is thus, "no part left behind." Everyone counts in the body of Christ, and God has a role for every part to play.

 **KEY IDEAS**

Everyone counts in the body of Christ, and God has a role for every part to play.

In 12:14–20, Paul addresses those who might wonder if they are part of the body of Christ because they do not have the gifts that others have. In contrast, 12:21–26 addresses those who might dismiss other parts of the body because they do not have their gift. It is deeply ironic that a few groups believe you cannot be a Christian if you do not have certain gifts of the Spirit. While the vast majority of charismatics believe you can go to heaven even if you do not speak in tongues, a few groups teach that speaking in tongues is an essential indication that you have received the Spirit and thus become a Christian. This position is clearly wrong, since it depicts exactly the kind of thinking Paul opposes in these verses.

The eye cannot say to the hand, "I don't need you!" And the head cannot say to the feet, "I don't need you!" (12:21).[4] We remember that Paul is talking about the spiritual gifts of 12:7–11 here. Thus no one with any of these gifts should dismiss someone with a different one. In the case of the Corinthians, this comment applied directly to those who would claim superiority over others in the community because of their wisdom or, as seems likely in this case, because of having the gift of tongues.[5]

On the contrary, those parts of the body that seem to be weaker are indispensable (12:22). Paul's message is clear: no one should think less of people in the church whose gifts *seem* less significant or spectacular than his or her own.

The language that Paul uses in verses 22–24 reminds us of things he has said in other places in 1 Corinthians. In chapter 8 he used the word "weak" in reference to those whose conscience did not allow them to eat food offered to idols (8:7–13). They may *seem* weaker because they do not have the gift of knowledge, but they are indispensable.

The mention of the "unpresentable parts" is an allusion to the parts of the body we keep covered to be modest. Does Paul allude to the women of the church, whom Paul's society believed needed to be "covered" and kept inside? We remember Paul's comments about modesty in worship in 11:2–16. If Paul referred to the women, Paul would be saying that the women in the church are just as valuable to the kingdom as anyone else. On the other hand, Paul could mean this comment somewhat sarcastically, since the prideful in the church were looking down at others as "unpresentable." Perhaps Paul's meaning is that those who are boasting about their spirituality should not look down on those they are ashamed to be associated with.

In 12:24–25, Paul thus harkens back to the opening of the letter (1:10–17) where he argued that division had nothing to do with Christ. We are all of equal honor in Christ. **If one part suffers, every part suffers with it; if one part is honored, every part rejoices with it** (12:26). The culture of the Mediterranean tended to function with the idea of "limited good." The idea is that there is only so much good in the world, so if someone gains, then someone else somewhere else must lose. Someone else's misfortune was thus a possible boon to you, and your success meant someone else's loss.

Paul rejects this idea within the body of Christ. The success of other Christians is your success, because they are you—you are both part of the same body. Similarly, their pain is also your pain, because you are both the same body. The behavior of the "uppity" Christians at Corinth had none of this mutuality to it. They did not "carry each other's burdens" (Gal. 6:2).

Paul ends the chapter with a list of some of the roles to which God calls various

LIFE CHANGE

The success of other Christians is your success—because they are you—you are both part of the same body.

Christians. The fact that the list does not exactly match the list of spiritual gifts in 12:8–10 warns us not to see these lists as absolute. We remember that Paul mentions these roles in dialog with the situation at Corinth and in the light of the forms of leadership that fit the culture of his own day. He never says that these are the only forms or the exact forms that would always apply throughout Christian history.

God has appointed first of all apostles, second prophets (12:28). Apostles included not only the twelve, but those like Paul who had seen Christ after His resurrection and thereby received a commission to take the message of the gospel to the world (1 Cor. 9:1, 15:7). In that sense there are no apostles of Paul's sort alive today.

The role of prophet is more foreign to us than it was to the church of Paul's day. The prophets of the early church were a significant enough group for Ephesians to include them within the foundation of the church.

First Corinthians 14:30 implies that prophets were individuals through whom God provided revelation to the church. Such revelations certainly at times involved the *foretelling* of future events (Acts 11:27, 21:10–11), but more likely involved encouragement and exhortation for the particular people at the current time.

Paul continues his list: **third teachers, then workers of miracles, also those having gifts of healing, those able to help others, those with gifts of administration, and those speaking in different kinds of tongues** (12:28). It is noticeable that Paul places tongues at the end of this list. This position in the list is significant because Paul will similarly nudge the Corinthians away from tongues and toward prophecy in worship when he gets to chapter 14.

Again, we should not think of these gifts as the only types of gifts that God gives to His people. We should also notice that (with the possible exception of tongues) the gifts Paul mentions all build up the church as a whole rather than individuals. Miracles demonstrate God's power to others and serve an evangelistic purpose, while also fortifying the faith of the church. Healing does the same while having an obvious physical benefit to someone else as well. Helping clearly builds up others, as does good leadership. Tongues can build up the church if they are interpreted (14:4, 13), but apparently such interpretation was not taking place at Corinth.

Paul endorses pursuing spiritual gifts, especially prophecy (14:1). But he clearly does not think that everyone will have every gift, and he sees no problem with this fact (12:29–30). The way Paul words these questions in Greek expects the answer "no." "All are not apostles, are they?"

Everyone simply will not have every kind of giftedness or fill every role in the body of

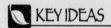

KEY IDEAS

When spiritual gifts are used properly, they build up the church, not just the individual.

Christ. This fact provides a strong word of caution to groups that think all Christians will speak in tongues if they are truly spiritual. Paul does not have this expectation, nor does he think that would happen in a perfect world. The diversity of gifts within the body of Christ is not only

acceptable; it is God's own plan for how the body of Christ would function. "All do not speak in tongues, do they? (No)."

Some Christian groups believe that the gift of tongues is like the gift
of faith: all Christians must have faith, but not all have the "gift" of faith.
Similarly they argue that all true Christians speak in tongues at some
point because tongues are the *evidence* of the Spirit in addition to being
a *gift* a person might have on a more extensive level.[6] But Paul says
exactly the opposite. He does not use the word *gift* in 12:28–30. He does
not say that all do not have the *gift* of tongues (12:30) or that God
appointed some with the *gift* of tongues. Paul says that God appointed
first apostles, second prophets, third teachers, then… *kinds* of tongues.
He starkly implies that all will not *speak* in tongues.

Paul concludes this section with encouragement: **eagerly desire the
greater gifts** (12:31). A great deal of disagreement exists among scholars
over what Paul exactly had in mind by this advice. For example, you
cannot eagerly desire to be an apostle—Paul was the last person to whom
Christ appeared (15:8). Paul's whole point is that *all* the gifts have honor.
How could he now "rank" them?

But Paul does rank them. He has numbered them in 12:28. While they
all share equal honor, they are not all equally authoritative nor do they all
have the same scope of impact on the body as a whole—some benefit the
body of Christ more than others. In the end, we have to pick up Paul's train
of thought in 14:1 to understand what he is really thinking. There he
resumes his discussion of spiritual gifts and points to prophecy as a "greater
gift" than tongues. This fact points us to see prophecy as a "greater gift," in
contrast to tongues.

Apparently tongues had become divisive at Corinth. Some were
thinking themselves more spiritual than others because they had the gift
of tongues. But in reality they were only building themselves up (14:4).
While 1 Corinthians 12 is great theology, its purpose was much more to
lay the groundwork for a course of action Paul wanted the Corinthians to
take in chapter 14. He wanted them to stop being so self-centered and
arrogant in their exercise of spiritual gifts, particularly tongues.

ENDNOTES

1. J. M. Bassler suggests interestingly that Paul was thinking of his own attitude before he became a Christian, "1 Corinthians 12:3—Curse and Confession in Context," *Journal of Biblical Literature* 101 (1982): 415–18.

2. This verse is the closest Paul comes to a reference to "baptism in the Holy Spirit."

3. The mention of "Jews or Greeks, slaves or free" reminds us of Gal. 3:28 and other places in Corinthians with similar categories (7:18–23). We remember the suggestion that these words may have been part of the baptismal ceremony and note the baptism context of 12:13.

4. Colossians and Ephesians will alter this imagery slightly. Here the whole body is the body of Christ, and some members of the body are the head. In Col. 1:18 and Eph. 1:22–23 Christ is the head of the body and the body is the church.

5. See the comments on 1 Corinthians 14 below.

6. This interpretation involves splicing a particular interpretation of Acts into Paul, as we will discuss in 1 Corinthians 14. But when we read these books in context, we have to deal with the fact that each book has its own unique way of using words and talking about things.

18

WHAT ABOUT SPIRITUAL GIFTS:
THE LOVE CHAPTER

1 Corinthians 13:1–13

First Corinthians 13 is one of the most familiar chapters in the New Testament, the "love chapter" of the Bible. This "hymn to love" rightly makes its appearance at countless weddings as a reminder of what true love really is. We read its description of love in 13:4–7 and the distance between the ancient Corinthians and our current context seems to disappear completely. These words jump out at us with a freshness that is as new as today and as enduring as tomorrow.

But it is no coincidence that we find these words at this particular point in the argument of this letter. This chapter is not only the answer to the Corinthians' attitude toward spiritual gifts. It is the answer to the division and divisiveness that was the root of almost all their problems. After he has told them that the whole body of Christ is important and has honor and after he has argued that no part is insignificant, he will now show them **the most excellent way** (12:31)—in contrast to their way.

First Corinthians 13:1–3 puts all the spiritual gifts into their proper perspective. **If I speak in the tongues of men and of angels, but have not love, I am only a resounding gong or a clanging cymbal** (13:1). Given the fact that the

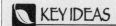

KEY IDEAS

The "love chapter" of 1 Corinthians 13 is not only Paul's answer to the Corinthians' spiritual gift problem. It was the answer to the division and divisiveness that was the root of almost all their problems.

sounds they are making are unintelligible (14:9), the mention of "tongues of angels" is probably an allusion to what some Corinthians were doing in worship. Whether they thought of them as *angelic* tongues or not, they certainly thought they were communicating with the spiritual realm in a special way (14:2). Paul says such a gift is useless if a person is not loving toward others in the church.

The same is true of the other gifts. **If I have the gift of prophecy and ... but have not love, I am nothing** (13:2). These words are reminiscent of the issues at Corinth. Some of the women there apparently have the gift of prophecy (11:5), and Paul will encourage the Corinthians to seek this gift in chapter 14. But all these great spiritual gifts and achievements mean nothing if we do not have the love of Christ.

Paul's overall meaning is also clear in 13:3, even if some of the details are unclear. He clearly refers to acts of great selflessness here, such as giving all your possessions **to the poor**. The second phrase is less clear. To our knowledge, no Christian had yet burned at the stake when Paul wrote these words. Some earlier copies of 1 Corinthians read, "surrender my body that I may boast," perhaps referring to the practice of selling oneself as a slave to pay for debts.

 KEY IDEAS

We do not have the original copies of any biblical book. In a few cases, the copies we have differ on what Paul originally wrote. In those cases, we have to decide which words we think were the original ones, using what we know about how copies were made.

First Corinthians 13:4–7 give us a description of how love operates. While these concepts apply to love in general, many of the words Paul uses echo things he has said previously in the letter about the "fleshly-minded" Corinthians. **Love is patient, love is kind** (13:4). God demonstrates these aspects of love toward us all the time. While we were still sinners and His enemies, He sent His Son to die for us (Rom. 5:8). The Greek word for kind (*chresteuetai*) has connotations of bestowing benefits or grace. These simple truths about love are the key to healthy relationships and lives. Yet for some ironic reason, it seems easiest for us to be least patient and least kind to those we profess to love the most.

It does not envy, it does not boast, it is not proud (13:4). Paul has told the Corinthians that we are one body as Christians. If one part of the body hurts, the whole body suffers with it. If one part rejoices, the whole body rejoices. This is the nature of love. When we love, we are happy for each other's successes. We do not value ourselves more than those who are not experiencing the same triumphs or rub it in their faces.

It is not rude . . . self-seeking . . . easily angered, it keeps no record of wrongs (13:5). In the words of Philippians 2:3, love leads us to "consider others better than yourselves." If patience is victory, venting your anger at someone else's expense is defeat in the Christian contest. If forgiveness is Christ-like (Matt. 18), then holding grudges is Satan-like. These behaviors are not only contrary to God's desire for us; doctors tell us they eventually cause our bodies to rebel against us.

Love . . . rejoices with the truth (13:6). Love should not rejoice that someone we love has gotten away with injustice or pretense. Love would do whatever is in its power to see its beloved become right with God and in line with the truth. Sometimes love must be tough to lead the beloved away from unrighteousness and to the truth. Love is not just about the beloved feeling good or not feeling pain. The highest love works for the greater and ultimate good of the beloved. Our love of God itself leads us to hate the evil and love the good (Rom. 12:9).

It always protects, always trusts, always hopes, always perseveres (13:7). Remembering that Paul directs these comments at the Corinthian situation, we will not fall into the trap of thinking that love must be gullible or always let others run over it. Love indeed "bears all things," as the KJV translates the first statement. But there is also a time for love to let the fledgling try its own wings, and even fail. This is part of learning and growing up. Sometimes "love must be tough."

Similarly, love does not focus on the negative or constantly second guess the beloved. But we also know there is a time for love to question. For the sake of love we hold our beloved accountable to what is true and right, not because we want to find failure but because we trust for success. We always hope for them; we always hang in there for them, even long after we would normally have given up. Perhaps Paul has himself in mind as he says these things. He is bearing suffering and even dishonor from them, trusting in what God is doing in them, hoping that they will come around, enduring till he sees them through to salvation.

In 13:8–13 Paul continues to put their spiritual gifts and virtues into perspective. **Love never fails** (13:8). In contrast, the things in which they are boasting will: prophecies, tongues, and knowledge. In the rest of the chapter Paul probably has the end times primarily in view, the time after the transformation of our bodies and the resurrection. He says that love will continue to be the operative principle for the Christian not only throughout our lives but also long after the current form of this world has passed away.

Not so with the other gifts. **[P]rophecies . . . will cease . . . tongues . . . will be stilled . . . knowledge . . . will pass away** (13:8). The prophecies of today are only as useful as this age, as is the knowledge of this world. Some prophecies are not even of God (14:32; 1 John 4:1). The "knowledge" of some often turns out to be misunderstanding (Rom. 10:2) or counterproductive (1 Cor. 8:1–2). Tongues, or languages, come and go—how many people today speak Akkadian or Latin? All these things pertain to this age, while love is timeless.

Some have used verses 9–10 to argue that gifts like tongues and prophecy only applied to the age of the apostles. But Paul gives not even a hint of such an interpretation. Did knowledge end with Paul's death? Who would be willing to say that the church today has entered its time of perfection? We cannot wish away the fact that Paul spoke of tongues and prophecy as legitimate gifts of the Spirit simply because they do not appeal to us in an age of rationality.

Perfection in this sense has to do with completion and fullness. Our knowledge in this age is only incomplete: it will only become full after Christ's return and our transformation. Even prophecies are often incomprehensible to the prophet him or herself. As Matthew and Mark looked into the future predicted by Jesus, they saw it **as a poor reflection as in a mirror** (13:12). Both Mark 13 and Matthew 24 mix together predictions, some of which relate to the destruction of Jerusalem in A.D. 70 (Matt. 24:2–3; Mark 13:1–4) and some of which are about the second coming of Christ (Matt. 24:30–31; Mark 13:24–27). In other words, as they conveyed these prophetic words to us, they themselves were unable to see exactly how God would fulfill them.

Paul is once again putting the gifts of the Corinthians into an eternal perspective in verse 11. The tongues they now speak are like the talking of a child. The prophecies they make now are like the thinking of a child. The knowledge they now have is like the reasoning of a child. Eternity, when we are perfected, is when we will truly grow up and put our childish, human ways behind us.

Ancient mirrors were made of polished metal. If you think of trying to see yourself in a reflection on a piece of metal, you will immediately realize how poorly ancient mirrors provided an image of their viewers in comparison to ours today. The comments in verse 12 make it fairly clear that Paul has been speaking of the end times in this paragraph. The course of our lives on earth presently is one of partial knowledge and understanding. All the things that the haughty Corinthians valued were the wrong things, things that were destined to pass away.

The language and imagery Paul uses here is close enough to Num. 12:6–8 for us to know he had it in mind. In that passage God contrasts the way He speaks through prophets and the way He spoke to Moses. The prophets hear God's message in riddles, but Moses spoke to God **face to face**.[1] After Christ returns, then we will see God face to face, and we will have no need for tongues or prophecies. Then we will have true and clear knowledge, more like the knowledge God has of us now.

In the meantime, **now these three remain: faith, hope, and love. But the greatest of these is love** (13:13). Of the three, only love will continue from this age to the next. We will have no need for hope when that for which we hope has come. We will have no need for faith when we can see face to face that in which we are now only trusting. But the love of God and of each other pertains not only to this present time, but also to all eternity.

ENDNOTES

1. The NIV's translation makes the parallel hard to see. A more wooden translation of 13:12 is "For we see now through a mirror in a riddle, but then face to face."

19

WHAT ABOUT SPIRITUAL GIFTS:
THE UNEDIFYING USE OF TONGUES IN WORSHIP

1 Corinthians 14:1–40

1. BASIC POINT: BETTER TO PROPHESY (14:1–5)

Paul now gets down to business. What he does in 1 Corinthians 12–14 is somewhat like what he did in his discussion of meat sacrificed to idols in 1 Corinthians 8–10. There, he began tactfully and generally in chapter 8, gave an illustration in chapter 9, and finally got down to the particulars in chapter 10. He follows a similar pattern here.

Paul continues his train of thought from chapter 12. Paul had interrupted his argument there to talk about love, the "most excellent way" in terms of the exercise of all spiritual gifts (12:31). He had told the Corinthians to *"eagerly desire* the greater gifts" (12:31), a comment that made him think of love, which is greater than *any* spiritual gift. Now Paul picks up where he left off by repeating the phrase **eagerly desire** (14:1). We now find out what the "greater gift" was that he primarily had in mind at the end of chapter 12. The greater gift is clearly **prophecy**.

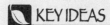 KEY IDEAS

The thrust of 1 Corinthians 14 is generally to discourage the use of tongues in Corinthian worship, although Paul clearly allows for its use if interpretation is possible.

Prophecy often did have an element of *fore*telling, prediction of things that would happen in the near future. But such foretelling usually also related to *forth*telling, to some word from God about things going on in the present or that had gone on in the past. The Old Testament prophets typically did talk about the future, but it was usually the near future of Israel in terms of its current and past actions. Thus one significant aspect of prophecy is to warn of what will happen if sin does not stop. A prophet might also serve to reveal new directions in which God wants His people to go.

In this particular argument, Paul seems to consider all the gifts "fair game" for every Corinthian, since he allows for some choice in what gifts they pursue. Paul may thus in some cases have seen spiritual gifts as specific "giftings" by God at particular times and places more than permanent abilities a person might have.

Similarly, the context pushes us to see tongues as the "lesser gift" he has in mind (14:2). Paul makes a clear contrast between verse 1 and verse 2. Seek spiritual gifts in general, but more to prophesy (14:1), for (in contrast to prophecy) tongues build up only the speaker him or herself rather than the church as a whole (14:2–4). Paul has a worship setting in mind in these words, so this chapter does not directly address the exercise of tongues in private devotion.

Many in the holiness movement have noted that we might translate the word *tongues* as "languages." It is one and the same word in Greek. Accordingly, many have argued that Paul was strictly speaking of human languages in this chapter, something like what we see taking place in Acts 2 on the Day of Pentecost. We sometimes hear stories of missionaries who unexpectedly and miraculously find themselves able to communicate to others in languages they have never studied.

It is true that the tongues spoken on the Day of Pentecost appear to be human languages. On that day the apostles "began to speak in other tongues as the Spirit enabled them" (Acts 2:4). Those who were staying in Jerusalem at that time, "God-fearing Jews from every nation under heaven" (2:5), each "heard them speaking in his own language" (2:6). The response of this incredibly diverse group of Jews and converts to Judaism was "we hear them declaring the wonders of God in our own tongues!" (2:11).

The most straightforward reading of Acts 2 is thus that the tongues in which the disciples were speaking was the ability to speak in foreign languages they had not learned. While someone could argue that they were speaking in ecstatic tongues and that the foreign born Jews only received the gift of interpretation, the text does not say this. The text implies that the visitation of tongues they received was the ability to speak in foreign, human languages. While it is certainly possible that the two other incidences of tongues speaking in Acts were angelic and not human tongues (Acts 10:46, 19:6), Acts 2 points us toward seeing them as human languages as well.[1] In other words, in the only place where Acts indicates the nature of these tongues, they are human languages.

The situation is different in 1 Corinthians 14. We have already seen that the mention of "tongues of angels" in 13:1 is likely linked to the treatment of tongues in the surrounding chapters. Since the thrust of the overall discussion of spiritual gifts is aimed at tongues, 13:1 probably alludes to the tongues the Corinthians were speaking in their worship—not human but "angelic."[2] First Corinthians 14:10 confirms this impression if indeed Paul there is distinguishing the tongues of the Corinthians from all the languages of this world.

Another difference between Acts and Corinthians is the relationship between tongues and unbelievers. The tongues of Acts 2 are an evangelistic tool that opens the door for

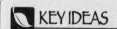 KEY IDEAS

The tongues of Acts and the tongues of 1 Corinthians 14 are interestingly different. The tongues of Acts serve an evangelistic purpose and are human languages. The tongues of Corinthians would turn off unbelievers and do not seem to be human languages.

unbelievers to come to Christ. However, in 1 Corinthians 14 Paul discourages the use of tongues in worship because of the potentially negative impact they might have on an unbeliever in their assembly (14:23). This contrast between Acts 2 and 1 Corinthians 14 pushes us toward seeing the two instances of tongues-speaking as different in character.

Finally, the tongues of 1 Corinthians 14 are clearly ecstatic rather than a matter of thought, meaning that the tongues speaker at Corinth did not use his or her mind when speaking in them (14:14). They seemed to be having religious experiences in which they uttered unrecognizable sounds that they perhaps interpreted to be the "tongues of angels" (13:1). These were non-rational experiences that by-passed their minds and their thinking. A non-believer might have compared them to the frenzies of the Dionysian festivals or the mysteries of Eleusis, a town about fourteen miles northeast of Corinth. The word the NIV translates as "out of your mind" in 14:23 (*mainomai*) may refer to these kinds of religious experiences.

Tongues is apparently a phenomenon that has occurred in many different religions in the history of the world. You could argue that the non-Christian incidences are counterfeit experiences. But a more likely suggestion is that certain human brains are "wired" in this way while others are not. This possibility leads us to wonder whether at times some spiritual gifts are instances of God magnifying aspects of who we are naturally rather than God gifting us completely "from scratch." Is the gift of faith God magnifying some aspect of us that was already there before we came to Christ? Is the gift of leadership the magnification of certain gifts that we had even before God sanctified them as His own?

If God sometimes sanctifies a predisposition for tongues, this fact might explain why we find them in other cultures and religions without us having to consider them demonic in those instances. It would not change the fact that a person speaking in tongues was in fact being blessed by God.

We actually find an example of non-Christian tongues in the Judaism of Paul's day. It shows a Jewish interest in speaking in the tongues of angels. A book of Paul's day called the *Testament of Job* depicts one of Job's daughters speaking "in the angelic dialect, sending up a hymn to God in accord with the hymnic style of the angels." Another daughter speaks "in the dialect of the cherubim."[3] While this story is clearly fictional, it indicates that some Jews must have valued such an idea and practice. An example might be the Jews to which Col. 2:18 refers. Notice that the Corinthians apparently sang as well as spoke in tongues (14:15).

Paul does not forbid the use of such tongues in Corinthian worship if they are interpreted (14:39), but the overall thrust of his argument is to discourage or at least qualify their use. His reasoning is very similar to his reasoning elsewhere in the letter and in his other writings. The way the Corinthians are using tongues is self-centered. It does not contribute to the rest of the church and even distracts from proper worship.

The one who speaks in a tongue **does not speak to men but to God. Indeed no one understands him; he utters mysteries with his spirit** (14:2) or perhaps better, "by the Spirit." Paul implies that such tongues do have personal, spiritual benefit. Although it is possible he made this comment with unexpressed doubts, it seems more likely that Paul really accepted ecstatic tongues as spiritual communication with God. But because these "angelic" languages were unintelligible to others, they were not helpful to the assembly of Christians as a whole. In contrast, **[h]e who speaks in a tongue edifies himself, but he who prophecies edifies the church** (14:4). This seems to be Paul's overall feeling toward the way tongues were being used at Corinth—they were detrimental rather than helpful to the church.

Paul's next comment has the form of a statement someone makes when you know there is a "but" coming. **I would like every one of you to speak in tongues,** Paul affirms those who are gifted by God in their ability to speak in tongues. **But I would rather have you prophesy** (14:5). We tend to focus on what we want to hear in Scripture, and it is thus no surprise that some focus on statements like "I want everyone to speak in tongues" and "I speak in tongues more than all of you" (14:18). Indeed, we in the holiness tradition probably do not take Paul's affirmation of tongues as seriously as we should. At the same time, both of these comments lead up to a "but." In both cases, the "but" is a discouragement of the use of tongues in public worship.

He who prophesies is greater than one who speaks in tongues, unless he interprets, so that the church may be edified (14:5). In this comment we have the chapter in a nutshell. Charismatics understandably often focus on the line "unless he interprets" in their appropriation of this chapter. It is certainly true that Paul allows for two or three instances of tongues in worship if interpretation is present (14:27). However, Paul dedicates the bulk of the chapter to dissuading the Corinthians from tongues in worship.[4]

2. PROPHECY BETTER THAN TONGUES IN WORSHIP (14:6-25)

The point to which Paul returns again and again in this section is that tongues are not generally appropriate for Christian worship, particularly in contrast to prophecy. Verses 6–14 argue that tongues are not helpful to others and conclude that the Corinthians should seek other gifts that build up the church. Verses 15–19 urge anyone who speaks in tongues to seek for interpretations so that they can use their mind in their prayers and can thus benefit the minds of others. Verses 20–25 present tongues as a potential obstacle to non-believers and urge prophecy instead.

Throughout, Paul assumes that the tongues in use at Corinth are uninterpreted. Consequently, the overall thrust of his argument discourages their use in worship. **[W]hat good will I be to you, unless I bring you some revelation or knowledge or prophecy or word of instruction?** (14:6). We may not all speak in tongues today, but Paul's words here are amazingly relevant to much contemporary American worship. How often do we treat church as a one-on-one between me and God without even thinking about it? Sometimes it seems during contemporary worship that the whole church is just a sea of individuals each in his or her own world talking one-on-one with God, waiting for an individual zap from heaven. Paul implies that worship should involve the body building up the body.

First Corinthians 14:7 and 8 both compare tongues to meaningless . . . **lifeless things that make sounds.** These comparisons seem to reflect a fairly negative feeling on Paul's part toward the ecstatic tongues speaking going on at Corinth. Paul says that the sounds the Corinthians are making are not helpful because their message is unclear. He makes no argument for interpretation here; he actually portrays *the act* of ecstatic tongues speaking *itself* as unprofitable.

Paul does not say, "Speak in tongues and then someone will interpret the ecstatic speech." Instead, he says it would be better if their words were intelligible in the first place (14:9). In my opinion, these comments reveal a fairly negative view toward the tongues speaking at Corinth: it is like **speaking into the air**. While Paul wants to affirm the Corinthians in their spiritual gifts, he himself has a fairly negative attitude toward its use in public worship in the manner of the Corinthians.

He continues with another illustration from human languages. **If then I do not grasp the meaning of what someone is saying, I am a foreigner to the speaker, and he is a foreigner to me** (14:11). Paul makes a simple but profound argument here. Languages are about communicating meaning. Further, people who are of the same kind, of the same race, speak the same language. To speak in language someone does not understand is to indicate that you are not of them. You are not of the same group or the same race.

We are undoubtedly more open to foreigners today than the people of Paul's world were. Ancient groups tended to divide the world into "us and them": Jews and Gentiles, Greeks and barbarians. Indeed, it is the word for barbarian that the NIV here translates as "foreigner" (*barbaros*). To be a foreigner to someone else meant that you were not in the same group as them and had a strongly negative connotation. It precluded you from being in the same family and usually even the same religion.

It was therefore insulting to be speaking in a language that had no meaning to those who should be your family. In a sense, the way the Corinthians were speaking in tongues was a little like the way they were eating the Lord's Supper. They were treating the others in the congregation as if they were not a part of their family or their race. They were treating them as foreigners.

[T]ry to excel in gifts that build up the church (14:12). With this comment Paul ends the first argument against the use of tongues in Corinthian worship. In this entire paragraph (14:6–12), he has not mentioned the need for interpretation once but has instead highlighted the intrinsic confusion and alienation that is a part of ecstatic tongues speaking in worship. Nevertheless, Paul does not deny that those who speak in tongues are actually experiencing messages from the heavens. Indeed, he almost treats tongues as angelic languages that the Corinthians might learn. He thus tells the tongues speakers to pray so that God will reveal to them the meaning of their tongues.

He begins his next line of thought. **[A]nyone who speaks in a tongue should pray that he may interpret what he says** (14:13). If you speak in tongues, pray that you will be able to convey what you mean. Notice in this instance that the tongues speaker is the person Paul wants to have the interpretation. Someone else is not interpreting for him or her.

Paul now substantiates this instruction. In 14:14–15, Paul is urging the person speaking in tongues to gain the ability to understand these angelic messages. He wants to close the gap between speaking tongues and understanding tongues, so that the person can pray with understanding.[5] Paul talks as if these really are languages of some sort. He seems to say that if these are really angelic languages, then these words have a meaning they should be able to share with the rest of the church.

If you are praising God with your spirit, how can one who finds himself among those who do not understand say "Amen" to you thanksgiving, since he does not know what you are saying? You may be giving thanks well enough, but the other man is not edified (14:16–17). This comment is an interesting window into the worship practices of the early church. Evidently they had times of free prayer where anyone might pray (including women: 11:5). Much of this prayer must have involved thanksgiving and praise to God. After each prayer, the rest of the church apparently said "Amen" in agreement. The problem with un-interpreted tongues is that no one knows whether to say "Amen" because they cannot understand what the person has prayed.

Paul's next comment is one of the most controversial in the chapter: **I thank God that I speak in tongues more than all of you** (14:18). This comment is very difficult for us in the holiness tradition. Is Paul really claiming to speak in tongues? On the one hand, it is possible that Paul is being "tongue in cheek" here. Paul spoke countless languages, and he used the word for tongues (*glōssa*) equally for both human and angelic ones (13:1). This comment might be nothing more than an affirmation that he speaks languages like Greek, Latin, Aramaic, and Hebrew, languages he spoke.

Further, Paul makes this comment as a concession on his way to a rather large "but." I speak in more tongues than all of you… **But in the church I would rather speak five intelligible words to instruct others than ten thousand words in a tongue** (14:19). He makes the contrast large: five words with my mind in church are better than ten thousand in tongues without my mind. This comment is rather strongly against the use of tongues in worship that do not involve the use of the mind, for we would better translate the phrase the NIV gives as "intelligible" as "with my mind." In church Paul would rather speak five words with his mind, thus in a known language, than ten thousand in an ecstatic tongue or un-interpreted angelic language.

On the other hand, we cannot dismiss the real possibility that Paul himself spoke in tongues in private prayer. In 14:19 he speaks of praying (1) in church and (2) with his mind. By contrast, the most natural way to take 14:18 is thus that Paul is claiming to speak in tongues (1) in private and (2) without his mind. He seems to assume in 14:19 that the tongues in question are not "with my mind." We simply do not have enough background information to know for certain what he meant by this comment.

Some scholars have taken Rom. 8:26 as a reference to Paul's own practice of tongues speaking.[6] Paul says that "the Spirit helps us in our weakness. We do not know what we ought to pray for, but the Spirit him-self intercedes for us with groans that words cannot express." If ecstatic tongues were an important part of Paul's private religious experience, it is surprising that the practice only comes up clearly in 1 Corinthians—and only then because of a Corinthian problem. Indeed, tongues does not appear on Paul's list of spiritual gifts in Rom. 12:6–8, nor are they men-tioned in Eph. 4:11. Further, we wonder if the fact that Paul did not speak in tongues like the Corinthians was actually one of the reasons they looked down on him. Is the fact that he did not speak in angelic tongues part of why he felt he should mention the religious experiences of 2 Corinthians 12. In the end, we simply do not have enough information to demonstrate conclusively whether Paul spoke in ecstatic tongues or not.

Brothers, stop thinking like children (14:20). The self-centered use of tongues at Corinth was immature. The Corinthians should start putting their childish ways behind them (13:11). First Corinthians 14:20–25 explores the negative impact tongues speaking might have on a non-believer who might join the Christian assembly. His argument is somewhat difficult for us to follow, but the basic thrust is that tongues give the wrong impression to non-believers and may actually hinder their coming to Christ.

He begins with a spiritual interpretation of Isa. 28:11–12. **Through men of strange tongues and through the lips of foreigners I will speak to this people** (14:21). Paul takes this verse to mean that tongues rein-force the disbelief of unbelievers.[7] **Tongues, then, are a sign . . . for**

unbelievers (14:22). While scholars have heavily debated the meaning of this comment, the best interpretation probably sees the word *sign* here as a sign of unbelief rather than a positive sign. Paul speaks of tongues as a kind of indicator of a person's unbelief. Tongues immediately have a negative effect on an unbeliever that reinforces his or her unbelief.

The idea that you are **out of your mind** (*mainomai*, 14:23) probably carried overtones of divine insanity such as the Greeks associated with certain pagan festivals like the Dionysian or Eleusinian mystery religions. If an unbeliever walked into a worship setting where everyone was speaking incomprehensible sounds, they might mistake the assembly for some similar religious experience of divine madness.

The word the NIV translates as **some who do not understand** (14:23) refers to someone who is illiterate in a particular language (*idiotēs*). With this word Paul seems to have in mind individuals who are not exactly unbelievers, but Christianity is "foreign" to them—they do not speak our language yet. Perhaps he wants to protect such individuals from being turned off to the Christian community because of the disorderly use of tongues.

In contrast, Paul believes prophecy is much more likely to benefit both believers and unbelievers in the Christian assembly. **[P]rophecy . . . is for believers, not for unbelievers** (14:22). Paul here refers to words from God to the congregation delivered within the worship setting. If tongues reveal that sinners do not speak God's language, prophecy provides signs of God's will and correction to believers.

The comments in 14:24–25 remind us a little of the experience of the woman at the well when Jesus set forth all the hidden secrets of her heart (John 4). She was amazed that a man could tell her everything she had ever done (John 4:39). His prophetic words convinced her that she was a sinner, and she believed that "this man really is the Savior of the world" (John 4:42).

3. SPECIFIC GUIDELINES FOR THE USE OF SPIRITUAL GIFTS IN WORSHIP (14:26–40)

Now Paul sets down specific guidelines for the use of tongues and prophecy in worship. **When you come together, everyone has a hymn, or a word of instruction, a revelation, a tongue or an interpretation**

(14:26). We can see from this comment how apparently unstructured and participatory the worship at Corinth was conducted. It was a truly "charismatic" styled church rather than one with a clear cut order of worship or sermon time. Surely it stands at one end of the spectrum in terms of its worship style, for Paul had to instruct a church like Thessalonica not to despise prophecy (1 Thess. 5:20). A slightly better translation of 14:26 is "let everything be for edification." In other words, Paul was not saying that all these things needed to take place but that whatever they did in worship, it should edify the body.

He now works to create order out of their chaos. **If anyone speaks in a tongue, two—or at the most three—should speak, one at a time, and someone must interpret** (14:27). He does not forbid the use of tongues in worship, but he significantly limits it and gives it order. **If there is no interpreter, the speaker should keep quiet** (14:28). Paul does not want any spiritual self-indulgence in the service. If no one has an interpretation for the tongues, the person must keep silent. We can wonder if Paul thought placing this stipulation on tongues speaking at Corinth would effectively shut down its use in their worship. Perhaps the tongues speakers there were so self-preoccupied that few interpretations would take place.

Paul's instructions for prophecy are similar. Ultimately, *interpreted* tongues and prophecy receive the same weight in the worship setting. The fact that Paul limits prophecy as well as interpreted tongues shows that worship, in the end, is more than the exercise of spiritual gifts. If we mention just a few activities Paul brings up in 1 Corinthians alone, we have prayer, singing, teaching of a more conventional sort, and fellowship.

With regard to prophecy, **[t]wo or three prophets should speak, and the others should weigh carefully what is said** (14:29). But no single prophet has absolute say: **if a revelation comes to someone who is sitting down, the first speaker should stop** (14:30). Beside his principal goal for the edification of the church, Paul has two further goals in these guidelines. The first is order: **you can all prophecy in turn so that everyone may be instructed and encouraged** (14:31). The second is accountability: **The spirits of prophets are subject to the control of prophets** (14:32). Just because someone claims to have a word from God does not mean that he or she truly does.

An important tension exists in Paul's words here between the need to hear the messages God brings to specific individuals and the need for authority and control in the church. In our current context, a pastor is usually the one through whom God speaks prophetic words to a congregation. From time to time there are other individuals who believe they know how God wants to lead a particular church. We also find any number of prophetic voices in broader Christianity as well, like Billy Graham. I believe that even an entire denomination can be a kind of prophetic voice on an issue, such as many holiness denominations are to conservative Christianity on the issue of women in ministry.

But all prophetic voices are subject to the "control of the prophets." It may take some time for the church to figure out which voices truly represent God and which do not, but ultimately all prophetic voices in the church must be subject to the prophets in the church as a whole. One key difference between a Billy Graham and a David Koresh (the sexually perverse "prophet" of the Waco, Texas, cult), is that the church ultimately affirmed the anointing of Graham, while it rejected individuals like Koresh as prophets.

 LIFE CHANGE

The key for Paul is that worship be orderly so that God is glorified by everything that takes place, and unbelievers will find Christianity attractive rather than distasteful. This should also be our goal in our worship today—the glorification of God. All other debates are ultimately counterproductive.

We should not feel compelled to set up our worship experiences like those of the Corinthians. If we could sit in on one of their meetings, we would immediately realize how different their culture was from ours. Just because they met in houses does not mean that all Christians should meet in houses. Indeed, some early Christian groups probably met in synagogues (James 2:2). At other times Christians may have met in something like our store front churches today (Acts 19:9).

In the same way, it is unlikely that all the early churches were as "charismatic" as the church at Corinth. Thus it does not seem likely that Corinth had a single church leader when Paul, Apollos, or Timothy were not in town. Most of the churches seemed to be led by a group of elders (Phil. 1:1). Paul's general principle is order: **For God is not a God of**

disorder but of peace (14:33).[8] In contrast, the Corinthians acted like they were the only Christians on the planet. **Did the word of God originate with you? Or are you the only people it has reached?** (14:36). No, the Corinthians were a part of something much bigger, and as such they needed to submit themselves to God's will for the church as a whole.

Paul thus saw the importance for charismatic prophecies to be tested and tried. **If anybody thinks he is a prophet or spiritually gifted, let him acknowledge that what I am writing to you is the Lord's command** (14:37). Here Paul interestingly asserts his authority over any prophet who might claim not to be subject to his rules. Not all who think of themselves as spiritual are truly spiritual, and not all who think they are prophets are truly prophets. Paul's apostolic and spiritual authority ultimately trumped their prophetic claims to authority. **If he ignores this, he himself will be ignored** (14:38).

Paul now concludes the chapter and gives his "final answer." **Therefore, my brothers, be eager to prophesy, and do not forbid speaking in tongues. But everything should be done in a fitting and orderly way** (14:39–40). Again, notice the way he steers the Corinthians toward prophecy and away from tongues in public worship. He refuses to forbid tongues, for he accepts it as a valid gift from God. He does not wish to "put out the Spirit's fire" (1 Thess. 5:19). But he clearly finds prophecy far more profitable by its very nature. The key for him is order in worship, so that God is glorified by everything that takes place and so that unbelievers will find Christianity attractive rather than distasteful.

It makes perfect sense that the concepts of order and peace would play themselves out differently in different cultures, as well as in different groups and denominations today.

We should not judge too quickly those groups that do not follow Paul's instructions exactly as he set them down for the Corinthians. After all, Paul was giving these instructions *to the Corinthian church* rather than to all Christians everywhere—even in his own day. When he told the Corinthians not to forbid speaking in tongues, the "you" he addressed was the Corinthian church. Paul himself might have given slightly different instructions to a church in Jerusalem or Rome—or charismatic churches, holiness churches, or liturgical churches today. No matter what the style of worship, it should unify and edify the particular congregation as it glorifies God.

ENDNOTES

1. However, Paul probably did not make as great a distinction between human languages and "angelic" languages as our worldview might push us to make. It is thus possible that Luke similarly did not distinguish strongly between human and angelic tongues. Acts 10 probably mentions tongues to highlight that the Gentile "Pentecost" was no different from that which fell on the disciples in Acts 2. You could similarly argue that the reason Acts singles out tongues and prophesy at Ephesus is to show the clear distinction between baptism by John and Christian baptism—the former was not sufficient in itself to make a person a Christian.

2. We cannot tell for certain whether Paul really believed their tongues to be angelic languages, whether they considered their tongues angelic, or whether Paul was speaking hyperbolically.

3. Testament of Job 48:1 and 50:2. The testament of Job may date either to the century before Christ or the century after and may have been a product of Egyptian Judaism. Translation from R. P. Spittler, *The Old Testament Pseudepigrapha*, vol 1, J. H. Charlesworth, ed (New York: Doubleday, 1983).

4. I might admit that many Pentecostal groups today do seem to be edified by the use of un-interpreted tongues in their worship. It is not clear to me that Paul would write the same things to them today as he wrote to the Corinthians.

5. As a side note, we see also that some of the Corinthians must have sung in tongues as well, like Job's daughter in the Testament of Job mentioned above.

6. For example, K. Stendahl, *Paul Among Jews and Gentiles* (Philadelphia: Fortress, 1976), 110–111.

7. As is often the case, Paul is not reading the words for what Isaiah originally meant, but for what he believes God is saying to the church through the words.

8. It is possible that the clause "as in all the congregations of the saints" goes with 14:34. The NIV divides up the paragraph this way: "As in all the congregations of the saints, women should remain silent in the churches" (the NIV translates the same word in two different ways—as in all the *churches*, let women be silent in the *churches*). Since some Greek manuscripts have 14:34–35 in a different place in the text, I have opted to see this comment as the final clause of 14:33: "God is not a God of disorder but of peace, as in all the congregations of the saints." Here we should remember that the original manuscripts did not have punctuation or even spaces between the words. Where this clause goes is a matter of interpretation since the original Greek text would not have told us.

20

AN ASIDE:
DISRUPTIVE WOMEN
1 Corinthians 14:34–35

You may have noticed that our analysis of the train of thought in the previous chapter bypassed two of the most controversial verses in the New Testament. Our translations of 1 Corinthians unexpectedly make an aside about women in the assembly at 1 Cor. 14:34–35.

Given that Paul has already presumed that women *can* pray and prophecy in church (11:5), these two verses are a bit startling. They also run counter to our spiritual common sense, since we know that women today are some of the most spiritual and discerning people in our churches—Christians from whom we *need* to hear.

As we follow the argument of 1 Corinthians 14, verses 34 and 35 seem somewhat out of place. Indeed, I by-passed them in my commentary earlier so that Paul's train of thought about prophets would be clearer. The flow of that argument makes more sense if we momentarily pass over 14:34–35, leaving the following: "The spirits of prophets are subject to the control of prophets. For God is not a God of disorder but of peace, as in all the congregations of the saints. Did the word of God originate with you? Or are you the only people it has reached? If anybody thinks he is a prophet or spiritually gifted, let him acknowledge that what I am writing to you is the Lord's command" (14:33, 36). Indeed, this is the way a fifth century manuscript called Codex Bezae (D) reads. Paul had been discussing the use of prophecy and tongues in worship, and this line of thought continues after 14:34–35 in our current Bibles.

It is therefore somewhat puzzling to find this aside on women in the middle of this section. When you consider that some Greek manuscripts actually put these verses in a different place (after verse 40), you will understand why several scholars wonder if these two verses were even in the original text of 1 Corinthians.[1] Gordon D. Fee, a conservative evangelical scholar, suggests that they were written in the margin of a very early copy of 1 Corinthians and then put into two different places in the text in subsequent copies.[2] As a scholar, I also take this position on these verses.

Nevertheless, we should be very careful about such decisions, especially when the manuscript evidence is so weak. There is some variation among manuscripts with regard to these two verses, but all existing manuscripts have the verses somewhere in the text of chapter 14.[3] Since we find similar statements elsewhere in the New Testament (1 Tim. 2:12), we will discuss these verses as if they were a part of the original text.

If they are original, we must read them very carefully in the context of 1 Corinthians 14. That is, we must read them in relation to Paul's discussion of prophetic speech in the church. Reading them in context forces us *not* to take it as an absolute statement or as a rule without exception. For example, take the comments that **women should remain silent in the churches** (14:34) and that **it is disgraceful for a woman to speak in the church** (14:35). First Corinthians 11 *assumes* that women can pray and prophecy in the Christian assembly. In that chapter, Paul is addressing public worship where a woman might dishonor her husband, her "head," by not covering her hair *while speaking* in public (11:5). If Paul really meant 14:34–35 as an absolute prohibition of women speaking in church—let alone prophesying—then he has seriously contradicted himself in the space of four chapters.

The conflict between the comments in 14:34–35 and 11:3–16 is very strong indeed. If 14:34–35 was in the original text of 1 Corinthians, it presumably does not mean that *all* women must remain silent, especially those to whom God has given the gift of prophecy (Acts 2:17–18, 21:9). Can we really picture Paul excluding someone like Priscilla from speaking in church, this exceptional woman who helped disciple Apollos? (Acts 18:26). Surely he must refer to a particular "stereotypical" woman of his day who caused disorder in worship by speaking inappropriately.

Verse 35 points to such disturbances: **If they want to inquire about something, they should ask their own husbands at home.**[4] If we read these verses in the context of 1 Corinthians 14, we see the main problem coming from

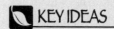

KEY IDEAS

Since Paul assumes that women can prophesy in 1 Corinthians 11, 1 Corinthians 14:34–35 cannot prevent women from speaking of a spiritual nature.

women interrupting prophecies or the worship service, particularly with questions. Paul had been arguing for the orderly use of prophecy in worship and for the appropriate testing of prophecy. As such, these verses would picture women who were disgracing their husbands by comments and inquiries that demonstrated ignorance and were disturbing the worship meeting.

It is possible that Paul's churches increasingly saw the involvement of such women in worship as a problem. Some have even suggested that Paul himself added this note later in the margin because of such increased trouble with the women at Corinth. They wonder if the women of 1 Corinthians 11 did not yield to his instructions and became more and more disgraceful in their worship conduct.

Without some scenario of this sort it is difficult to see how the Paul who said "There is neither . . . male nor female, for you are all one in Christ Jesus" (Gal. 3:28) could say it was a disgrace for a woman to speak in church. Paul elsewhere was very affirming of his female coworkers, women like Priscilla (16:19), Junia (Rom. 16:7), Euodia, Syntyche (Phil. 4:3), and Phoebe (Rom. 16:1).

Indeed, some other aspects of these verses seem uncharacteristic of Paul if they are original. It pushes us to see them as responses to specific issues that were really bothering him.[5] For example, Paul had been addressing the church (singular) at Corinth. He does not think of Corinth as a group of churches but as a single church (1:2). Suddenly Paul says not to let women speak "in the churches." Who is he now addressing? The Corinthians have no influence on how women speak anywhere else. If these verses belong here, then the worship of the Corinthians has suddenly triggered his thought on an issue bothering him in other places beside Corinth. He interrupts his train of thought to vent on the frequent disruption of Christian worship by a certain type of woman he has seen in several places.[6] I personally think that this shift to speaking of churches, plural, is a very strong indicator that these verses are not, in the end, original.

What are we to make of his argument from the Jewish law: women **must be in submission, as the Law says** (14:34). At first glance, it seems odd that Paul would use the Law as the basis for an argument, since he so often emphasizes that Christians are "not under law, but under grace" (Rom. 6:14; Gal. 3:23, 4:21, 5:1; Eph. 2:15). But Paul is thinking of the Pentateuch here, the Law as a section of Scripture (Rom. 3:21).[7] Genesis 3:16 tells us that wives are subordinate to the rule of their husbands as a consequence of Eve's sin. This is probably the verse from the Law to which this statement refers.

But even then, this argument is very peculiar. Genesis 3:16 places wives in subordination to their husband's rule as a result of Eve's sin. But Christ atoned for *all* sin, including the sins of Eve. In other words, it is an offence to Christ to say that women are still living under this particular law, unless we simply mean that women still experience painful childbirth (1 Tim. 2:15). It so much as says, "Jesus, there are a few sins your death did not take care of." In short, if we do not see this comment as an example rather than a principle, we find Paul making a blasphemous statement. I would rather think that Paul is simply giving an example from the old covenant.

If these verses are original, the most attractive way to resolve such issues is to suppose that the need for order in the church and the desire to avoid unnecessary persecution pushed Paul's churches increasingly in the direction of greater restriction on the role of women in worship. By the time Colossians, Ephesians, and 1 Timothy were written, we are no longer hearing the phrase "neither male nor female" that Paul earlier used in Galatians (Col. 3:11). The instructions become ever more male oriented (1 Tim. 3:2, 3:8; Titus 1:6), and we find hints here and there that some women were facilitating false teaching by supporting false teachers (2 Tim. 3:6).

But as with the issue of slavery, we are in a position today to see the implications of the gospel played out even further than the early church was able to play them out. In their world, any leadership of men by women was seen as disgraceful. It would seem that they could scarcely let women take too much leadership without hurting their witness to the world, especially as Christianity increasingly came under persecution. When a bully is standing over you, you do not do things that will make the bully upset. Accordingly, books like 1 Peter are like "defensive strategies" for living in a world that is looking for an excuse to persecute Christians.[8]

We find ourselves in the opposite situation today. We live in a world that wants to afford women the same status as men. In a remarkable turn of events, the respectable position in our culture is actually the one that best fits the spiritual truth that God values both men and women equally and that God speaks to men and women

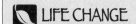 LIFE CHANGE

In a remarkable turn of events, the respectable position in our culture is actually the one that best fits the spiritual truth that God values both men and women equally and that God speaks through both men and women. We honor God most when we work to see this heavenly principle played out to the full in the church and in the cultures of the world today.

equally. In the first century there was nothing uniquely Christian about placing women in subordination to men. This was exactly the position the world had on the issue. Christianity was unique when it afforded worth and value to women, when it moved in the direction of empowerment and spiritual equality. It was at this point that Christianity was being uniquely Christian. Today we can work out these spiritual principles more fully than the early church did in their day, just as we did when we abolished the institution of slavery.

ENDNOTES

1. For example, G. D. Fee, *The First Epistle to the Corinthians* (Grand Rapids: Eerdmans, 1987), 699–705. For some reason, several manuscripts in what scholars call the "Western text" place the verses after verse 40. While I will attempt to interpret these verses as they appear in most Greek manuscripts, I find Fee's arguments that they were an early addition very convincing.

2. The Greek text behind the NIV and almost all other contemporary trans-lations have resulted from painstaking study of the different variations that occur in the over five thousand Greek manuscripts at our disposal. When the Greek text behind the King James Version (KJV) was edited in the 1400 and 1500s, almost all the documents at their disposal were late ones, dating from the 900s on. With the discovery of much older manuscripts, ones that date to as early as the second century, we are now in a position to know the original wording more accurately than the 1611 KJV scholars could. Anyone who uses a translation like the NIV, NLT, or almost any other modern version enjoys the fruits of these labors. Similarly, most conservative churches accept the practice of such textual study, a fact born out by faith statements that locate the inerrancy of the Bible *in the original manuscripts* (*The Wesleyan Discipline* 218).

3. It is possible that we will one day find a manuscript that does not have them at all.

4. Notice here also that Paul presumes that these women are wives. Therefore, the matter of husband-wife relationship may also be involved.

5. Given comments like Gal. 5:12, we cannot doubt that God allowed the anger of inspired authors to come through at times in Scripture.

6. This sudden change of addressee is a strong argument that these verses were not in the original text. Others have noted that in Paul's comment that the word of God had not come to them "alone" (14:36), the word "alone" is mascu-line in Greek, not feminine. Some argue that if 14:34–35 were original, the word "alone" would be feminine, in reference to the women he would have been addressing. This latter argument is far from conclusive.

7. Genesis, Exodus, Leviticus, Numbers, and Deuteronomy.

8. I take this concept from S. McKnight, *1 Peter* (Grand Rapids: Zondervan, 1996), 29.

21

CHRIST'S RESURRECTION

1 Corinthians 15:1–11

1. LOCATING THIS PART OF THE LETTER

First Corinthians 15 is another one of those instances where the problems of the Corinthian church are a boon for us. Paul has heard that some of the Corinthians do not believe in the resurrection of the dead (15:12), a situation that leads him to present the argument of this chapter. It is the most detailed argument for resurrection in the New Testament, and it provides us with important information about the appearances of Christ after His death. Our Christian understanding would be greatly diminished if we did not have this chapter.

Scholars have suggested a number of different explanations of what the Corinthians were thinking and on the precise meaning of Paul's response. On the whole, the best suggestion is that some of them believed in an afterlife but rejected the notion of a bodily resurrection. Here we need to remind ourselves that there is a difference between the idea that we have an immortal soul and the idea that our corpses will be resurrected in the future. It is the resurrection of the dead that has stood historically at the heart of Christian belief, particularly New Testament Christian belief. While it seems possible to synthesize these two beliefs together in some way, the focus of New Testament teaching lies squarely with the idea of resurrection.

The resurrection of the dead is the bodily rising of the dead at a specific point in future history. The New Testament is not completely clear about whether the resurrected return to the earth or to heaven. Aside from Christ and perhaps the anonymous individuals of Matt. 27:52–53, no one has yet been resurrected from the dead in the way Christians believe we will at the end of history.[1] The word for the dead used in 1 Corinthians 15 (*nekros*) implies that our dead bodies are involved with this resurrection in some way. It seems that only Jews had this belief in Paul's time, and not all Jews even then.[2] It was no doubt one of the many things that the "wise" of that day found ridiculous, as we see in Acts 17:32.

In contrast, the concept of the immortality of the soul was perfectly respectable, even if it was not widely believed by the culture at large. Famous philosophers like Plato and Pythagoras thought that our souls— at least the souls of the virtuous—continued to exist at death. In contrast, the body was a hindrance to virtue and wisdom. Most philosophers had no desire to get their bodies back after death. Philosophers like these thought of death as the liberation of your soul to a better reality.

It is worth reminding ourselves that the way most of us think about death and the afterlife is not the primary way the New Testament authors thought about these things. We tend to think that you die and then go immediately to heaven or hell. This idea has some merit. But as we have seen in our discussion of 1 Corinthians 7, the early Christians focused much more on the idea that we would come back from the dead in a body. They were very vague about where or what we would be in the meantime. They did not focus on heaven or hell and had very little to say about the state of the dead—both righteous and wicked—between death and the resurrection.[3] What they preached was that God would bring wrath on the earth at some point in the *near* future.

2. PAUL REMINDS THEM OF CHRIST'S RESURRECTION (15:1–11)

Paul begins by reminding the Corinthians of the basic Christian gospel: **By this gospel you are saved** (15:2). This comment is extremely helpful. It tells us we are about to hear the essential content of the good news, the gospel. These are the things in which we must trust if we are to be saved and escape God's wrath when He judges the earth.

For what I received I passed on to you as of first importance: that Christ died for our sins according to the Scriptures, that he was buried, that he was raised on the third day according to the Scriptures, and that he appeared to Peter, and then to the Twelve (15:3–5). It is possible that some form of these verses was actually a kind of early Christian confession of faith. Herein we can identify at least three, perhaps as many as five, basic beliefs: (1) that Christ's death was a part of God's plan, (2) that Christ was buried, and (3) that God raised him from the dead as a part of God's plan. We can also infer that (4) there is an implicit trust in the prophetic worth of Scripture and (5) the appearances of the resurrected Christ to Peter and the other disciples were significant events as well.

Among these five points, the two that fulfilled Scripture seem particularly important. The first is the atoning death of Christ, which Paul likely saw as the fulfillment of Old Testament passages like Isa. 53:5. We remember from the first chapter of 1 Corinthians that the cross of Christ stood at the heart of the gospel Paul preached. It was the path to reconciliation with God because Christ had paid the price for sin (2 Cor. 5:21).

But Paul also saw the resurrection as a central element in the equation of salvation. He likely believed that Christ's resurrection was the fulfillment of passages like Ps. 16:10, Hos. 6:2, or Jon. 1:17. On the one hand, the resurrection represented God's vindication of Jesus. It validated the atoning death of Christ. Yet it was also the hope of all Christians for life beyond this present world. If the Day of Salvation was the day when Christians escaped God's wrath, then resurrection was the path to salvation for those Christians who died before Christ returned.

Many Christians today are wondering what the bare minimum of Christian belief is, the absolute core of what we must believe in order to be saved. Paul's "short list" is very helpful. We may disagree on many, many things, but these

 GREAT THEMES

1 Corinthians 15 gives us the absolute, rock bottom, core beliefs of Christian faith: the atoning death of Christ as a part of God's plan and His victorious resurrection from the dead.

are the absolute, rock bottom, core beliefs of Christian faith. If we deviate from this list, we are in trouble.

Paul reminds the Corinthians that he is passing along universal Christian traditions. In other words, these beliefs preceded his entrance into the faith. He mentions Peter and the Twelve. We remember that the Corinthians were aware of who Peter was and the position of prominence he had in the Christian movement (1 Cor. 9:5). Some at Corinth probably considered Peter even more authoritative than Paul (1 Cor. 1:12). Paul even uses Peter's Aramaic name throughout 1 Corinthians: Cephas.[4] This fact implies that Paul knew Peter personally, not as someone people talked about.

Some have argued over the years that Paul invented Christianity and that his teachings had little to do with Jesus or His first followers. But it is clear that Paul and Peter were on the same page when it came to the essentials of Christian faith. For example, someone might argue that Peter was lying when he said he had seen Jesus alive after His death on the cross. Someone might argue that Peter was mistaken in his belief that he had seen Jesus. But you cannot argue that Paul made it all up. First Corinthians removes this possibility from the table.

It also does not seem likely at all that Peter or the disciples were lying. We remember that most of these individuals paid for their faith with their lives. Peter in particular was probably crucified in Rome during the reign of the Emperor Nero (1 Clement 5). If he had made up his experience of the resurrected Christ, surely he would have confessed his lie as he faced death. But he did not, because he was not lying. He truly believed he had seen Christ after His death on the cross.

Indeed, we can probably identify two points when the continued existence of the Christian movement was most vulnerable. The first was immediately following the crucifixion. Other Jewish messianic movements would come and go, their messiahs crucified by the Romans or otherwise lost to time. But this movement survived despite the death of its Messiah. The resurrection is the reason. It turned a group of scared, hiding followers into bold proclaimers of a renewed message.

The other point was when the first disciples were dying off and Jerusalem was being assailed and destroyed by the Roman army. If the faith of Peter and Paul had not been so strong, if they had not conveyed such firm conviction of Christianity's truth to their converts, surely the Christian movement would have died out then. But apparently their faith was unassailable, a proof of their conviction in these things.

Someone might suggest that Peter and Paul were hallucinating. If they were, they were not alone. Paul notes not only that Peter had seen the resurrected Christ, but that the other disciples had as well. The list did not stop here: **more than five hundred of the brothers . . . James . . . all the apostles, and last of all he appeared to me** (15:6–8).

Paul's mention of the five hundred brothers amounts to a challenge for someone to check his sources. If you think Peter is crazy, check out these five hundred individuals. They are still around. Jesus also appeared to His half-brother, James. This fact explains why James went from questioning his brother's mission (John 7:3–5) to leading the Jerusalem church (Acts 15:13–21).

Apparently there was another group of individuals to whom Jesus also appeared: the apostles. We unfortunately do not know much about who these individuals were. To call them apostles probably means they received a commission from God to bring the message of the resurrection to the world. It is possible that people like Barnabas had seen Christ after He rose from the dead (1 Cor. 9:5–6), and perhaps the Andronicus and Junia of Rom. 16:7 as well.

Paul considered himself the last apostle, the last one to whom Jesus appeared in this way after His death on the cross. [I] **do not even deserve to be called an apostle, because I persecuted the church of God** (15:9). Certainly we should make no mistake about it—Paul thought he was an apostle. Not only does he defend his apostleship elsewhere in 1 Corinthians (9:1), but he ultimately did not view himself as any less of an apostle than Peter or anyone else (Gal. 2:2, 6, 9; 2 Cor. 12:11).

But he also recognized his ultimate unworthiness: **But by the grace of God I am what I am** (15:10). Paul was extremely misguided before he came to Christ. He persecuted God's church. But he must have done so out of a heart of true devotion, for God stopped long enough to tap him on the shoulder and show him the right direction. Paul was ever thankful for this graciousness on God's part, this undeserved favor.

The result was an incredible ministry, as God's grace worked through Paul (15:10). Here we remember the vigor with which Paul fought for his authority in certain sectors of the early church. We will hear the specifics of how hard he worked for the gospel—and suffered—when we get to 2 Corinthians 11 and 12.

[T]his is what we preach (15:11). Paul ends this section where he began: the resurrection of Christ is a central element of Christian faith. It stands at the heart of what Paul had preached to them, and it was something in which they had faith. In other words, while some Corinthians apparently questioned whether there would be a future resurrection, they accepted the resurrection of Christ in some way.

ENDNOTES

1. We do find a number of people who are resuscitated from the dead in the Old and New Testament, but these individuals went on to die again. They also will be resurrected at some point in the future.

2. Although some would say some Persians did as well.

3. See the discussions of 1 Cor. 15:18 and 2 Cor. 5:8.

4. Although the NIV translates it as Peter.

PAUL'S ARGUMENT FOR A FUTURE RESURRECTION

1 Corinthians 15:12-34

P aul's argument for a future resurrection works because Christ's resurrection is connected with our resurrection. Christ's resurrection was the beginning of *the* resurrection, a resurrection of which we will also be a part one day. In fact, our resurrected body will actually be the same as Christ's resurrected human body.

This is a difficult concept for some: that our resurrected body will be like the resurrection body of Christ. We tend to think of Christ as so different from us that we can hardly imagine that

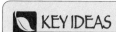
KEY IDEAS

Christ's resurrection was the beginning of *the* resurrection, a resurrection of which we will also be a part one day.

our future bodies would be the same. We have a hard time accepting the full humanity of Jesus. But Paul's argument proceeds with this assumption. **If there is no resurrection of the dead, then not even Christ has been raised** (15:13). The word for dead (*nekros*) implies an empty tomb, since we might just as well translate the phrase a "resurrection of corpses." In other words, Christ's resurrection was not just a matter of His spirit continuing to exist after death or the immortality of His soul. Christ's body somehow returned from the dead to the land of the living.

The first part of this section presents what is called a "contrary to fact" argument (15:13–18). In other words, Paul explores what the consequences would be if Christ was not truly raised from the dead. **[O]ur preaching is useless and so is your faith** (15:14). Paul does not spell out how the resurrection validates the atoning significance of Christ's death, but for him the two were connected. He will tell them a few verses later that they would still be in their sins if Christ had not risen (15:17).

More than that . . . if the dead are not raised, then Christ has not been raised either (15:15–16). To be an apostle was to be a witness to Christ's resurrection (Acts 3:15, 4:33; 1 Cor. 9:1). But if there was no resurrection, then they were guilty of breaking the ninth commandment, bearing false witness by claiming something in God's name that was not true. If the Corinthians accepted the validity of Christianity or of its leaders, then they would need to accept the truth of resurrection.

Paul reiterates the unhappy conclusion again: **And if Christ has not been raised, your faith is futile; you are still in your sins** (15:17). Even worse, **those also who have fallen asleep in Christ are lost** (15:18). We remember that Paul wrote his first letter to the Thessalonians in part because of this issue. Some of the Thessalonians wondered whether Christians who died would miss out on the kingdom of God. Paul assured them that "we who are still alive, who are left till the coming of the Lord, will certainly not precede those who have fallen asleep . . . the dead in Christ will rise first" (1 Thess. 4:15–16).

But if there is no resurrection, Paul says, then those Christians who have died are lost. Some aspects of Paul's thinking are unclear here. For example, if the alternative to resurrection is to be lost, then Paul sounds like he does not believe in any other kind of afterlife at all. In other words, he does not even consider the possibility that our spirits might continue to exist somewhere other than the earth. Further, what does he mean by "sleep"? Normally a sleeping person is not aware of anything. Did Paul think that we are unconscious between the time of our death and our future resurrection?

Thankfully, other passages in the New Testament, as well as the later history of the church, clarify these issues for us. If Paul had any of these thoughts at this point, he does not show it in his later writings. In Philippians 1:23 he indicates that a Christian goes to be with Christ at death. Further, Luke gives us two clear passages where the dead are conscious after death (Luke 16:19–31, 23:43). The most appropriate Christian belief is thus that we are somehow conscious in between our death and resurrection.

As Paul brings this paragraph to a close, we can feel the emotion in his words. He draws the logical conclusion if there is no resurrection: **If only for this life we have hope in Christ, we are to be pitied more than all men** (15:19). When we read passages like 1 Cor. 4:11–13 or 2 Cor. 11:23–29, we understand Paul's feelings. If this life is all there is—and Paul faced such constant distress—then his only existence was truly miserable.

So the first paragraph of this section (15:12–19) presents a number of undesirable conclusions that would follow if there were no resurrection. But thankfully, **Christ has indeed been raised from the dead** (15:20). In 1 Cor. 15:20–28, Paul looks at Christ's resurrection from the perspective of history and God's ultimate plan for humanity. He begins with a theme we will see him explore more fully in Romans 5, namely, the idea that Christ solves the problems that Adam brought into the world through his sin.

Death, Paul tells us, **came through a man** (15:21), namely, Adam. Paul will later put it this way in Romans: "sin entered the world through one man, and death through sin, and in this way death came to all men, because all sinned" (Rom. 5:12). Paul does not explain exactly how Adam's sin brought death to humanity, but he clearly considered him the culprit. Because of Adam, all humans are destined to die.

But everything that Adam did wrong, Christ did right. "Since death came through a man, **the resurrection of the dead comes also through a man** (15:21). Paul is not espousing universalism here—the idea that everyone will eventually be saved, even the Hitlers of the world. First Thessalonians 4 makes it clear that it is the dead *in Christ* who rise. When he says all will be made alive he either means (1) everyone has the *possibility* of resurrection in Christ, (2) everyone *in Christ* will be made alive, or (3) everyone will rise because of Christ, some to everlasting life and others to everlasting judgment. My personal inclination is to option 2. Paul indicates that all of those who become incorporated into Christ will rise.

The idea of being in Christ is a key concept for Paul that runs throughout his writings. To him, baptism symbolized dying with Christ

KEY IDEAS

The idea that we are in Christ is a key concept for Paul that runs throughout his writings.

(Rom. 6:3; Gal. 2:19–20). As we participate in His death, we die to sin (Rom. 6:6–7). It is like our mortal body and our flesh is dead, just as Christ's body died (Rom. 8:10). But while we are on earth, our spirits become alive because of Christ, as God's Spirit lives within us (Rom. 8:11). We are enabled to "live a new life" (Rom. 6:4) that involves victory over sin and temptation (Rom. 8:1–4; 1 Cor. 10:13).

But when Paul says that we who "have been united with him like this in his death . . . will certainly also be united with him in his resurrection" (Rom. 6:5), he is not referring to something that takes place while we are on the earth, although we do live life in a new way (Rom. 6:4). In this comment, as in 1 Cor. 15:22, he is thinking of the future resurrection when the "dead in Christ will rise first. After that, we who are still alive and are left will be caught up in the clouds to meet the Lord in the air" (1 Thess. 4:17). As in Adam all died, so all those who become incorporated into Christ will rise from the dead one day.

Some have called Paul's idea of dying and rising with Christ "mystical." From our perspective, Paul is not clear about how it all works. But in some way, our old self dies with Christ when we become baptized (Rom. 6:3–6). This death alone means that we die to sin in some very real way—we are actually freed from the power of sin. But one day, "he who raised Christ from the dead will also give life to your mortal bodies through his Spirit, who lives in you" (Rom. 8:11). We will find out later in the chapter that our new body will not be made of flesh and blood, but it will be a spiritual body at the resurrection yet to come (1 Cor. 15:44, 50).

Paul's words in 15:23 mark a new twist on Paul's beliefs as a Pharisee. As a Pharisee, Paul had no doubt believed that one day in the future, at the dawn of eternity, God would raise the dead and reward those who had trusted in Him. But he would have thought this resurrection would take place all at once. Everyone to be raised would be raised at the same time.

Now that Paul was a Christian, God showed him two important new truths. The first and most important was that the end of time had already begun. Christ's resurrection was nothing less than the beginning of the end. Paul was now in the time of fulfillment when all of God's promises would come to pass. This was the good news, the gospel that was the "power of God for the salvation of everyone who believes" (Rom. 1:16).

Yet God had done something very surprising. Rather than raise all the righteous dead of Israel when He raised Christ, God had set aside a period of history for Gentiles to come to Him, as well as for the rebellious of Israel to repent. "Israel has experienced a hardening in part until the full number of the Gentiles has come in. And so all Israel will be saved" (Rom. 11:25–26). A process that Paul had previously seen as a single event would now take place as a two step process. Christ was the beginning of the resurrection, the **firstfruits** of the dead. Then at some point in the future when Christ returned, the dead in Christ would rise.[1]

What would happen after this resurrection of the dead in Christ? **Then the end will come** (15:24). These next few verses reflect Paul's understanding of Christ's role in the end of the ages. The ultimate goal of history is for everything to return to submission to God. For whatever reason, the sovereign God has allowed the vast majority of His creation to live in a state of rebellion against Him for a very long time. This rebellion includes not only humans, but some angels as well (6:3). Obviously God will not allow such a state of affairs to continue forever. At some point in His mysterious will He will bring judgment on this rebellion and bring everything once again under His rule in the "kingdom of God."

For Paul, Christ was God's agent for bringing this submission into effect. As messianic king, Christ would judge the earth (Rom. 8:34). God confirmed Christ's lordship over the world when He raised Him from the dead (Acts 2:36; Phil. 2:9–11). In heaven He now reigns **until he has put all his enemies under his feet** (15:25). Paul thus does not picture Christ's job of quelling the rebellion as quite finished yet.[2] The final enemy **is death** (15:26). At the resurrection, when Christ has conquered death once and for all, then the rebellion will have finally ended for good.

Throughout this passage, Paul is drawing on rich Christian interpretations of the Old Testament. For example, when he alludes to Christ as King and mentions putting His enemies under His feet, Paul is thinking of Ps. 110:1. This verse was very important for the early Christians: "The

LORD says to my Lord, 'Sit at my right hand until I make your enemies a footstool for your feet.'" Jesus even quoted this Scripture about himself (Mark 12:35–37). It also played a significant role for Acts, Paul, and Hebrews (Acts 2:34–35; Rom. 8:34; Eph. 1:20; Heb. 1:13). I personally wonder if the early Christians in fact started calling Jesus "Lord" on the basis of this verse.

For Paul, this verse had a whole story behind it, a plan that God was working out on the earth. This story began when God created humanity. His goal for humanity was for us to rule the earth. As Psalm 8 says, God intended to "put everything under his [humanity's] feet" (Ps. 8:6), God intended to crown humanity "with glory and honor" (Ps. 8:5). But it did not happen because of humanity's sin. "At present we do not see everything subject to him [humanity]" (Heb. 2:8). Instead, "all have sinned and fall short of the glory of God" (Rom. 3:23), the glory for which God created humanity.

God's solution to this problem was to send Jesus to lead us to this glory (Heb. 2:10). "[W]e see Jesus, who was made a little lower than the angels, now crowned with glory and honor" (Heb. 2:9). To fulfill God's intention for humanity, God has now **put everything under Christ** (15:27) in fulfillment of Ps. 8:6. Christ defeated death, the ultimate challenge to humanity's glory. Christ "suffered death, so that by the grace of God he might taste death for everyone" (Heb. 2:9). Paul's subtle move from Ps. 110:1 in 1 Cor. 15:25 to Ps. 8:6 in 1 Cor. 15:27 likely has this whole story of redemption in mind.

In any case, Paul makes it clear **that this does not include God himself, who put everything under Christ. When he** [God] **has done this** [put everything under Christ's feet], **then the Son himself will be made subject to him** [God] (15:27–28). Christ is Lord, but God is King (1 Cor. 8:6; Eph. 4:5–6). Paul pictures Christ here as the agent to whom God assigns the task of "cleaning up" the mess that is the world. After Christ has defeated God's enemies, God will resume His rightful role as King of the creation.

In the last part of this section, 15:29–34, Paul mentions a few more problems that would follow if there were no resurrection.

His first comment is very puzzling to us. **If the dead are not raised at all, why are people baptized for them?** (15:29). Paul does not say that he approves of such baptism for the dead, but clearly both he and the Corinthians know of some group that practices such baptism. Scholars have spilled a great deal of ink

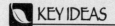

KEY IDEAS

After Christ has defeated God's enemies, God will resume His rightful role as king of the creation.

over this verse, and it is tantalizing to wonder what exactly was going on. We simply do not have enough information to know for sure what stands behind this comment.

In my opinion, we can infer first of all that some group existed who baptized others so that these others could be resurrected or at least could have a good afterlife. Paul presumes they are doing it in the hope of resurrection. Since baptism was involved, it would seem to be a Christian group. The Corinthians must have known about this group and apparently had some regard for them.

We can only speculate about the precise motivation these Christians had for such baptism. From our current perspective, it must have come from misunderstanding on some level or another. The act of baptism implies that the dead individuals in question had not believed on Christ. Had they disbelieved in Christ while alive? Or had they just never heard about Christ? Were these Gentiles who had died before Christianity came to town? Were they Jews who had lived before Christ came to earth? Baptism implies that they were trying to incorporate them into Christ after the fact, to atone for their sins after their death.[3]

Again, Paul does not commend this practice. But he does argue that those Corinthians who respect the practice are inconsistent if they do not believe in the resurrection. We are scarcely in any position to baptize for the dead today, as Mormons do. Whatever was going on exactly, it was not likely baptism for people who had rejected Christ while they were alive. Nor was it a baptism for Christians who had "backslid." That only leaves those who have died without ever knowing of Christ. Like children before the age of understanding, we can trust the souls of these individuals to God, the righteous judge. Whatever He does, He will do what is right (Gen. 18:25).[4]

Paul also returns to his own plight if there is no resurrection: **why do we endanger ourselves every hour . . . If I fought wild beasts in**

Ephesus for merely human reasons, what have I gained? (15:30–31). This comment is similar to the one Paul made in 15:19. Paul underwent a lot of hardship in the course of his ministry. He will lay out a list of them in 2 Corinthians 11. What an incredible waste if there was nothing after this life!

Some have speculated that Paul might have been imprisoned at some point during his stay at Ephesus, although not when he was writing 1 Corinthians. Particularly in 2 Cor. 1:8–11, he indicates some extreme hardships he encountered while he was in Asia, the region in which Ephesus was located. Some scholars actually think he may have written some of the prison epistles, particularly Philippians, while imprisoned there during this period.[5] Paul would have written 1 Corinthians before that imprisonment. Paul's mention here of fighting wild beasts makes us wonder whether he had faced some sort of imprisonment even before that point.

It does not seem likely that Paul actually faced wild animals in an arena at Ephesus. Doubtlessly we would hear somewhere of a miraculous delivery from them if he was speaking literally here! Rather, it seems more likely that Paul had already had a run in with the authorities at Ephesus by the time he wrote 1 Corinthians. The wild beasts could be a reference to Roman soldiers. For example, the early Christian Ignatius, writing in the early second century, referred to the Roman soldiers who escorted him as "leopards."

No, if there was no resurrection, then it would be ludicrous for Paul to live the way he was. Instead, he would adopt the philosophy of some of the Epicureans of his day:[6] **"Let us eat and drink, for tomorrow we die."** What was the point of suffering, if there was no accountability? What was the point of virtue, if everything was pointless anyway? Why not live for pleasure?

But this is not what Paul believed, and he strongly instructed the Corinthians to stay away from people with such a philosophy. **Do not be**

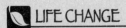

LIFE CHANGE

To Paul, a world without God is a world without meaning, a world where we should all be living for pleasure and ourselves. We must always remind ourselves of what true meaning is, and we must view the present through the lens of eternity.

mislead: **"Bad company corrupts good character"** (15:33). The Corinthians should avoid the people who were telling them things like these. **Come back to your senses as you ought, and stop sinning** (15:34). Paul strongly chastises them for even listening to people who thought things like these. How could they draw on people who did not even know God for their thoughts on such matters? The Corinthians were sinning by turning from the truth and needed to stop. They needed to turn back to the path and the traditions that Paul had first delivered to them and that they had apparently accepted.

ENDNOTES

1. Paul's writings know nothing of a seven year tribulation, a millennium, or the two resurrections of Revelation (Rev. 20:5, 12). To be faithful to his part of Scripture, we cannot impose these ideas from other places into his words (Revelation itself actually never mentions a seven year tribulation or associates any period of time with the great tribulation of Rev. 7:14. These concepts are impositions of Daniel on Revelation itself). It is possible that those who weave the quite distinct messages of these different books together may turn out to be spiritually inspired. But they (perhaps unintentionally) sacrifice the specific meanings of each individual passage in their quest to create an overall picture. This picture is actually none of the individual meanings, but a new meaning of their own making!

With regard to the book of Revelation, we should remember that it is so symbolic that it may not mean to give us a straightforward presentation of how events will unfold. This is at least one way to listen to what Paul has to say while not denying the inspiration of Revelation as well. One might also argue that the book of Revelation represents a more developed understanding of end time events than Paul yet did. But it does not honor Scripture to ignore its meaning at one point because we want it to fit with its meaning at another point. Such harmonizing tendencies only show that our *idea* of Scripture is more important to us than what the Bible itself actually says.

2. Contrast the imagery of Eph. 1:22, where it was more appropriate to speak of all authorities already under Christ's feet.

3. Something of this sort takes place in the Jewish book 2 Maccabees 12:39–45, where sacrifices are offered to atone for the sins of certain soldiers who died in battle so that they can be part of the resurrection.

4. We know that Jesus is "the way and the truth and the life," that no one comes to the Father except through him (John 14:6). The debate is whether God

sometimes applies the atoning significance of Christ's death to children who are not old enough to understand Christ, as well as to those who have responded to the light they had without having heard of Christ.

5. However, the traditional location from which Christian tradition saw Paul writing these four letters (Ephesians, Philippians, Colossians, Philemon) was Rome.

6. Although this approach was not that of Epicurus himself, the founder of Epicureanism.

WHAT KIND OF BODY WILL WE HAVE?

1 Corinthians 15:35-57

1. SPIRITUAL BODIES

Paul now deals with the greatest objection Greeks had to the idea of a resurrection, the idea that we will somehow get our bodies back at some point in the future. To the Greeks, the body was not something a person would want to get back. One Jewish writing shows the influence of such Greek thinking when it says that "a perishable body weighs down the soul, and this earthly tent burdens the thoughtful mind."[1] We remind ourselves that Paul's teaching focused on the resurrection of our bodies rather than on the survival of a soul after death. There is really only one place where Paul gives us any reason to believe that he thought a person could exist without a body of some sort after death (Phil. 1:23–24). This one instance makes it clear that Paul did believe we would be conscious in between our deaths and our resurrection. But Paul barely even mentions this fact.

In contrast, the Greeks thought the liberation of their souls from the body was a good thing. Why would I want a decrepit body back? It is no doubt for this reason that we see the Epicureans of Acts 17 mocking Paul when he begins to talk about resurrection (Acts 17:32). Epicureans did not believe in any kind of afterlife.

So Paul heads their objections off at the pass. **With what kind of body will they come?** (15:35). We notice that for Paul, resurrection presupposes a body of some sort. He cannot conceive of resurrection apart from some kind of body. In all his writings Paul is unclear about what a disembodied spirit might be—God apparently did not give him a definitive revelation on this subject (2 Cor. 12:2–3). But he was sure that whatever the resurrected body was, it would not be a body made up of flesh and blood (15:50). It would be a different sort of body, a "spiritual body."

In 15:36–41, Paul explores how many different kinds of bodies exist and how God gives to each thing a body appropriate to its purpose and His will. For example, **[w]hen you sow, you do not plant the body that will be, but just a seed** (15:37). What comes out of the ground does not look like what goes in, but **God gives it a body as he has determined** (15:38).

Paul notes a similar phenomenon with regard to living things. **All flesh is not the same** (15:39). God has an order to His creation, and he appropriates different kinds of bodies as He sees fit. Paul proceeds to heavenly bodies: **the splendor of the heavenly bodies is one kind, and the splendor of the earthly bodies is another. The sun has one kind of splendor, the moon another and the stars another** (15:40–41). Paul's purpose here is not to give us a chemistry or astrophysics lesson. He is not arguing about the chemical composition of stars or planets. His argument is simply that God apportions different forms to different objects in His creation.

These analogies now lead him to the nature of our resurrection body in comparison to our physical bodies (15:42–49). Again, Paul's purpose is not to tell us precisely what the composition of our resurrection body will be, only to contrast it with our current earthly body and associate it with heaven. As we have seen that God apportions different bodies to different things in His creation, so **will it be with the resurrection of the dead** (15:42).

For one thing, the earthly body that is buried in the earth, that is "sown," **is perishable. But it is raised imperishable** (15:42). Our resurrection body will never die but will last for all eternity (2 Cor. 5:1). Our earthly bodies are part of our groaning on earth (2 Cor. 5:2); my body is buried **in dishonor. But it is raised in glory** (15:43), the glory to which Christ is leading many sons (Heb. 2:10). **[I]t is raised in power . . . it is raised a spiritual body** (15:43–44).

Paul returns to the distinction some Corinthians were making between "natural/soulish" and "spiritual" (see commentary on 1 Cor. 2:14–15). **The spiritual did not come first, but the natural** (15:46). There is a natural/soulish body and a spiritual body that Christians potentially can have

(15:44). The natural/soulish body corresponds to the body of Adam, whom God made a living soul. In contrast, the spiritual body pertains to Christ, **the last Adam**, who is a **life-giving spirit** (15:45).

Paul is not talking in 15:47 about where Christ came from, but about the nature of His resurrection body. Adam's body was of the dust of the earth, Christ's resurrection body was made of heavenly materials. **As was the earthly man, so are those who are of the earth** (15:48). When Jesus was on earth, He had the kind of body we all have here on earth. More difficult is the second concept: **just as we have borne the likeness of the earthly man, so shall we bear the likeness of the man from heaven** (15:49).

Since Jesus is fully human, He retains His full humanity even in heaven alongside His full divinity. Paul teaches the difficult concept that our resurrection body will be of the same type as His. At the resurrection Christ "will transform our lowly bodies so that they will be like his glorious body" (Phil. 3:21). This teaching is in keeping with the fact that Christ is just the "firstfruits of those who have fallen asleep" (1 Cor. 15:20). Christ begins the resurrection, but when He returns the second time, He will also bring back the dead who belong to Him (15:23).

Paul concludes this section in glorious anticipation of our transformed bodies (15:50–57). **[F]lesh and blood cannot inherit the kingdom of God, nor does perishable inherit the imperishable** (15:50). Whatever our transformed bodies are like, they will not be like the corruptible flesh and blood with which we currently live. Flesh and blood die; our spiritual bodies will never die.

Listen, I tell you a mystery (15:51). When Christ returns to judge the world, we will be saved from God's wrath. We will meet Christ in the air before the judgment begins. **For the trumpet will sound, the dead will be raised imperishable, and we will be changed** (15:52). As Paul said in 1 Thessalonians,

> [W]e who are still alive, who are left till the coming of the Lord, will certainly not precede those who have fallen asleep. For the Lord himself will come down from heaven, with a loud command, with the voice of the archangel and with the trumpet call

of God, and the dead in Christ will rise first. After that, we who are still alive and are left will be caught up together with them in the clouds to meet the Lord in the air. And so we will be with the Lord forever (1 Thess. 4:15–17).

First Corinthians fits exactly with what Paul had told the Thessalonians. **For the trumpet will sound, the dead will be raised imperishable, and we will be changed** (1 Cor. 15:52). This change has to take place because **the imperishable must clothe itself with the imperishable** (15:53). If our bodies did not change, we could not live with the Lord forever.

Paul saw the resurrection as the spiritual fulfillment of several Old Testament verses. With the transformation of our bodies, **then the saying that is written will come true, "Death has been swallowed up in victory." "Where, O death, is your victory? Where, O death, is your sting?"** (1 Cor. 15:54–55). Using spiritual glasses, he sees that **the sting of death is sin** (15:56). Sin is what brings death on us, and death entered the world through the sin of Adam (Rom. 5:12). On the other hand, **the power of sin is the law** (15:56). "For when we were controlled by the sinful nature [flesh], the sinful passions aroused by the law were at work in our bodies, so that we bore fruit for death" (Rom. 7:5). "Once I was alive apart from law; but when the commandment came, sin sprang to life and I died" (Rom. 7:9). Without the Spirit, the law gives power to sin over my flesh, a force that leads me into sin.

Paul will speak of victory over these forces in this life in verses like Rom. 6:18, 7:6, 8:2; and Gal. 5:16. But in 1 Corinthians 15, he has in mind the ultimate victory over death and sin that we will have at the resurrection. Then we will no longer be made of the flesh that dies. Then we will no longer be made of the flesh over which sin can have such awesome power. In the prospect of that day, **thanks be to God! He gives us the victory through our Lord Jesus Christ** (15:57).

2. CONCLUSION (15:58)

If we realize that we are headed toward a future of this sort, then we will want to **stand firm** (15:58). We will want to heed Paul's words to **[l]et nothing move you** so that we can be a part of the glorious resurrection. We know that at the end of our lives, our **labor in the Lord is not in vain**. Accordingly, we should **give ourselves fully to the work of the Lord**.

It is worth reminding ourselves that Paul and the New Testament strongly believe in a literal return of Jesus to the earth and a literal resurrection of the dead with a subsequent judgment. Like the Corinthians, many of us live mostly for this life and do not take too seriously the New Testament claim that God will at some time break through the normal routine of life to judge the earth and set everything aright. Paul reminds us that our lives today are conditioned by an eternal hope. While it is easy enough for us to remember this hope when we are having difficulties, let us not fall into the trap of the Corinthians in thinking that we have already arrived spiritually and are already ruling on the earth (4:8). We must always view our present through the lens of eternity.

ENDNOTES

1. Wisdom of Solomon 9:15, New Revised Standard Version.
2. Philo was from Alexandria, curiously Apollos' home town as well (Acts 18:24).

24

FINAL QUESTIONS AND FAREWELLS

1 Corinthians 16:1–24

1. QUESTION 4: WHAT ABOUT THE COLLECTION? (16:1–4)

aul answers one or two more final questions from the Corinthians in chapter 16. The first one concerned a collection he had apparently set in motion in all the churches he had founded: **Now about the collection for God's people** (16:1).[1] He intended this collection for the church of Jerusalem. He does not make clear the exact reasons for the gift. Some scholars hypothesize that Jerusalem had never fully recovered from the famine of A.D. 46 mentioned in Acts 11:27–30. Paul himself on that occasion had taken relief from Antioch of Syria to Jerusalem, along with Barnabas. Paul wrote these words some eight years after that famine.

Persecution is yet another reason sometimes given for Paul's offering. Perhaps Paul was trying to bring relief to the churches of Judea that were suffering for Christ (1 Thess. 2:14–15). Paul wrote 1 Thessalonians three to four years before 1 Corinthians, so hardship in the Jerusalem community because of persecution may stand as another reason for Paul's desire to bring them an offering.

But all in all, we may find one of the most important reasons for Paul's offering in a comment James, Peter, and Paul made to him when his mission to the Gentiles was just beginning. Before Paul had ever come to Greece, he had presented the message he preached to the leaders of the Jerusalem church (Gal. 2:2). On that occasion they had not rejected Paul's "gospel." But they had asked that he continue to remember the poor (Gal. 2:10). They may have specifically had the poor of Jerusalem in view.

At that time Paul told them he was already eager to help in this way. Paul's offerings for Jerusalem may have grown out of this conversation. We have three clear comments scattered in Paul's writings that relate to these offerings: the current one in 1 Corinthians 16, Paul's extensive treatment in 2 Corinthians 8–9, and some side comments Paul makes in Rom. 15:25–28. We will thus give a fuller discussion of the offering when we come to 2 Corinthians 8–9.

For the moment, we can note at least three positive motivations behind the offering. The first and most obvious was to help the poor of Jerusalem. The impetus for the offering may have come from Jerusalem itself, when James asked Paul to remember the poor (Gal. 2:10). Paul told the Romans that the collection was "for the poor among the saints in Jerusalem" (Rom. 15:26).

A second purpose for the offering was perhaps as a kind of "peace offering" between Paul and the Jerusalem church. At least some in the Jerusalem church viewed Paul with suspicion (Acts 21:20–24), and Paul himself sometimes used combative language in relation to them (Gal. 2:6, 9). Paul asked the Romans for their prayers so that "my service in Jerusalem may be acceptable to the saints there" (Rom. 15:31). He knew that it was not a foregone conclusion that the church would even accept the offering.[2]

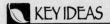 KEY IDEAS

While he knew tensions were an inevitable part of human interrelationships, Paul's theology could not live with unending disunity.

Related to the idea of fuller reconciliation with Jerusalem is a theological concept Paul valued: the unity of the church universal. While he knew tensions are an inevitable part of human interrelationships, Paul's theology could not live with unending disunity. Galatians 3:28 expresses a foundational dimension to Pauline theology: "There is neither Jew nor Greek, slave nor free, male nor female, for you are all one in Christ Jesus." As Ephesians puts it, "There is one body and one Spirit—just as you were called to one hope when you were called—one Lord, one faith, one baptism; one God and Father of all" (Eph. 4:4–6). Christ had "destroyed the barrier, the dividing wall of hostility, by abolishing in his flesh the law with its commandments and regulations" (Eph. 2:14–15). The offering was thus likely an expression of the unity of Jew and Gentile for Paul.

In the course of this brief conversation Paul gives us a good indication that the Christians of Corinth met together on Sunday, the Lord's Day, rather than on the Jewish Sabbath, Saturday. **On the first day of every week, each one of you should set aside a sum of money in keeping with his income, saving it up, so that when I come no collections will have to be made** (1 Cor. 16:2). Paul's entire way of dealing with money reflects a deep understanding of how divisive the subject could be. Paul did not want to take up any offerings in his own presence. We will discuss his reasoning in more detail when we come to 2 Corinthians 8–9.

By taking up the offering over time, the church would raise a greater amount of money. As we will find in 2 Corinthians 8–9, the Corinthian church was a comparatively wealthier church than many others (2 Cor. 8:2, 14). Paul asks them to set aside in keeping with their income. He does not ask for a tithe, a strict tenth of their intake. He only expects giving *proportional* to their income. The more God blesses, the more one should give.

This was a special offering with a specific purpose. The Corinthian church did not have a senior pastor on a salary. Nevertheless they were expected to support any visiting apostle for the duration of

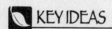

KEY IDEAS

Paul expected the Corinthians to give in proportion to their resources. This is the fundamental principle of Christian giving today as well.

the stay (1 Cor. 9:4–12). Paul and Barnabas themselves chose to work for a living so that the issue of finances did not interfere with their ministry.

Paul also did not want to handle the money from these offerings without the express permission of the church in question: **I will give letters of introduction to the men you approve and send them with your gift to Jerusalem** (16:3). Paul did not want anyone to confuse him with the increasing number of traveling "Christian" teachers who were using the gospel as an opportunity to make money (1 Tim. 6:10). He did want anyone to think he was like so many who "peddled" the word of God for profit (2 Cor. 2:17).

He wanted the offering to come from the churches themselves, and Paul would write letters of introduction for the representatives of each church, much as Romans 16 seems to have served for Phoebe to the Romans. When Paul finally made his way to Jerusalem with the offering—about a year later than he had initially planned (2 Cor. 8:10)—he traveled with a large delegation of individuals representing the gamut of his churches (Acts 20:4–6). Upon receiving this letter, the Corinthians were initially eager to contribute, although perhaps not as much the second time (2 Cor. 8:10).

2. PAUL'S PLANS (16:5–18)

As Paul begins to bring the letter to a close, he makes some personal remarks relating to his current situation and his coming plans. Second Corinthians gives us the benefit of knowing how some of these plans played themselves out. For example, Paul's plans at this point were to **go through Macedonia** (16:5). He planned perhaps **to stay with you awhile, or even spend the winter** (16:6). He did not want to make a quick visit. **I hope to spend some time with you, if the Lord permits** (16:7).

But events did not play themselves out quite the way Paul planned. Paul did visit them, perhaps after Pentecost as he said (16:8), but it was not a pleasant visit or a long one (2 Cor. 2:1). When he wrote 1 Corinthians 16, he had planned to come down through Macedonia to Corinth and then perhaps to go elsewhere. All we know is that he had a painful visit to Corinth, perhaps an emergency one, after which he apparently returned to Ephesus. On the whole it seems doubtful that he visited Macedonia on that trip.

He did **stay on at Ephesus** (16:8), the place from which he wrote 1 Corinthians. He apparently had his most fruitful work there. As he said, **a great door for effective work has opened to me, and there are many who oppose me** (16:9). We will discuss this opposition when we get to 2 Cor. 1:8 and speculate whether Paul eventually was imprisoned at Ephesus for several weeks. We have already mentioned that 1 Cor. 15:32 may allude to a first imprisonment there. All in all, Acts mentions about two years and three months Paul spent at Ephesus (perhaps late 52 to early 55, Acts. 19:8).

At this point Paul may have sent Timothy ahead to represent Paul in his absence. **If Timothy comes, see to it that he has nothing to fear** (16:10). The church may not have received Timothy as well as Paul had hoped. Paul would send Titus the next time (2 Cor. 2:13, 7:6–7). Timothy, along with Silas, had helped Paul found the church there (2 Cor. 1:19), and perhaps Timothy was a target of the same disdain some had for Paul.

Paul instructs them to receive Timothy. **No one, then, should refuse to accept him** (16:11). Paul may have sent Timothy along with those who were delivering 1 Corinthians to Corinth. These brothers may thus have included Stephanas, Fortunatus, and Achaicus, individuals from Corinth Paul mentions in 16:17. On the other hand, it is also possible that by "the brothers" Paul refers to individuals with him in Ephesus who eagerly await Timothy's return. We can see in Paul's instructions that he has a little bit of fear for Timothy. It is a hint of just how much opposition Paul may have faced at Corinth.

Paul also urged **Apollos** to go. Paul introduces the subject of Apollos with the same "Now concerning" with which he answered the other questions of the Corinthians, so it is possible they had inquired in their letter about him. Paul's response is that **he will go when he has the opportunity** (16:12).

We remember from the first four chapters of 1 Corinthians that a group loyal to Apollos stood at the heart of the divisions in the city, and we have speculated throughout our discussion that Paul himself may gently correct Apollos and some of his positions at various points in the letter (3:10, 4:6, 8:4). We do not know what Apollos himself really thought of Paul. Perhaps he honestly disagreed with Paul on some matters. Perhaps he neither wanted to go to Corinth in full submission to Paul, nor did he want to go and undermine Paul's authority or foment disunity. From where we stand it is almost impossible to know for certain.

First Corinthians 16:13–14 give five short instructions whose value for us is self-evident. **Be on your guard** against temptation, against Satan, against false teaching, against bad influence. The world is full of influences and forces that are potentially detrimental to our faith. Thus, **stand firm in the faith**, the first instruction is negative; this one is positive. Standing firm involves spiritual discipline and resolve, as well as a strong sense of what the faith is. We stand ready on our guard against attack and we stand firm when it comes.

The battle theme continues: **be men of courage**. "[A]fter you have done everything, to stand" (Eph. 6:13). Do not shrink back from the conflict with Satan. Do what you know is right despite the opposition it may bring. Thus **be strong** in the battle, putting on the armor of God and allowing the power of God to flow through you in the conflict.

For some of us, the battle is what we are all about: vanquishing the enemy. Paul's final injunction puts a distinctively Christian twist on this "fight verse." **Do everything in love** (16:14). How do we fight *in love*? We fight in love when we are defending our brothers and sisters in Christ. We fight in love when we are not fighting for ourselves but for the Lord. We fight in love when we make fighting itself the very last option. We remember from 1 Corinthians 13 that love is the solution to all the Corinthians' problems.

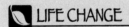

LIFE CHANGE

We fight in love when we are defending our brothers and sisters in Christ. We fight in love when we are not fighting for ourselves but for the Lord. We fight in love when we make fighting the very last option.

First Corinthians 16:15–18 give us an interesting glimpse into the details of Paul's ministry to the Corinthians. There we learn of three men who had recently come to Ephesus from Corinth to Paul: **Stephanas, Fortunatus, and Achaicus** (16:17). It was probably this group that brought to Paul the letter that he answers in the last nine chapters or so. Paul tells us that **the household of Stephanas were the first converts in Achaia** (16:15), in southern Greece including Corinth. We learn that **they have devoted themselves to the service of the saints** (16:15). Given the way Paul interrupts the flow of his comments on who he baptized in 1:14–17, he may have written those verses before they came. Stephanas then reminded him that he had baptized them first of all.

The household of Stephanas was apparently loyal to Paul in the community, and they also apparently were some of the leaders of the church. Perhaps Stephanas was one of the church's elders. Paul tells the Corinthians to **submit to such as these and to everyone who joins in**

the work, and labors at it (16:16). These men probably carried 1 Corinthians back to Corinth and perhaps had it read to the assembly there.

Stephanas, Fortunatus, and Achaicus may have brought some support for Paul from Corinth: **they have supplied what was lacking from you. For they refreshed my spirit and yours also. Such men deserve recognition** (16:17–18). While Paul did not receive support from his churches while he was there ministering to them, he seems to have accepted patronage when he was away from a church. But whether these men brought material support or not, they encouraged Paul by reinforcing his bond with the church.

3. FAREWELL (16:19–24)

Paul now gives his customary letter closing. As he so often does, he gives greetings from the church where he is at: **in the province of Asia** (16:19). The Christians here included **Aquila and Priscilla** who had a **church that meets at their house** (16:19). Perhaps in keeping with the fact that some of the women at Corinth are shaming their husbands, Paul here puts the husband first, Aquila. Elsewhere he mentions Priscilla first (for example, Rom. 16:3, 2 Tim. 4:19, Acts 18:18–19, 26). We remember that Priscilla and Aquila had founded the church at Corinth along with Paul (Acts 18:2) and had led Apollos himself to Christ (Acts 18:26).

In addition to Priscilla and Aquila—individuals the Corinthians knew— **[a]ll the brothers here send you greetings** (16:20) —family members that the Corinthians did not know by name, but who were family members all the same. Paul encourages the Corinthians to **[g]reet one another with a holy kiss** (16:20), a sign of kinship and a reflection of the fact that the church is in fact our truest family. The early church met in homes, and they understood the church as a new kind of family more intimate than any blood relations.

I, Paul, write this greeting in my own hand (16:21). If Paul had already written 2 Thessalonians by this time, we realize that some letters may have floated around falsely in his name (2 Thess. 2:2). He ends 2 Thessalonians with a resolve to "write this greeting in my own hand, which is the distinguishing mark in all my letters. This is how I write"

(2 Thess. 3:17). Paul in fact ends 1 Corinthians in this way, taking up the pen of his amanuensis or secretary, possibly Sosthenes (1 Cor. 1:1), and writing this one sentence greeting. In this way he authenticates the letter with his "signature."

He ends with four short wishes. First, **If anyone does not love the Lord—a curse be on him** (16:22). It is astounding to us to think that there may be individuals in our churches who would not love the Lord, but we get the feeling that Paul suspects this is the case at Corinth. He wonders if there are some who are into Christianity to explore its potential to help them advance. Perhaps they can rub shoulders with some important people in the city, perhaps they can get power over a small group of people and exert their will on them. Paul reminds any such individuals that Christianity is about serving the Lord, not about advancement. He curses any Ananias or Sapphira who might be hiding among God's people (Acts 5).

His second wish is an Aramaic affirmation. Aramaic was the language of Palestine at this time in which Jesus spoke and preached. It was a cousin to Hebrew, the language of most of the Old Testament. *"Marana tha,"* Paul says, **Come, Oh Lord!** (16:22). This worship affirmation must have come from the earliest churches in Judea, for Paul would scarcely use an Aramaic phrase among the Greek speaking Corinthians if it did not have a significant history behind it. Clearly Jewish Christians from the very earliest days considered Jesus Lord, perhaps on the basis of Ps. 110:1: "The LORD said to my Lord, 'Sit at my right hand until I make your enemies a footstool for your feet.'"

Paul's third wish is that the **grace of the Lord Jesus be with you** (16:23). God's grace is always with us, every moment and day of our lives, whether we realize it or not and whether we are Christians or not. God has given us so much of which we are not even aware. But Paul wishes the special gifting of Jesus on the Corinthians as well, all the blessings that are potentially ours in Christ Jesus, not least the forgiveness of our sins.

Finally, he gives them his love: **My love to all of you in Christ Jesus. Amen** (16:24). In 2 Corinthians we will see just how much Paul loved this church. There we will see that he stuck by them even when they rejected him. He was even willing to die for them (2 Cor. 7:3). He would love them even when they did not submit to his authority.

ENDNOTES

1. The wording of Paul's comment on Apollos in 16:12 could indicate that they had asked about Apollos as well ("now concerning" in the Greek).

2. Interestingly, while this offering was clearly of great significance for Paul, Acts does not mention it.

2 CORINTHIANS

INTRODUCTION TO 2 CORINTHIANS

DATE AND PLACE OF WRITING

The situation at Corinth worsened before it improved. In the introduction to 1 Corinthians, we told about how Paul founded the church at Corinth during a one and a half year stay in the city around A.D. 50–51. He then returned to Jerusalem and to Antioch in Syria, the starting point for all his journeys in Acts. He then spent the bulk of his "third" missionary journey in the city of Ephesus on the western coast of Asia Minor, in what is now Turkey. He stayed there well over two years and had a very fruitful ministry (1 Cor. 16:9), although he also faced serious opposition as well (Acts 19; 2 Cor. 1:8–9).

It was from Ephesus that Paul wrote a letter to the Corinthians that has not survived, a letter before 1 Corinthians that dealt with issues like shunning sexually immoral Christians (1 Cor. 5:9).[1] Paul also wrote 1 Corinthians to answer some of their questions, as well as to address problems about which he had heard rumors. We suggested Paul may have written 1 Corinthians early in A.D. 54.

Unfortunately, some of the Corinthians apparently did not accept Paul's assertion of authority in 1 Corinthians. He apparently made a visit to them that Acts does not record, a "painful visit" (2 Cor. 2:1; 13:1). While he had initially planned to spend some time there later in the year (1 Cor. 16:6–7), perhaps he had to make an emergency visit instead. At the very least he did not stay as long as he had initially planned. One person in particular appears to have strongly opposed Paul (2 Cor. 2:5–6).

Paul then told the Corinthians he would come, perhaps in part to take care the matter. His new plans initially included two visits, one on the way to Macedonia and a second time on his way back (2 Cor. 1:16). This plan may have aimed in part at giving the Corinthians an opportunity to give twice to Paul's collection for the poor in Jerusalem (2 Cor. 1:15).

But for whatever reason, he wrote another letter instead of the first visit he planned, a letter that hurt the Corinthians (2 Cor. 7:8). He wrote the letter "out of great distress and anguish of heart" (2 Cor. 2:4) drawing a line in the sand for them: either they would obey Paul and punish the sinner or apparently Paul would wash his hands of them (2 Cor. 2:9).

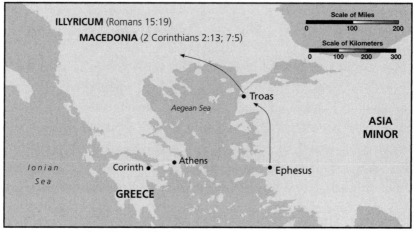

Paul's Travels from Asia Minor to Macedonia

Paul left Ephesus and made his way north to Troas on the northwestern tip of Asia Minor, then he jumped across the Bosporus into Macedonia at the north of Greece, where cities like Philippi and Thessalonica were located (2 Cor. 2:12–13, 7:5–6; Acts 20:1; see map above). All the while he was nervous to know how the Corinthians had responded to his ultimatum. He had sent Titus on his behalf to take care of the situation (2 Cor. 2:13, 7:6). Titus finally met up with Paul in Macedonia, and Paul's relief is clear from 2 Corinthians. The sinner had repented; the church had submitted to his authority (2 Cor. 2:5–11, 7:8–12).

It is in this context that Paul writes 2 Corinthians, perhaps early in the year A.D. 55. For at least the first nine chapters of 2 Corinthians, the sense of reconciliation and comfort Paul feels is overwhelmingly evident. Hidden in this letter are incredible gems of comfort for the discouraged and alienated. Paul may have felt such relief from the situation that he spent some extra time to the north of Greece. He mentions in Rom. 15:19 that he had spread the gospel as far west in the north of Greece as a region called Illyrium (see Fig. 4). This period gives us the most likely time when he visited this region.

Against the overall tone of reconciliation in 2 Corinthians 1–9, the last four chapters take on a surprisingly different tone. In 2 Corinthians 10–13 we find Paul defending himself once again in some of the most aggressive language of all his letters.[2] Indeed, some of the things Paul says seem so incredibly different in attitude

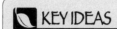 KEY IDEAS

Paul wrote 2 Corinthians to Corinth from Macedonia perhaps early in the year A.D. 55.

from the first chapters that some have suggested these chapters are an excerpt from the missing harsh letter Paul mentions in 2 Cor. 7:8. They would thus serve as a kind of appendix to 2 Corinthians 1–9 and give some background about the harsh letter.

Others suggest these chapters are yet a fifth letter Paul wrote very shortly after 2 Corinthians in relation to new issues that quickly arose after he had sent the first nine chapters. Perhaps Titus delivered 1–9 in preparation for the offering but encountered renewed opposition. Paul then wrote 10–13 shortly thereafter in response. The majority of Pauline scholars lean toward this option at the moment.

While they do not have any theological objection to this kind of theory, a number of commentators are hesitant to speculate in this way when we do not have any manuscript evidence that 2 Corinthians was originally two distinct letters. Those who take the text as it stands have several suggestions for Paul's change in tone. Some suggest he received new information before he had sent the first nine chapters and so added on the last four. Many think 10–13 simply address a different segment of the church than the first part of the letter does. Some have even suggested we can explain the difference in tone by the different mood a person can have from one day to the next. We will consider these theories a little further when we reach 2 Corinthians 10.

THE LAYOUT OF 2 CORINTHIANS

It is easy enough to see that 2 Corinthians divides into two main sections. The first nine chapters have a basically peaceful and conciliatory feel to them that binds them together (2 Cor. 1–9). The last four chapters (10–13) have a very defensive tone that binds them together.

It is much more difficult to determine the flow of thought in the first major section of the letter, 1:12–7:16. Chapters 8 and 9 clearly stand on their own as a discussion of the offering Paul was taking up for the poor in Jerusalem. But in the other chapters, Paul seems to start a topic, then set it aside for a while, only to pick up these topics again in reverse order at the end of the section.

For example, at 2:13 he interrupts telling about his trip to Macedonia only to pick up his train of thought again four chapters later at 7:5. In 3:1–6 he introduces the idea that he is a minister of a new covenant, someone who does not need a letter of recommendation. Then in 5:11–6:2 he seems to return to the idea that he is a minister of reconciliation who does not need to commend himself to them. That makes 3:7–5:10 the heart of the letter, perhaps the richest expression in the New Testament of the paradox between our glorious hope and our current distress in this world. See the outline that follows the introduction.

2 CORINTHIANS IN A NUTSHELL

Paul has reconciliation on his mind throughout 2 Corinthians. His opening prayer mentions or alludes to the comfort of God and Christ no less than ten times in the space of five verses (1:3–7). This theme alludes to both the comfort we have in the gospel as well as to the comfort Paul now feels because the Corinthians have submitted to his authority and repented of their sin. The heart of the letter, 3:7–5:10, not to mention 5:11–6:2, gives us perhaps the most uplifting and comforting words in the entire New Testament. The comfort of these passages comes in a discussion of Paul's intense suffering and persecution.

One important purpose behind the letter is the offering Paul was taking up for the poor of Jerusalem. He will spend two chapters giving them instructions in relation to this topic (8–9). As we all know, tensions often become greatest when money is involved. Some may have thought Paul was just trying to get rich off their offering (2 Cor. 2:17, 12:17).

Even though 2 Corinthians has an immensely comforting and reconciling tone on the whole, we can still feel tension even in the first nine chapters. Paul spends a great deal of the letter defending his recent conduct, particularly a change of plans he made in relation to a visit to Corinth (1:12–2:4). Despite the fact that the sinner repented and the community submitted to Paul (2:5–11, 7:8–16), Paul clearly indicates that the hearts of the Corinthians were not fully open to him yet (6:12–13).

Second Corinthians 10–13 make this fact overwhelmingly clear. Whether Paul receives new information or is simply letting go of his restraint in the earlier chapters, 2 Corinthians 10–13 constitute the most intense and sustained defense of the fact that he is an apostle in all of his writings. Apparently some traveling Christian missionaries were influencing the Corinthians against Paul, individuals Paul sarcastically deems "super-apostles" (11:5). So Paul reluctantly decides to present his spiritual credentials and defend his spiritual authority.

It is unfortunate that the last correspondence we have between Paul and the Corinthian church ends with a question mark. Did the church finally submit to him fully? At least we know he went on to stay there and write Romans. His words about them at that time are cordial (Rom. 16:23). But this conflict was probably part of a series of struggles that lead him to feel that "there is no more place for me to work in these regions" (Rom. 15:23). At least the memory of him was positive enough at Corinth for Clement of Rome some forty years later to use Paul's example to spur the Corinthians on again to the proper course of action.[3]

ENDNOTES

1. We will mention below that some think 2 Cor. 6:14–7:1 is an excerpt from that first letter, an interesting but unprovable theory.

2. Only Galatians could make any claim to match it in vigor and combative feeling.

3. 1 Clement 47:1–4.

OUTLINE OF 2 CORINTHIANS

I. Greetings (1:1–2)

II. Prayer of praise (1:3–11)

III. Tales of reconciliation (1:12–9:15)

    A. Paul recounts recent events: Part one (1:12–2:11)

    B. Paul: Authentic minister of a new covenant (2:12–3:6)

        1. Celebration of reconciliation (2:12–17)

        2. Paul: Minister of the new covenant (3:1–6)

    C. The paradox of the ministry's glory and suffering (3:7–5:10)

        1. The glory of the new covenant (3:7–18)

        2. Beaten bodies, renewed spirits (4:1–5:10)

    D. Paul: Authentic minister of reconciliation (5:11–7:1)

        1. Be reconciled to God (5:11–6:2)

        2. We have not wronged you (6:3–13)

        3. Avoid the wicked (6:14–7:1)

    F. Paul recounts recent events: Part two (7:2–16)

    E. The offering for Jerusalem (8:1–9:15)

        1. Paul encourages the Corinthians to give (8:1–15)

        2. The logistics of the collection (8:16–9:5)

        3. The principles behind the collection (9:6–15)

IV. A vigorous defense of Paul's apostolicity (10:1–13:10)

    A. Paul's appeal for full obedience (2 Corinthians 10:1–18)

    B. Paul makes a fool of himself by boasting
       (2 Corinthians 11:1–12:10)

    C. Worry about his third visit (2 Corinthians 12:11–13:10)

V. Farewell (13:11–14)

GREETING AND PRAYER

2 Corinthians 1:1–11

1. PAUL'S GREETING (1:1–2)

The opening of the letter we call 2 Corinthians is short and to the point.[1] **Paul ... To the church of God in Corinth** (1:1). Paul greets them along with other Christians in the region, which would have included the church at Cenchrea, the port village of Corinth where Phoebe lived (Rom. 16:1). We notice that Paul still addresses the Corinthians as a single church, probably implying a rather small number of Christians there (about forty to fifty). Paul now identifies his co-writer as Timothy, rather than Sosthenes. Perhaps Sosthenes had returned to Corinth (Acts 18:17). Perhaps Timothy was serving as Paul's secretary in the writing of this letter.[2]

2. PRAYER OF PRAISE (1:3–11)

After his greeting, Paul usually thanked God for the church in question and assured them of his regular prayers for them. In 2 Corinthians he takes a slightly different tact: he begins with a kind of doxology of praise to God.[3] As we saw in 1 Corinthians, this part of Paul's letters often anticipates some of the main themes that will show up later in the letter. This is the case with 2 Corinthians. In particular, this idea of comfort or encouragement inundates this opening prayer.

251

The word *comfort* appears in some form ten times in the space of the next five verses.

Paul praises **the God and Father of our Lord Jesus Christ** (1:3) in particular because God is the origin of **compassion and the God of all comfort,** who *comforts* **us in all our troubles, so that we can** *comfort* **those in any trouble with the** *comfort* **we ourselves have received from God** (1:3–4, *italics* mine). These words anticipate the reconciliation with the Corinthians that Paul celebrates in the first seven chapters of this letter. Paul himself has also been comforted recently by God after a time of persecution and possibly imprisonment. Now that the Corinthians are repenting of their sins he wants to share some of the comfort he has experienced with them.

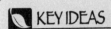

KEY IDEAS

The word *comfort* appears in some form ten times in the space of ten verses.

It is sometimes difficult to understand why God allows some things to happen to us in this world. But we can always see good things that God raises from the ashes of suffering and disaster (Rom. 8:28–29). One is the ability we gain to comfort others who are undergoing suffering. Because we have suffered, we are better able to help others who are suffering (Heb. 4:15). We often become better people through suffering, and our love for others usually increases.

Christ's sufferings should have the same effect on us. **[T]hrough Christ our** *comfort* **overflows** (1:5, *italics* mine). We may not always be able to understand why God allows us to suffer, but we can take solace in the fact that God himself was willing to identify with our suffering. The sufferings of Christ are in part a demonstration to us that God understands and cares about our plight. The degree of God's love for us is great comfort (Rom. 5:7–8).

If we are distressed, it is for your *comfort* **and salvation; if we are** *comforted***, it is for your** *comfort* (1:6, *italics* mine). Paul sees his sufferings as a benefit to his churches. If for no other reason, Paul was doing the hard work of the gospel for them. If Paul himself were not suffering for the gospel, then someone else would need to take his place.

Paul also saw his sufferings as an indication of God's judgment on the wicked and yet of salvation for him and others who suffered (Phil. 1:28).

He does not give us the details of his thinking, but some Christians today would say that Satan's opposition sometimes increases the more good you are doing. Some would say you can tell when God is doing something significant through you because of the intensity of the opposition and persecution.

In some such way suffering vindicated for Paul the truth of the story of salvation and indicated that God would bring His people through. What truly valuable thing does not come with effort and struggle? Colossians 1:24 seems to say that one Christian's sufferings can even have a redeeming effect on other Christians: "I fill up in my flesh what is still lacking in regard to Christ's afflictions." Clearly righteous suffering has "redeeming" value on some level.

The apostle Paul certainly paved the way for others to endure persecution. Observing his successful endurance **produces in you patient endurance of the same sufferings we suffer . . . as you share in our sufferings, so also you share in our comfort** (1:6–7). Here is a sobering word for Christian leaders: the way we survive the challenges of our lives is either a help or a hindrance to those who are under our care, watching us.

In 1:8–11 Paul alludes to some serious persecution he endured at Ephesus, which was **in the province of Asia . . . far beyond our ability to endure, so that we despaired even of life** (1:8–9). He does not tell us the details. Whatever these pressures were, they took place after Paul had already written about fighting "wild beasts in Ephesus" in 1 Corinthians (15:32). His statement in 1 Corinthians refers to difficulties Paul had with the Roman authorities in Ephesus even before he wrote 1 Corinthians.[4]

But the tone of 2 Cor. 1:8–9 seems even more desperate than his comment on "wild beasts" did in 1 Corinthians, more truly life-threatening. It also seems fresh on his mind, which would explain why he did not mention it in his earlier letter. It is possible that Paul was imprisoned once or twice while he was at Ephesus, particularly at the very end of his time there. Acts does not mention any imprisonments at Ephesus, but we know from elsewhere that Acts does not tell us everything that happened to Paul.[5]

Second Corinthians 11 mentions frequent imprisonments (11:23), severe floggings, five lashings from Jews, three beatings with rods, a stoning, and three shipwrecks. All of these had taken place before Paul wrote the letter. But at the equivalent point in Acts, we have only heard for certain about the stoning at Lystra (Acts 14:19), about one of the floggings and about one imprisonment at Philippi (Acts 16:23).[6]

Acts does tell us about a significant crisis that occurred near the end of Paul's time at Ephesus (Acts 19:23–41). A silversmith named Demetrius tried to cause Paul trouble because of the way Christianity was cutting into his idol making business. Enough people had apparently turned to Christ that those in the business of making idols were increasingly losing money. The guild conspired against Paul and, at one point, caused a riot in the famous theater of Ephesus. If Paul's friends had not prevented him from entering the theater, he almost certainly would have been killed. Perhaps this crisis is enough to explain Paul's comments in 2 Cor. 1:8.

In addition, some would suggest that Paul also experienced an imprisonment of several weeks around this time. Imprisonments were never punishments in the Roman world; they were times of holding until the appropriate official could try a person. Some scholars think that Paul may have written Philippians from Ephesus during such an imprisonment. Paul's comments in Philippians would fit the tone of 2 Cor. 1:8. Paul certainly was facing the possibility of death when he wrote Philippians: "Christ will be exalted in my body, whether by life or by death. For to me, to live is Christ and to die is gain" (Phil. 1:20–21).

When he wrote Philippians, Paul planned to visit Philippi if he was released (Phil. 2:24). Further, Paul almost certainly had recently visited Philippi when he wrote 2 Corinthians (2 Cor. 7:5). In short, the suggestion that Paul wrote 2 Corinthians soon after he wrote Philippians also makes sense of the evidence we have.[7] While we cannot have absolute certainty on this question, we will dialog with this possibility throughout our time in 2 Corinthians.

But this happened that we might . . . rely . . . on God . . . and he will deliver us (1:9–10). Here Paul anticipates a theme that we will find repeatedly in 2 Corinthians: weakness is not a bad thing or a sign of God's disapproval, for God's strength is complimented by our weakness (12:9). Apparently some at Corinth saw Paul's problems as a sign that he was not a true apostle, that he was not truly God's representative. Even in Philippians he mentions Christians who apparently preached in a way that made him out to be the bad guy with the wrong message (Phil. 1:17).

But God always brought Paul through, and his trials gave his churches an opportunity to see prayer work. **On him we have set our hope . . . Then many will give thanks** (1:10–11). While no one wants to suffer, few would deny the strength we gain as we go through suffering, not to mention the strength that others gain as they witness God bringing us through. This effect is surely not the only reason God allows suffering, but it is a significant benefit.

All of those who prayed for Paul saw their faith strengthened when God answered their prayers and delivered Paul. Such experiences build our faith and hope that God can bring us through. True enough, God does not always choose to

LIFE CHANGE

God strengthened and matured Paul through his sufferings, while giving churches like the Corinthians a chance to strengthen their faith by participating in Paul's struggles. This is the attitude we should have toward the suffering we may endure for Christ.

deliver us from suffering. But we have confidence that He can and does. Then when He visits us with His grace, we give Him thanks. Paul hoped that many, many Christians would be able to give thanks to God for the way He kept delivering Paul from his trials.

ENDNOTES

1. Second Corinthians is actually the fourth letter Paul sent to Corinth. See the introductions to both letters in this commentary.

2. See our discussion of the opening of 1 Corinthians for the typical features of an ancient letter, as well as the format Paul typically followed. These two verses constitute the "prescript" of 2 Corinthians.

3. Ephesians is the only other Pauline letter where we see this kind of opening doxology.

4. Paul probably does not mean he actually faced lions in an arena. Ephesus was a "free" city that ran to a large degree by its own laws and such. Nevertheless, it was the main city of Asia and had a Roman governor. A second century Christian named Ignatius referred to his Roman guards as "leopards," perhaps a hint that Roman soldiers were sometimes likened to beasts.

5. For example, Acts does not mention Paul's argument with Peter at Antioch (Gal. 2:11–14) or the circumstances that led to the writing of Galatians. Acts does not tell us that the Arab ethnarch of Damascus was trying to arrest him (2 Cor. 11:32), only that the Jews of the city were. Indeed, one of the implicit themes of Acts is that Christians are not troublemakers, although many others made trouble for them.

6. It is possible that Paul was held in prison for a short time in relation to the events at Athens (Acts 17:19) and Corinth (Acts 18:12). Note that the shipwreck mentioned in Acts 27 was after Paul had written 2 Corinthians.

7. Traditionally Paul wrote Philippians from Rome. While a number of evangelicals prefer Ephesus as the place from which Philippians was written, I suspect others think Acts would have told us about such an imprisonment if it had actually taken place.

2

PAUL RECOUNTS RECENT EVENTS:

PART ONE

2 Corinthians 1:12–2:11

For about the length of a chapter, Paul now gives his perspective on some recent events that had taken place in his relationship with the Corinthians. First of all, Paul had told the Corinthians he was coming to visit them at a certain time, but then he had changed his plans. At the end of 1 Corinthians, Paul mentions certain plans to visit them (1 Cor. 16:5–7), and he had. But this "second visit" to Corinth had apparently not gone well (2 Cor. 2:1, 13:1). He may have even gone under emergency circumstances (1 Cor. 16:10–11). He had planned for this visit to last for some time, perhaps even over a winter (1 Cor. 16:6–7), but in the end he did not stay long.

Paul had apparently left them with new plans to visit them again: **on my way to Macedonia and . . . from Macedonia, and then to have you send me on my way to Judea** (2 Cor. 1:16). But he did not follow his original plan. Instead of going straight to Corinth and then up to Macedonia, he started the trip in Macedonia (2:12–13). While he had **planned to visit you first so that you might benefit twice** (1:15), in the end he skipped the first visit until he heard from Titus what the attitude of the Corinthian church had become toward him.

Instead of going himself, Paul sent Titus with a "harsh letter" to the Corinthians (2:3, 9, 7:8). This letter dealt in particular with a problem person at Corinth. The exact nature of this person's offense is not completely clear. Was it the person sleeping with his step-mother in 1 Corinthians 5? Was it those taking others to court in 1 Corinthians 6? Second Corinthians 7:12 implies that an individual had done wrong to another party, but Paul does not tell us the specifics. Any number of scenarios are possible, including the idea that some Corinthian might have offended Timothy during his previous visit.

Whatever the "trigger" issue was, it led to a showdown between Paul's authority and the offensive individual, with the church and its leaders apparently in the middle. Paul's letter must have amounted to an ultimatum of sorts: take care of this individual or consider yourself severed from me. It was a test of obedience to his authority (2:9, 7:12). Perhaps Paul's change of plan amounted to such an ultimatum: I will not visit you again until you take care of this unrepentant sinner.

The Corinthians submitted, at least on the surface, and Paul was delighted. The individual was punished by the majority (2:6). He repented, as did the community as a whole (2:7, 7:9). But the community was also hurt (7:8), and some who supported him may even have felt abandoned by his failure to come and help them with the matter (1:17). Some remaining hard feelings over the whole series of events may have contributed to the need for Paul to write 2 Corinthians 10–13.

[W]e have conducted ourselves . . . in the holiness and sincerity that are from God (1:12). Some manuscripts of 2 Corinthians read "genuineness" rather than "holiness," a reading that fits the context better.[1] Paul is emphasizing to the Corinthians that he has not been playing political games with them. His actions have been genuine and his words sincere. His conscience is clear. He told the Corinthians the same thing in 1 Cor. 4:4.

When people look you straight in the eye and tell you they feel no guilt about something you think should make them feel guilty, there are four possibilities. The first is that they are lying—they really do feel guilt but they are pretending not to. The second is that their conscience is "seared," that they are so far from God that they cannot even hear His chiding voice. Thirdly, their head may be wrong but their heart right. Perhaps they are wrongly convinced in their mind even though their intentions are correct (Rom. 14:22). Finally, *you* yourself may be wrong or partially wrong.

On more than one occasion Paul looked his opponents "straight in the eye," so to speak, and claimed a free conscience (Acts 23:1). On this occasion, he assures the Corinthians of his sincerity—he is not lying. Surely his conscience was not seared. That means either he is mistaken or they are. The unwavering nature of Paul's "look" no doubt would have caused self-doubt in anyone who questioned him.

He alludes to a theme from 1 Corinthians: **not according to worldly wisdom but according to God's grace** (2 Cor. 1:12). He reminds them what the true criteria are for success and a clear conscience—not intellectual excellence, but spiritual dependence on God's grace. This theme will recur throughout 2 Corinthians as well: God's strength is made perfect in our weakness (2 Cor. 12:9).

Paul hopes that one day they will stop being embarrassed by him and will **boast of us just as we will boast of you in the day of the Lord Jesus** (1:14). Paul will boast of them on the Day of the Lord, for they represent the fruit of his labor, the "interest" he has made on the "talents" the master left him (Matt. 25:14–30). He hopes that one day they will be proud to say they come from one of the churches founded by Paul.[2]

Paul's initial plan to visit them first was based on this confidence (1:15) that they remained on the whole positive toward him. When he told them his plans, he was completely sincere. Paul words his initial plans somewhat curiously. **I planned to visit you first so that you might benefit twice** (1:15). It is not exactly clear what he meant for the word the NIV gives as "benefit" is the word for grace (*charis*).[3] He may simply mean that they would have the benefit of two visits from him. However, he may also have meant that they would have the opportunity to give twice to the offering he was collecting (2 Cor. 8–9): they could have two opportunities to show their graciousness toward Jerusalem. The souring of his relationship with them may have led him not to irritate them by asking for money twice.

When I planned this, did I do it lightly? (1:17). Clearly either some Corinthians claimed that Paul was insincere in his promises, or Paul suspected some thought so. These would think that Paul spoke "out of both sides of his mouth." Paul's response is two-fold. In 1:23–2:4 he will give his side to the story. But in 1:18–22 he talks about a surety even more significant. Human beings fail, and while Paul does not claim failure here, he makes it clear that it would not matter even if he did. As he will say in Rom. 3:4: "Let God be true, and every man a liar." Setting the issue of his conduct aside for a moment, he makes it clear that his *message* is not in question.

[O]ur *message* to you to you is not "Yes" and "No" . . . in him it has always been "Yes" (1:18–19, *italics* mine). Jesus is the key to everything that is truly significant and meaningful in life. He is the eternal "yes" to all that is truly good and desirable. Even the "no's" that He gives are ultimately "yeses." **For no matter how many promises God has made, they are "Yes" in Christ** (1:20).

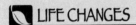

LIFE CHANGES

Jesus is the key to everything truly significant and meaningful in life. He is the eternal "yes" to all that is truly good and desirable. Even the "no's" that He gives are ultimately "yeses."

What are some of these promises? Paul alludes to several in his letters. For example, Paul saw the salvation of the Gentiles as the fulfillment of God's promise to bless all the nations through Abraham (Gal. 3:6–9). God kept this promise and brought justification by faith to the Gentiles through Christ. Our commentary on 1 Corinthians 15 argued that Paul believed God had planned to give humanity glory and honor in the creation (Ps. 8, 1 Cor. 15:27, Heb. 2:5–9). Although all humanity sinned and is currently lacking this glory, Christ has made this glory finally possible for us. God made both of these important promises possible through Christ, the one "through whom all things came and through whom we live" (1 Cor. 8:6). Not long after he wrote 2 Corinthians Paul wrote the Romans that he was "not ashamed of the gospel, because it is the power of God for the salvation of everyone who believes" (Rom. 1:16).

God did not promise that we would not suffer on earth. Indeed, much that Paul says in 2 Corinthians relates to the incredible sufferings he experienced in his life. But Ephesians also speaks of great spiritual blessings God has already given us here on earth. He has "blessed us in the heavenly realms with every spiritual blessing in Christ" (Eph. 1:3). All these great things are just a sampling of the "yes" that is in Christ.

And so through him the "Amen" is spoken by us to the glory of God
(1:20). Paul mentioned in 1 Corinthians the Christian practice of saying
"Amen" after a prayer in worship (1 Cor. 14:16). We say this "Amen"
through Christ, this affirmation of our praise and thanksgiving to God. This
is what we mean when we pray "in Jesus' name." It is only because of what
God has done for us through Christ that even He allows us to approach the
throne of grace at all, let alone with boldness (Heb. 4:16).

Regardless of what they might think of Paul, **it is God who makes
both us and you stand firm in Christ** (1:21). This is an important, yet
all too easily forgotten truth. The "yes" of Christianity does not ride on
my faithfulness or the consistency of a pastor or church leader. It is not
my effort that makes me holy or righteous in God's sight. It is only God
who makes anyone stand firm. Because it all rides on God, Christianity
will indeed stand firm no matter what challenges it or we may face.

To make it possible for us to stand firm, God has **anointed us** (1:21),
He has set His purposes on us and empowered us to accomplish them. He
has given us this commission and empowerment by setting **his seal of
ownership on us**, namely, He has **put his Spirit in our hearts as a
deposit** (1:22). It is through the Holy Spirit in us that God marks us out
as His own and empowers us to stand firm in Christ.

We in the holiness tradition have often so emphasized the perfecting
work of the Holy Spirit that we
have missed some of the more
obvious roles He plays in the
life of the believer. For Paul, it
is the Holy Spirit who more
than any other factor makes
the difference between

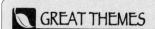

GREAT THEMES

The Holy Spirit in us is what truly makes
us a Christian. He guarantees our salvation on the Day of Judgment and is a
foretaste of glory divine.

someone who is a Christian and someone who is not. As he says in
Romans, "if anyone does not have the Spirit of Christ, he does not belong
to Christ" (Rom. 8:9).

In 2 Cor. 1:22 Paul once again points out that the Holy Spirit is God's
seal of ownership on us, like a seal a notary public puts on a document
to signify its authenticity. The Holy Spirit is this kind of a seal in us, a
clear indicator that we belong to God.[4]

Paul also uses a word in 1:22 that the King James Version translated as an "earnest" (*arrabōn*). We still use the idea of "earnest money" when buying a house. The buyer puts down such money (1) to guarantee that the seller will not negotiate with anyone else and (2) to put a down payment toward the purchase of the house. Since the word *earnest* is so rarely used today, the NIV tries to spell out clearly what Paul is saying: the Holy Spirit is **a deposit, guaranteeing what is to come**. Here we have the two functions of an earnest. The Holy Spirit guarantees that God will give us salvation on the Day of Judgment. Yet the Spirit is also a "foretaste of glory divine," a little bit of heaven inside us. The Holy Spirit is a taste "of the powers of the coming age" (Heb. 6:4–5).

After he makes it clear that in God the word is always "yes," Paul goes on to defend his own conduct toward the Corinthians (1:23–2:4). He tells them that he did not come back to Corinth **in order to spare you** (1:23). His previous visit had been crisis-filled, and he **would not make another painful visit** (2:1). He decided to send a letter with Titus to pave the way for his next visit, **so that when I came I should not be distressed by those who ought to make me rejoice** (2:3).

Had Paul given the Corinthians an ultimatum: "Submit to our authority or your salvation is in jeopardy"? Paul tells them that he was not dealing tyrannically with their faith, but **we work with you for your joy** (1:24). He would not play games with their faith, **because it is by faith you stand firm** (1:24).

If he had gone as planned, perhaps he would have had to condemn them for their failure to submit to his authority. Perhaps he would have pushed them out of the faith. On the other hand, by not coming, he ran the risk of being thought weak or a coward. As some said of him, "His letters are weighty and forceful, but in person he is unimpressive and his speaking amounts to nothing" (2 Cor. 10:10). Clearly they needed confrontation, but Paul wrestled with the best way to accomplish it.

So Paul sent a letter through Titus. He decided to let the church itself take responsibility for its problems. If he came, punishment would take on a finality to it. He thought it was more appropriate for the church to demonstrate its submission to his authority. He tells them he was confident that they would do the right thing, that **you would all share my joy**

(2:3). He wanted the church to know **the depth of my love for you** (2:4). He did not want to grieve them.

But in the meantime he wrote **out of great distress and anguish of heart and with many tears** (2:4). Despite his ultimate confidence, he must have had significant doubts as well. Who would he lose in the process? If the sinner did not repent, what would the repercussions be for the community? The spiritual fate and the loyalty of the Corinthian church to Paul were of tremendous importance to him. From Romans we get the impression that Paul's options for ministry in the east were increasingly diminishing (Rom. 15:23). He did not plan to minister in Asia any more (Acts 20:25) and perhaps was even forbidden from entering Ephesus. He did not want to lose Corinth too. He waited anxiously for Titus to bring him news of the Corinthian reaction to his letter.

Thankfully, the news was good. The church obeyed Paul rather than siding with the troublemaker. But for reasons that will become clearer as we go along, by this point of the letter Paul may be having second thoughts that the sinner of 2:5–11 was really repentant after all.

If anyone has caused grief, he has not so much grieved me as he has grieved all of you (2:5). Paul does not want the Corinthians to think that the problems they have experienced were all about him. His insistence on submission and repentance had not caused them the trouble, but the sinner had brought these struggles on them. He does not want them to think that the situation was all about him getting what he wanted. The sinner was the problem—for them as much as for him.

The church had submitted to Paul's ultimatum for obedience. They had punished the sinner. We know the punishment even less than the sin. First Corinthians 5 implies expulsion from the assembly as a consequence of sexual immorality. Perhaps for a time a portion of the church disassociated from the individual or shunned him. He apparently repented, and the church itself largely repented for its disobedience to Paul. Paul was pleased.

The punishment . . . is sufficient for him. Now instead you ought to forgive and comfort him (2:6–7). Here is proof that Paul did not use church discipline to exact vengeance on "sinners." The punishments Paul saw the church administering were meant to be redemptive, to lead the sinner back to Christ. Paul now urges the church to **reaffirm your love for him** (2:8). Paul was not interested in the person getting his "just desserts," only in getting the sinner into the Kingdom.

KEY IDEAS

Paul did not use church discipline to exact vengeance on sinners. Rather, discipline was meant to be redemptive, to lead individuals to repentance and restoration.

Paul's letter had thrown down the gauntlet of his authority. **The reason I wrote you was to see if you would stand the test and be obedient in everything** (2:9). Paul was satisfied with their response. Forgiveness was now in order. **If you forgive anyone, I also forgive him** (2:10). The slate was clean with him. He has forgiven the congregation if they truly did anything needing his forgiveness. The sinner was now forgiven because he had repented.

We breathe a sigh of relief (for the moment). We can only wish that all church conflicts ended as quickly as this one seems to end. He closes the subject **in order that Satan might not outwit us** (2:11).

Paul here recognizes a sobering truth about the way Satan works. When Satan is done leading someone to do wrong to someone, he can then lead the victim to do just as much wrong in return. How many people does Satan manage to string out with bitterness over the years over some wrong that was done to them? We sometimes waste years in disgruntlement that we could have passed serving the Lord with joy. Satan can play both sides, and he can trick people who were genuinely wronged to play right into his schemes. Paul did not want to play such a game with the Corinthians to the joy of the devil.

ENDNOTES

1. Although the better manuscript evidence favors "holiness," the context favors "genuineness." This variation in different ancient copies of 2 Corinthians is a good example of the kinds of errors that happened occasionally in copying the New Testament. The difference between the two words in Greek is small (*haplotēti*, "in genuineness," versus *hagiotēti*, "in holiness") and resulted from the mistake of a copyist's eye.

2. We have here again the tension we saw in 1 Corinthians where Paul says "What, after all, is Apollos? And what is Paul? Only servants, through whom you came to believe" (1 Cor. 3:5). Yet Paul also claims a certain priority or honor as the "father" of the Corinthian church (4:15).

3. Although once again there is a textual issue. Many manuscripts read "joy" here (*charan*) instead of "grace" (*charin*).

4. Some holiness preachers mistakenly used the picture of a seal in terms of sealing a jar or an envelope, emphasizing the idea of completion and finishing something. Paul however does not use the word in this way.

PAUL: AUTHENTIC MINISTER OF A NEW COVENANT

2 Corinthians 2:12–3:6

1. CELEBRATION OF RECONCILIATION (2:12–17)

Paul suddenly digresses from his discussion of recent events when he gets to 2 Cor. 2:14. If he had stayed on topic, we would no doubt consider 2:12–13 as part of the section we have just treated (1:12–2:11). The paragraph begins with Paul recounting more recent events.

Paul had left Ephesus, probably under duress and under the threat of his life in some way. He went north to **Troas**, and might have stayed there longer if he had not been worried about the Corinthians. But his concern for the Corinthians drove him west to **Macedonia**, across the Bosporus, the path that would eventually lead him to Greece and down to Corinth. He had apparently told Titus to go north from Corinth and then east toward Troas, clockwise around, while Paul himself would go counterclockwise. They would meet somewhere in the middle.

But after Paul begins this train of thought, at 2:14 he unexpectedly starts ruminating on the confidence he has in the reconciliation provided in God's new covenant with humanity. Paul's reconciliation with the Corinthians is just a small sample of the overall reconciliation available through Christ. For the next four chapters or so he will give us some incredibly rich words on the hope he has in the midst of challenges and trying times. The themes of the section reinforce Paul's claims about his relationship with the Corinthians in several ways. Then as if he had not digressed at all, Paul just as unexpectedly picks up his train of thought again about recent events at 7:5.[1]

So at 2:14, after Paul mentions his anguish as he entered Macedonia, after he mentions his anticipation of Titus' return from Corinth, he suddenly breaks out into thanksgiving. **[T]hanks be to God, who always leads us in triumphal procession in Christ and through us spreads everywhere the fragrance of the knowledge of him** (2:14). Although he does not tell us now what happened next, we know from what Paul has said thus far that Titus brought good news. This fact pushes Paul into celebration mode.[2]

Paul uses the imagery of a triumphant military procession in Rome where a Roman general leads a sampling of the defeated nation through the streets of Rome, individuals who were then mostly killed, although some were sold as slaves. He used the same imagery in 1 Cor. 4:9 to describe how he felt as someone who was constantly under attack and persecution for his preaching. He identified with the prisoners on their way to the arena.

What he means in this passage is not as clear. We know God is leading the procession. Normally to be led in procession is to be one of the captives. But given the celebratory tone of this comment, some commentators have supposed that Paul is thinking of himself as one of the generals.[3] Unfortunately, we lack any evidence that this word (*thriambeuō*) was *ever* used in this way. Accordingly, most scholars today have felt compelled to take it as a reference to Paul's suffering in some way.

For these reasons we probably have to take Paul's statement as another one of his paradoxes. Just as true wisdom is foolishness to the world, so God's victory is human suffering. God may lead Paul through this life with suffering, but that suffering is in fact his ultimate victory. The Corinthians thought the opposite, that his suffering indicated he was not authentic.

Paul's references to a fragrance and aroma are similarly puzzling. **To the one we are the smell of death; to the other the fragrance of life** (2:16). Some commentators have supposed that incense must have been involved in triumphal processions.[4] This interpretation is certainly possible.

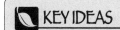

KEY IDEAS

Paul paradoxically celebrates the fact of his suffering in this world, for that suffering is ultimately a victory march.

The fragrance of the procession would thus have different connotations depending on whether you are one of the victors or one of the captured. For the victors and those looking on the procession, the aroma of the procession means you have been saved from the enemy. Similarly, those in Christ will escape the wrath of God that will come on the world. To them the message of Christ has a smell of salvation. But for those who have rebelled against God and refuse to submit to His will, the aroma of the procession smells of the doom they face in the arena. When they reach the arena, they will die. So it is with those who reject Christ, they will perish on the coming Day of Judgment.

On the other hand, Paul's comments may rather have overtones of sacrifice (Exod. 29:18; Lev. 1:9; Phil. 4:18). Paul's suffering, his "sacrifice," had brought the fragrance of the knowledge of God to countless places and individuals in the Mediterranean world. The smell of his sacrifice brought salvation to those who responded in faith. But it confirmed the judgment of those who rejected faith.

What an incredible task such a ministry is: victory through suffering! **And who is equal to such a task?** (2:16). He had told them earlier that they could trust in his genuineness (1:12). He reinforces this claim here by giving them a sense of the awesome charge God had given him. It would be insane to try to make money off the gospel given what the stakes were. Who would volunteer to suffer in this way and go to death in the arena?

Yet from this comment it is clear that even this early in the Christian enterprise, some preachers tried to make money off the gospel. Indeed, it is in the context of false teaching that 1 Timothy tells us that "the love of money is a root of all kinds of evil" (6:10). Sophists were individuals in Paul's day who hired themselves out as teachers. The wealthy would support such individuals from place to place.

The New Testament gives us good reason to believe that not long after the gospel reached Greek-speaking soil, Christian sophists of this nature began to become more and more common. These "itinerant evangelists" might vary from those like Paul who had integrity to many who were getting rich off the gospel. From scattered comments in the Corinthian letters, it is clear that some were accusing Paul of being such a gospel "peddler." In particular, they may have seen his offering for Jerusalem as a way for him to get rich.

We can wonder if there was some projection going on in those who accused Paul of being a Christian sophist. Perhaps they were some of the rich at Corinth who themselves were inclined to support false teachers, the "super apostles" Paul will mention in 11:5. Paul himself had not accepted patronage from the Corinthians. He had chosen to work rather than encumber the gospel with the strings that came with accepting money (1 Cor. 9:6, 2 Cor. 11:7–9). He might accept support from other churches, but not from the location where he currently preached (2 Cor. 11:9, Phil. 4:16). Yet some apparently had the gall to suggest his offering for the poor was an attempt to get rich on his part.

2. PAUL: MINISTER OF THE NEW COVENANT (3:1–6)

Second Corinthians 2:14–7:4 is like one long interruption of Paul's story about recent events. They are a rich interruption, with some of the most encouraging words in the New Testament. Nevertheless, we could almost put these chapters in parentheses, for Paul picks right back up where he left off after he is finished with his digression.

He begins by telling the Corinthians that they are in fact his "letter of recommendation" that prove that God has commissioned him as a minister of reconciliation. The Corinthian church should not too quickly forget that they would not even be Christians if it were not for Paul. Was this not proof enough that God had called Paul as a minister of the gospel, the fact that so many churches would not even exist if it had not been for him?

Perhaps there is a note of encouragement here for pastors with burdens for difficult churches. The letter of recommendation that proofed Paul's authenticity was **written on our hearts, known and read by everybody** (3:2). You could tell that Paul was concerned for the Corinthian church just by being around him and watching his ministry to them. He gives them double proof of his apostleship toward them: his burden is known by all and they became Christians as a result of his ministry. Even if they now did not want him as a minister, they were stuck because this letter of recommendation came **from Christ** (3:3).

Paul now begins to slide into the metaphor that will dominate the next few chapters: the new covenant. The letters of recommendation that God is now writing are **not with ink but with the Spirit of the living God, not on tablets of stone but on tablets of human hearts** (3:3). This contrast immediately evokes images of prophecies in Ezekiel and Jeremiah. In Ezekiel, we read verses like, "I will give them an undivided heart and put a new spirit in them; I will remove from them their heart of stone and give them a heart of flesh. Then they will follow my decrees and be careful to keep my laws" (11:19–20).[5] Even more important is Jeremiah 31, where God promises that He "will make a *new covenant* with the house of Israel . . . I will put my law in their minds and write it on their hearts" (31:31, 33). The fact that God wrote on the hearts of the Corinthians shows that Paul and his co-workers were **competent as ministers of a new covenant** (3:6).[6]

This fruit of Paul's ministry gave him confidence **through Christ before God. Not that we are competent in ourselves to claim anything for ourselves, but our competence comes from God** (3:4–5). Our competency comes from God. As the next few chapters will bear out, Paul could have become discouraged for so many different reasons at this point of his ministry. He was driven out of Ephesus. Meanwhile Corinth, the church in which he had invested the most effort, was only barely loyal to him. He was beginning to feel that his ministry in the east was like "scorched earth," that there was "no more place for me to work in these regions" (Rom. 15:23). In times like these, we look to God for our competence—we have reached the end of our own.

But his confidence in the "yes" of the gospel message (1:18–22), the message of Christ, had not waned. Far better than the old covenant, the covenant delivered to Moses on

GREAT THEMES

The early Christians understood themselves as the people of God under a new covenant arrangement, a covenant of Spirit rather than law.

"tablets of stone" (3:3) was the new covenant, the covenant of which he was a minister. This language ultimately comes from Jeremiah 31, which we quoted earlier. The idea of a new covenant probably came from Jesus himself (1 Cor. 11:25, Luke 22:20, Mark 14:24, Matt. 26:28). The fact that both Paul and especially Hebrews (Heb. 8) drew on the idea shows that the early Christians understood themselves as the new covenant people of God.

Paul and the author of Hebrews use this imagery to show that the new covenant was a covenant of spirit rather than of written law. By placing the Holy Spirit inside us, God wrote His laws on our hearts (Jer. 31:33, Heb. 8:10, 10:16). What an incredible upgrade, **for the letter kills, but the Spirit gives life** (2 Cor. 3:6). As Paul will say in Romans, the law did not bring life. On the contrary, "when we were controlled by the sinful nature [flesh], the sinful passions aroused by the law were at work in our bodies, so that we bore fruit for death" (Rom. 7:5). In contrast, "the law of the Spirit of life set me free from the law of sin and death. For what the law was powerless to do in that it was weakened by the sinful nature [flesh], God did by sending His own Son in the likeness of sinful man to be a sin offering" (Rom. 8:2–3).

ENDNOTES

1. Some scholars have even suggested that these chapters come from a different letter Paul wrote to the Corinthians and that they have been artificially spliced in here. But this position seems unnecessary and extreme, given the number of parallels between 2:14–7:1 and other parts of the letter. Most Pauline scholars believe that at least 2 Corinthians 1–9 belong together as a single letter Paul sent to the Corinthians.

Because Paul digresses, it is not entirely clear how he might have divided this part of the letter into sections. We have done our best to divide up the sections in a way that makes sense for expressing their meaning, but other divisions are possible.

2. Although it is possible that the "we" Paul uses throughout this section refers to him and his co-workers (for example, Timothy), Paul was probably more just referring to himself in the plural.

3. For example, C. K. Barrett, *The Second Epistle to the Corinthians* (London: A & C Black, 1973), 98.

4. For example, Barrett, 98.

5. Paul does not think of the "tablets of stone" as hard heartedness here.

6. The plural again may simply refer to Paul himself.

THE PARADOX OF PAUL'S MINISTRY:

THE GLORY OF THE NEW COVENANT

2 Corinthians 3:7–18

The next major section of 2 Corinthians runs from 3:7 to 5:10. In general, it explores the paradox of the ministry God entrusted to Paul. On the one hand, it was a glorious ministry with an incredible eternal destiny. Yet while Paul was on earth he repeatedly found himself suffering. But it was when Paul was suffering for the gospel that he felt closest to Jesus; he felt like he was participating in the sufferings of Jesus himself.

First of all, Paul acknowledges that **the ministry that brought death . . . came with glory** (3:7). As Paul says in Romans, the law itself is "spiritual" (Rom. 7:14), "holy, righteous, and good" (Rom. 7:12). But this glory was fading due to the arrival of Christ and the Spirit. The ministry of the letter may have been glorious, but **will not the ministry of the Spirit be even more glorious?** (3:8). Paul clearly means us to say yes.

The ministry of the Spirit in the new covenant **brings righteousness** (3:9). Now that we are "not under law but under grace" (Rom. 6:14, 15), we are no longer "slaves to sin, which leads to death" (Rom. 6:16). Now we are slaves "to obedience, which leads to righteousness" (Rom. 6:16). We can infer Paul's whole theology of sin and the Jewish law in these words in 2 Corinthians.

The Law told the Jews what sin was, and the Jews' inability to keep the Law pointed to their need for something more, namely, Christ and the

273

Spirit. Christ provides a true atonement for sins to which the Old Testament sacrifices only pointed (Heb. 10:11). The Spirit actually gives us the power to live victorious over sin, a victory they could only wish for in the Old Testament (Rom. 7:24–25).

With Christ and the Spirit on our side, what have we to fear? **[S]ince we have such a hope, we are very bold** (3:12). We are in such a better position now than anyone was under the old covenant! Paul looks at the story of the glory Moses had on his face after he met with God to receive the law (Exod. 34:29–35). But the radiance made the Israelites afraid to come near Moses (Exod. 34:30), so he veiled his face until he returned to speak to the Lord.

Paul presents a startling spiritual interpretation of this passage. Moses **put a veil over his face to keep the Israelites from gazing at it while the radiance was fading away** (3:13). The veil thus comes to represent the blindness of Israel to the fact that the glory of the old covenant has now faded in the presence of Christ. **Their minds were made dull** (3:14).

Paul argues that their minds were "veiled" to the fact that the glory behind the veil had faded. With the coming of Christ and the Spirit, the radiant glory never fades from our faces, for we are always in the presence of the Lord and the Spirit always dwells in our hearts. This is the glory of the new covenant! But **only in Christ is it** [the veil] **taken away** (3:14). **Even to this day when Moses is read, a veil covers their** [Israel's] **hearts** (3:15). Paul's unbelieving brothers and sisters in Israel could not see that because of Christ, the glory of the law had faded.

But whenever anyone turns to the Lord, the veil is taken away (3:16). In Paul's almost allegorical interpretation of Exodus 34, Moses would show Israel the glory as he gave the law, but he would then veil his face so they could not see that the glory was fading. Similarly, the veil represented for him the inability of the Jews of his day to see that the glory of the law had faded. But when Moses returned to the Lord in Exodus 34, he took the veil off. Similarly, any Jew who would turn to the Lord has taken the veil off.

This background is essential to understand what Paul now goes on to say in allegory. **[T]he Lord is the Spirit** (3:17) in the story of Moses, or to put it more clearly, the Lord in the story of Exodus *stands for* the Holy

Spirit. As Moses turned to the Lord, he took the veil off. So when we receive the Holy Spirit in our hearts, the veil of the old covenant is removed from us. The Spirit is the seal of God's ownership on us, the guarantee and deposit of what is to come (1:22). When we enter into the new covenant, we take off the covenant written on tablets of stone. We have turned to the Spirit, to a new covenant written on tablets of human hearts (3:3). It is like the removed veil in Exodus 34 when Moses turns to the Lord.

This situation brings freedom from the power sin had over us by way of the law (Gal. 3:23–24, 5:1; Rom. 4:15, 5:20–21, 7:9), although we are still under Christ's law (Rom. 3:31; 1 Cor. 9:21). **Where the Spirit of the Lord is, there is freedom** (3:17). This is not a freedom to sin (Rom. 6:1–2, 15). It is a freedom to serve the Lord in the way we wanted to serve Him previously, but we were unable to do so because of the power of sin over us (Rom. 7:7–24). Now through the Spirit we have the power to serve him in holiness and righteousness. **And we . . . are being transformed into his likeness with ever-increasing glory** (3:18).

This is a great text from which to reflect on the progressive dimension of a Christian's life. With the Spirit inside us, we are constantly becoming more and more like the Lord, a process that will culminate in the resurrection when our bodies will actually be transformed to be

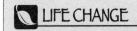

LIFE CHANGE

With the Spirit inside us, we are constantly becoming more and more like the Lord, a process that will culminate in our resurrection.

like His glorious body (1 Cor. 15:49; Phil. 3:21). In the meantime, the new covenant that brings the Spirit inside us makes it possible for the Spirit himself to "guide you into all truth" (John 16:13).

In this passage, Paul was specifically thinking of the inability of many Jews in his day to see the truth about Christ. Their love of the Jewish law for its own sake "veiled" their minds to the point where they could not see the wonderful freedom God was now bringing. If we expand on this concept, there is no doubt many things that we will not be able to see today if we have not turned to the Lord, who is the Spirit.

We are reminded of Paul's words in 1 Corinthians when he said that the "man without the Spirit does not accept the things that come from the

Spirit of God, for they are foolishness to him, and he cannot understand them, because they are spiritually discerned" (1 Cor. 2:14). For example, some philosophers have argued that selfishness is a virtue since the only option that makes any sense is for all of us to do what is in our personal best interest. But Christ teaches that we should always "consider others better than yourselves" (Phil. 2:3). Our human nature tells us that we should try to vanquish our enemies, but Christ tells us to love them (Matt. 5:44). We as Christians must let God remove the veils of human nature and cultural common sense so that we can see His spiritual will.

We should make one final note about this passage for those who encounter some of its more heretical interpretations. The idea of the Trinity has increasingly come under attack in certain Christian circles. The Trinity is the long standing Christian belief that although God is only one God, He exists as three persons: God the Father, God the Son (Jesus Christ), and God the Holy Spirit. Some have used 2 Cor. 3:17–18 to argue that Paul equated the Holy Spirit with the spirit of the risen Lord Jesus.

But as we have seen, Paul was not equating the Spirit with Jesus in this passage. Paul was allegorically equating the Holy Spirit with the Lord in the Exodus passage, who was literally God the Father. The persons of the Trinity thus remained distinct for Paul, although he clearly saw a close relationship between the three (2 Cor. 13:13). God would work out the details through the church in the centuries that followed.

5

THE PARADOX OF PAUL'S MINISTRY:
BEATEN BODIES, RENEWED SPIRITS

2 Corinthians 4:1–5:10

In 4:1–5:10 Paul expands on the paradox between the incredible glory and hope that is his as a minister of the new covenant and the sacrificial suffering he is currently undergoing. **Therefore . . . we do not lose heart** (4:1). Any minister or Christian who is discouraged should read this passage over and over again. The hope of glory kept Paul going, even in immensely trying times.

Rather . . . we do not use deception, nor do we distort the word of God (4:2). In 1 Corinthians Paul was mainly dealing with those in the church who wanted far more freedom than was appropriate. Now he seems to be getting criticism from those who think he is too "liberal"; that he distorts the word of God by disregarding too much of the Jewish law. Others apparently thought he was really taking up an offering for his own personal gain.

Most leaders and pastors have some sense of the direction in which they want the people under their charge to go. Many times their plans are indeed what they believe the Lord wants. Of course there are occasions where, as some Corinthians were apparently accusing Paul, a minister or leader may have selfish designs on the church.

Yet churches are sometimes carnal, and when they are not carnal they are often stubborn. We may be tempted to manipulate people, even for their own good. Deception of this sort is never the Christian path to reach even a good goal. We see in the case of the Corinthians that the very suspicion that Paul might be doing something of this sort destroyed their willingness to listen to him.

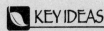 **KEY IDEAS**

We commend the truth to others most effectively when we set it forth plainly and without manipulation.

Paul recognized that his gospel might be veiled to some. If so, **it is veiled to those who are perishing** (4:3). Paul was highly suspicious even of many in the church who failed to see what God was doing in bringing Gentiles into the faith. It is possible that Paul considered some people "false brothers" (Gal. 2:4). At times Paul could wonder how discerning even James, Peter, and John were about God's plans for the Gentiles (Gal. 2:6).

Paul believed that some of those who opposed his message would make it, even if their work was burned up (1 Cor. 3:15). But Satan had clearly blinded those who could not see the truth of the new covenant **so that they cannot see the light of the gospel of the glory of Christ** (4:4). As Christians in the Wesleyan tradition, we do not take this statement to mean that those who are blinded have no responsibility in the matter of their blindness. Surely God enlightens everyone (John 1:9) enough to accept or reject the light (John 3:16; 1 Tim. 2:4). We must somehow hold in tension the twin, paradoxical truths of human responsibility to respond to God with the fact that spiritual forces are constantly at work on us.

The simple statement that Christ is the "image of God" implies the entire story of salvation. We have already seen in 1 Cor. 15:21–28 that Paul saw Christ as the "last Adam" (Rom. 5:12–19). God made Adam and Eve in the image of God (Gen. 1:27). He gave them authority over the created world (Gen. 1:28–30) and intended them to be crowned with glory and honor in the creation (Ps. 8:5–6).

But when Adam sinned, he lost this glory, and sin and death entered the world (Rom. 5:12). Because all people sin, we all lack the glory of God that God intended for humanity (Rom. 3:23; 5:12; Heb. 2:8). But by sending Jesus, God has solved our dilemma. Jesus became lower than the angels for a little while (Heb. 2:9). He was tempted in every way as we are, but did not sin (Heb. 4:15). As a result He was crowned with glory and honor, as God wished us all to be (Heb. 2:9). Now because He has tasted death for everyone, He can lead many more sons and daughters to glory (Heb. 2:9–10).

Christ is thus "the exact representation of his [God's] being" (Heb. 1:3). He is "the image of the invisible God, the firstborn over all creation" (Col. 1:15). He is the image of God in fulfillment of all God planned for humanity, the Lord of all creation who has made our salvation possible. For Paul, it was not himself he preached, **but Jesus Christ as Lord, and ourselves your servants** (4:5). To call Jesus "Lord" was to recognize that God had raised Him from the dead (Rom. 10:9; Acts 2:36; Phil. 2:9–11) and exalted Him as cosmic King at His right hand (Heb. 1:13).

The narrowness of the Corinthians' suspicions was almost mind-boggling in the light of Christ's awesomeness. How fearful for Paul to conduct a mission of selfishness when Christ stood in this position over him! No, Paul was on a mission for God and Christ, and he was the servant of the Corinthians because of the charge God had given him. **For God, who said, "Let light shine out of darkness," made his light shine in our hearts** (4:6). Paul could see—there was no veil on his face any longer after God appeared to him on the road to Damascus. He hoped the Corinthians would see as well.

The purpose God has in mind for us is **to give us the light of the knowledge of the glory of God** (4:6). Paul had experienced this enlightenment, and now he was bringing this knowledge of God's glory in the new covenant to others. The Corinthians were some of the recipients of this knowledge. Whose face was revealed behind the veil? It was not the face of Moses, but **the face of Christ** (4:6), and the glory in the face of Christ will never fade.

What an incredible treasure, the glorious knowledge God has given us and the glorious Spirit within us as a part of the new covenant! But for the moment, **we have this treasure in jars of clay**, earthen vessels (4:7). In the rest of the section (4:7–5:10) Paul contrasts his earthly body and its sufferings with the heavenly bodies we will receive at the resurrection. These verses anticipate what he will say in 2 Cor. 12:9 about how God's power is made perfect in weakness. If you are ever discouraged, Paul's words in these paragraphs are some of the most encouraging in the New Testament.

Our lives, our bodies, our "jars of clay" are so easily shattered. But this fact simply shows that **this all-surpassing power is from God and not from us** (4:7). In the earthly plane, **[w]e are hard pressed on every side . . . but not destroyed** (4:8–9). Even if someone were to kill our earthly bodies or if cancer were to eat them up, we have a hope that cannot be destroyed. We may not understand why God allows something to happen to us or to others, but it ultimately does not matter. Our hope and faith in our destiny is intact. Even if we go through a period of time when we cannot feel God's presence, He can enable us to continue in faith to the end.

 GREAT THEMES

"The better you dispose yourself to suffer, the more wisely you act and the greater is the reward promised you." Thomas à Kempis, *The Imitation of Christ*

On earth we **always carry around in our body the death of Jesus, so that the life of Jesus may also be revealed in our body** (4:10). As Paul will say in Romans, "if Christ is in you, your body is dead because of sin, yet your spirit is alive because of righteousness. And if the Spirit of him who raised Jesus from the dead is living in you, he who raised Christ from the dead will also give life to your mortal bodies through His Spirit, who lives in you" (Rom. 8:10–11). These words in 2 Corinthians and Romans are about the resurrection, the fact that God will one day bring life to our bodies no matter what fate they might face here on earth.

In Paul's day, and for many Christians around the world today, the life of the Christian is a life of suffering. **For we who are alive are always being given over to death for Jesus' sake** (4:11). Certainly Paul seemed to face trials wherever he went. But Paul's sufferings had a positive benefit for the Corinthians: **life is at work in you** (4:12). His ministry was **for your benefit, so that the grace . . . may cause thanksgiving to overflow to the glory of God** (4:15). Far from trying to rob them and take advantage of them, Paul was suffering to the point of death so that they might have life.

I believed; therefore I have spoken (5:13). In this verse, Paul quotes Ps. 116:10 where the psalmist fears for his life. "The cords of death entangled me, the anguish of the grave came upon me" (Ps. 116:3). The psalmist goes on: "you, O Lord, have delivered my soul from death, my eyes from tears" (Ps. 116:8). I believe Paul took this psalm spiritually as a prophecy about Jesus' death and resurrection.[1]

Paul believes that every Christian must have this same faith in the God who raises the dead. **[T]he one who raised the Lord Jesus from the dead will also raise us with Jesus and present us with you in his presence** (4:14). Paul seems to sense now that he will die before the Lord returns. I personally believe that his experiences at the end of his stay at Ephesus convinced him that he would probably die a martyr's death before the Lord's return.[2] Nevertheless, his wording holds open the possibility that the Corinthians might be alive and be remaining at the coming of the Lord (1 Thess. 4:17).

In the light of all these things, Paul reiterates what he said at the beginning of this line of thought (4:1): **we do not lose heart** (4:16). With the same encouragement we heard in

We can feel a special closeness to Jesus when we suffer in our bodies, particularly if we are to suffer for the sake of the gospel.

4:8–9, Paul affirms that **[t]hough outwardly we are wasting away . . . inwardly we are being renewed day by day** (4:16). What an incredible testimony Paul has given us in these words! We can pray these words even when we feel least like it. We can pray this prayer in faith that God will indeed soon refresh our spirits.

The key is to take an eternal perspective: **our light and momentary troubles are achieving for us an eternal glory that far outweighs them all** (4:17). My troubles today may not seem "light" or "momentary," but they certainly are in the light of eternity. To a child, a cut finger may seem like the end of the world, but the parent puts it into a more mature perspective. So it may seem preposterous to consider a painful death by cancer, torture, war, or disaster as "light." But we will no doubt see it this way when we are in eternity.

In the meantime, **we fix our eyes not on what is seen, but on what is unseen** (4:18). This perspective is the very nature of faith. "Faith is being sure of

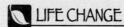

My troubles today may not seem "light" or "momentary," but they are in the light of eternity.

what we hope for and certain of what we do not see" (Heb. 11:1). We have this faith knowing that "our present sufferings are not worth comparing with the glory that will be revealed in us" (Rom. 8:18). Paul felt this way, and God can empower us to have this same faith in the time of crisis.

As Paul said in the first half of this section (4:1–15), we can face any trial in this life because we hope in our future resurrection. **[W]e know that if the earthly tent we live in is destroyed, we have a building from God, an eternal house in heaven, not built by human hands** (5:1).[3] Paul is not referring to some "mansion in the sky" here but to the resurrection body he already wrote to the Corinthians about in 1 Cor. 15:35–55. The context makes it likely that Paul is now contrasting our earthly body with our heavenly one yet to come.

Paul then expresses the tension between our current groaning and our longing for the resurrection. **Meanwhile we groan, longing to be clothed with our heavenly dwelling, because when we are clothed, we will not be found naked** (5:2–3). It is possible that Paul is referring to the state between death and resurrection as a kind of metaphorical "nakedness." We have our current body; we will have a resurrection body. In this interpretation, Paul is a little nervous about being naked in the meantime.

While it is difficult to read between the lines, Paul probably did not have this meaning in mind. The only place in all Paul's writings where he seems to speak clearly about the time in between death and resurrection is Philippians 1. Here Paul implies that going to be with Christ is a good thing, even before the resurrection when we will receive a glorious body. He does not think of it as a shameful nakedness to shun. Paul says that "to me, to live is Christ and to die is gain" (Phil. 1:21). Part of him desires "to depart and be with Christ, which is better by far" (Phil. 1:23). These comments push us away from seeing Paul's comments in 2 Corinthians on nakedness as a reference to the time between our deaths and our future resurrection.

A more likely interpretation of 2 Cor. 5:3 is thus that nakedness is what we have in store for us if we do not receive a resurrection body at the judgment.[4] **For while we are in this tent we groan and are burdened** (5:4). The mention of clothing and the swallowing of death remind us of what Paul has said in 1 Cor. 15:54: "When the perishable has been clothed with the imperishable, and the mortal with immortality, then the saying that is written will come true: 'Death has been swallowed up in victory.'" We are thus clothed with our heavenly dwelling at the time of the resurrection, the point in the future when we will forever return from the dead and receive a glorious, heavenly body. Paul's desire at that point is not to be unclothed, not to be among those who do not receive a resurrection body.[5]

This entire process is part of God's plan. **Now it is God who has made us for this very purpose and has given us the Spirit** (5:5). While it is difficult to know precisely how Paul conceived of our spiritual body, it seems clear enough that there is some connection between the Spirit and the heavenly "stuff" that will compose our spiritual bodies. The Spirit inside us is thus a foretaste of glory divine, a little bit of heaven inside us, a down payment toward the heavenly dwelling God will give us at the resurrection.

Confident in the coming resurrection, assured by the guarantee of the Holy Spirit inside us, we **know that as long as we are at home in the body we are away from the Lord** (5:6). In this in between time, we cannot see that for which we hope. **We live by faith, not by sight** (5:7). We would prefer for Christ to return now; we would prefer for the immediate transformation of our bodies and for the resurrection to take place as soon as possible. We **would prefer to be away from the body and at home with the Lord** (5:8). While it is possible that Paul has an intermediate state in view here, the context is pushing us to see this as a reference to the resurrection, when we will "be with the Lord forever" (1 Thess. 4:17).

The last two verses of this section seem to confirm this interpretation. **So we make it our goal to please him . . . For we must all appear before the judgment seat of Christ** (5:10). The things we do "in the body" are clear enough: we act in such a way while we are on earth so that we will be pleasing to God at the judgment.

On the other hand, what would it mean for us to be pleasing to God when we are "away from" the body? Paul gives us no indication anywhere in his writings that he thinks we are accountable for how we behave in some intermediate state after death. The best interpretation is that we want to please Him when we are away from the body at the point of judgment. That is, we want to please God at the judgment when we can receive our resurrection body. At that point we do not want to be naked or be unclothed. We want a heavenly dwelling.

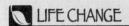

LIFE CHANGE

Despite the frailty of our earthly bodies, we can hope for the heavenly one God will give us at the resurrection.

The Corinthians were well acquainted with the idea of a judgment seat or *bēma*. Indeed, Paul himself stood before the *bēma* of Gallio while he was in Corinth (Acts 18:12; see map on p. 248). As in 1 Cor. 3:10–15, Paul reminds the Corinthians that they do not want to face God's wrath on the day when everyone's "work will be shown for what it is" (1 Cor. 3:13). Every knee will bow on that day (Rom. 14:10–11), including those "in heaven and on earth and under the earth" (Phil. 2:10). These are rare places where Paul indicates the destiny of the non-Christian dead. Like those alive, they will face God's judgment as well.

ENDNOTES

1. The Greek verb to believe (*pisteuō*) comes from the same root as the word for faith (*pistis*) and can in fact be translated as "to have faith."

2. I mentioned earlier in the commentary that I think Paul wrote Philippians while imprisoned at Ephesus (2 Cor. 1:8). See also Acts 20:25.

3. The NIV's choice of "now" makes it seem like 5:1 is the beginning of a new thought. The actual word is "for," and 5:1 is simply continuing the thought of 4:16–18.

4. So S. J. Hafemann, *2 Corinthians* (Grand Rapids: Zondervan, 2000), 213.

5. Our difficulty in following Paul's train of thought surely comes from the fact that we are far more preoccupied with the "intermediate state" we will be in than he was. Paul thought of Christ's return on far more immanent terms than we do. Whereas we almost expect to die first and for the resurrection to happen in the distant future, Paul expected Christ's return in the imminent future, but also apparently believed in some kind of intermediate state as well.

PAUL: AUTHENTIC MINISTER OF RECONCILIATION

2 Corinthians 5:11–6:13

1. BE RECONCILED TO GOD (5:11–6:2)

In 2 Cor. 5:11–6:13 Paul returns to the themes of the earlier section, the fact that he does not need to commend himself to the Corinthians (5:12) and that he is a minister of God's reconciliation (5:18). After this section he will return to recounting recent events and solidifying his relationship with the Corinthians. But Paul closes his digression by making clear to them the big picture of what he was all about. Because of the coming judgment of Christ and his solemn task as minister of the new covenant, he had a charge to keep. **Since, then, we know what it is to fear the Lord, we try to persuade men** (5:11). He has just mentioned the judgment seat of Christ, a fearful thing for those unprepared. This fearful event spurred Paul to persuade and "save" as many as possible.

He did not worry about convincing God of His genuineness, and he should not have to try to persuade the Corinthians. There were too many people that needed to be persuaded of the gospel. It is an unfortunate thing that churches often spend so much time dealing with internal squabbles, hard feelings, and conflicts when there is so much work to be done for the kingdom. Still others spend most of their time preoccupied with their own relationship to God and never get to the point where they can look to "persuade" those outside themselves. Paul brings our priorities into focus: we should aim to get beyond ourselves and our own individual worries. We should begin to minister to others in need of God.

We are not trying to commend ourselves to you again, but are giving you an opportunity to take pride in us (5:12). Here is the clearest indication yet in 2 Corinthians that some individuals were slandering Paul, perhaps in comparison to the "super apostles" he will mention in 11:5. These individuals took pride in exactly the wrong things: outward things that did not really count. Paul may allude to 1 Sam. 16:7 here: "Man looks at the outward appearance, but the LORD looks at the heart."[1] Some "apostles" and people in the congregation looked for things like eloquence (11:6), human wisdom (1 Cor. 2:1), nobility and influence (1 Cor. 1:26).

Perhaps some were saying Paul was a lunatic. The way he went about preaching the gospel was insane, given the suffering it brought him. **If we are out of our mind, it is for the sake of God** (5:13). If Paul appeared to behave in ways that made no sense from a worldly point of view, he was doing it for God. But in reality, Paul's thinking was as straight as an arrow (5:13). Paul was in his right mind. His message and mission came straight from God: **Christ's love compels us** (5:14).

What was that message? **[T]hose who live should no longer live for themselves but for him who died for them and was raised again** (5:15). These words are a condensed version of how Paul understood atonement to operate. First of all, Christ died as an atoning sacrifice for sins. "God presented him as a sacrifice of atonement" (Rom. 3:25), "to be a sin offering" (Rom. 8:3). "Christ, our Passover lamb, has been sacrificed" (1 Cor. 5:7). Therefore, those who become incorporated into Him pay the penalty for their sin through Him, by dying with Him. It is our faith in what God has done for us through Christ that ultimately saves us from God's wrath.

 GREAT THEMES

Those who enter into Christ participate in His death and resurrection. We die to sin; we will live to God.

Since we have died, **from now on we regard no one from a worldly point of view** (5:16) or more woodenly, "we know no one from now on according to the flesh." We have died, as Christ died. **Though we once regarded Christ in this way, we do so no longer** (5:16). Paul does not mean that he knew Christ personally while he was on earth. He is merely reiterating in a new way what he said before. Christ was alive on earth once, but now Christ has died for all—we no longer see Christ on earth. Since we have died with him, we no longer know the world from the point of view we had while we were "alive."

So we no longer live for ourselves. We are new people: **if anyone is in Christ, he is a new creation; the old has gone, the new has come!** (5:17). We now walk in newness of life (Rom. 6:4). Our "old self was crucified with him so that the body of sin might be done away with, that we should no longer be slaves to sin" (Rom. 6:6). We must no longer "let sin reign in your mortal body so that you obey its evil desires" (Rom. 6:12). You have "taken off your old self with its practices and have put on the new self, which is being renewed in knowledge in the image of its Creator" (Col. 3:9–10).

All this is from God, who reconciled us to himself through Christ and gave us the ministry of reconciliation (5:18). When you consider the awesomeness of this task, the lunacy of preaching for personal gain or selfish ambition comes into focus. After all, cosmic goals and forces are at play here. While some preachers might play games with the gospel, Paul was at work in the reconciling of the world to God. He was part of a process of remaking the entire universe.

Paul now gives us perhaps the clearest expression of his calling and mission in all his writings. **And he has committed to us the message of reconciliation. We are therefore God's ambassadors, as though God was making his appeal through us** (5:19–20). Although God walked the earth as Jesus Christ, He and Christ are currently in heaven. And while the Holy Spirit is with us, God has chosen the "foolishness" of a preached message to save those who come to have faith (1 Cor. 1:21).

Furthermore, Paul could boldly say to the Corinthians, **Be reconciled to God** (5:20). All the side issues of the Corinthians paled beside this ultimate concern. How could they respond with anything but wholehearted repentance and commitment?

Reconciliation to God is the very essence of Christianity. Christ is the one through whom God reconciles the world, the one "through whom *are* all things, and through whom we *live*" (1 Cor. 8:6, NKJV).

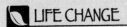

LIFE CHANGE

Reconciliation to God is the very essence of Christianity and a welcome message to a world filled with alienation.

God's eagerness to reconcile, even when we are uninterested, demonstrates God's "righteousness" as shown in 2 Cor. 5:21: **God made him who had no sin to be sin for us, so that in him we might become the righteousness of God**. The fact that Paul elsewhere emphasizes how God declares us righteous because of our faith leads me to wonder if Paul also had a second meaning in mind when he said that we *become* the righteousness of God.

Not only do we become a demonstration of *God's* righteousness, but we also become righteous too! This is the Wesleyan/holiness message: "For just as through the disobedience of the one man the many were made sinners, so also through the obedience of the one man the many will be made righteous" (Rom. 5:19). "May God himself, the God of peace, sanctify you through and through. May your whole spirit, soul and body be kept blameless at the coming of our Lord Jesus Christ" (1 Thess. 5:23), "[P]ut on the new self, created to be like God in true righteousness and holiness" (Eph. 4:24), "[That you] may be pure and blameless until the day of Christ, filled with the fruit of righteousness that comes through Jesus Christ—to the glory and praise of God" (Phil. 1:10–11), "You are witnesses, and so is God, of how holy, righteous and blameless we were among you who believed" (1 Thess. 2:10).[2]

But Paul adds a warning: **[W]e urge you not to receive God's grace in vain** (6:1). Indeed, who in his or her right mind would turn down such an offer? We do not know what particular influences were swaying the Corinthians away from God's grace. But clearly the right way to rely on grace involved repenting for the sins about which Paul had written them, as well as submitting to his ministry of reconciliation on their behalf.

Paul challenged them to make a choice for God and for the gracious forgiveness He had on offer. The longer you reject a deal of this sort, the harder it becomes to hear it; God's grace is not something you pass up. God has said, **"In the time of my favor I heard you, and in the day of salvation I helped you"** (6:2, quoting Isa. 49:8). Therefore, this choice is not something to postpone. Today is the day to accept God's grace and receive His Holy Spirit, the down payment and guarantee of what is to come.

2. WE HAVE NOT WRONGED YOU (6:3–13)

Since Paul and his coworkers have such an important and momentous charge, he would not want to undermine the possibility of accomplishing his mission in any way. **We put no stumbling block in anyone's path** (6:3). On the contrary, he has absorbed the brunt of the suffering that the Corinthians themselves might otherwise be responsible to endure for the sake of the gospel's furtherance. Paul's actions have done nothing but demonstrate the authenticity of his ministry. **[A]s servants** or ministers (*diakonoi*) **of God we commend ourselves in every way** (6:4).

Paul now gives a list of the many ways in which his actions have made it clear that he is serving God rather than his own self-interests. This list anticipates a more developed list of the hardships he has endured in 11:23–29. But here he mentions things like his **great endurance; in troubles, hardships and distresses; in beatings, imprisonments and riots; in hard work, sleepless nights and hunger** (6:5–6).

But Paul has not only commended himself as a minister of reconciliation in his sufferings. He has also commended himself in the positive characteristics of his ministry: **in purity, understanding, patience and kindness . . . in truthful speech and in the power of God** (6:6–7). Some Corinthians might be more doubtful of these, but they are Paul's consistent claims. He certainly wrote them regarding issues of purity in 1 Corinthians (1 Cor. 5). He has never flinched when they have accused him of untruthfulness in his speech (2 Cor. 1:12–24). He argues continually for his legitimacy on the basis of the power that accompanied him rather than his worldly wisdom or eloquence (1 Cor. 2:1–5; 2 Cor. 12:12, 13:3–4).

The time of his ministry brought **glory**, other times **dishonor** (6:8). Some times people gave him a **good report**; other times they slandered him (6:8). He knew that he and his coworkers were **genuine**, even though they were sometimes **regarded as imposters** (6:8). They were **known, yet regarded as unknown** (6:9), even by the Corinthians, whom Paul shames by asking whether they needed someone to write letters of recommendation so they would know whether they could trust him (3:1).

Some times it seemed like they were going to die at any minute, **and yet we live on** (6:9). He had many an occasion to be **sorrowful**, but he was **always rejoicing** (6:10). The letter to the Philippians is an excellent example of this attitude. Although Paul wrote it from prison, the theme of rejoicing permeates it (Phil. 1:4, 18; 2:18; 3:1; 4:4). His trials had made him **poor**, but it did not matter when he was **making many rich** (6:10). He may have **nothing**, but he possessed **everything** that mattered (6:10).

What a rich testimony! How many of us have come anywhere close to enduring so much for the sake of the gospel? Paul's example calls us to reexamine our priorities and set them in order. He calls us to lay aside the things that ultimately do not matter, especially any sins that might easily "beset us" (Heb. 12:1, KJV). He invites us not to worry about the fleeting pains and discomforts of this present world because in Christ we truly possess everything we need.

Paul now extends an invitation to the Corinthians: **We have spoken freely to you** (6:11). Paul has bared his soul to them. Some of them thought he was being "stand-offish." He assures them that this is not the case. He may have disciplined them, but even his discipline was administered out of love. **We are not withholding our affection from you**. On the contrary, **you are withholding yours from us** (6:12).

It is a shame that it can be so hard for two parties to reconcile when they have had "hard feelings" toward each other. In some instances, the entire matter could be resolved if just one of the two parties would take the initiative to approach the other. Paul makes this move in 2 Corinthians. **As a fair exchange—I speak as to my children—open wide your hearts also** (6:13). He has taken a first step toward laying aside past conflicts. Paul has opened his heart to them. He hopes that they will now reciprocate and fully open to him the hearts that they have already opened a little. He hopes they will proceed to open them all the way.

ENDNOTES

1. Both the Greek translation of 1 Samuel and Paul use the word for "face."

2. It is most attractive to see the exchange in a "tighter" manner. Christ is righteous, and I am sinful. Then Christ takes my sin, and I become righteous. Certainly these are true statements. But the history of the precise phrases—and the fact that God is also in this equation—probably makes Paul's original

meaning a little more complicated. God's saving righteousness is not demonstrated if He does not act to save. Meanwhile, there is the problem of our sin. Christ as a sacrifice without blemish takes on our sin, and thus the saving righteousness of God is demonstrated.

AVOID THE WICKED

2 Corinthians 6:14–7:1

In our breakdown of 2 Corinthians, the third and final section of the unit that stretches from 5:11–7:1 starts at 6:14. The words of this section are familiar to many Christians: **Do not be yoked together with unbelievers** (6:14). This is often applied to "evangelistic dating" of non-Christians as well as marriage to unbelievers. Paul does indeed say elsewhere that a Christian should not marry a non-Christian. He tells widows in 1 Cor. 7:39 that they are free to remarry whomever they wish—"but he must belong to the Lord."

At the same time, 2 Cor. 6:14–7:1 does not explicitly mention a marital relationship. The passage calls into question a person's motivation for intimate "fellowship" with unbelievers if in fact God is the very heart, center, and most essential part of them.

But also keep in mind, Paul told the church in 1 Cor. 5:10 that it was not wrong to *associate* with non-Christian sinners, even sexually immoral ones. He tells them they would have to leave the world not to come into contact with such people. He also tells any Christian who would find him or herself married to an unbeliever to stay with the spouse (1 Cor. 7:12–14). He must have very specific influences in mind.

Indeed, once we look beyond the words of this section and begin to ask how they fit into the flow of 2 Corinthians, we wonder more and more exactly what this section was all about. All the existing copies of 2 Corinthians have these words at this point of the text, so we have no manuscript basis to question whether they belong here.

At the same time, they do not fit this context very well. You could read straight from 6:13 to 7:2 and not realize you had missed any verses. For this reason, a number of Pauline scholars wonder if these words come from some other letter Paul wrote the Corinthians, and others question if they come from Paul at all. Some have even suggested they are an excerpt from Paul's very first letter to the Corinthians, one of the ones that has not survived (1 Cor. 5:9).[1]

We really do not have enough evidence to prove or disprove this idea. In general, our default inclination should be to take biblical texts as they stand in the absence of manuscript evidence or extremely compelling reasons.[2] As we move through these verses, we will read them as if they were originally a part of 2 Corinthians, although I am sympathetic to the other view. If in fact they come from some other letter of Paul's, they would have some similar meaning. Only the specific implications would differ.

In the current context, Paul has just told the Corinthians that they have been withholding their affection from him (6:12). He implores them to open their hearts wide to him (6:13). Against this background, the text drives us to see the influence of non-believers as a major reason for the Corinthians withholding their affection from Paul. If the verses belong at this point of the text, Paul seems to imply that it is some non-Christian influence that is ultimately pulling them away from him. Perhaps we should also remember that Paul sometimes thought of people in the churches as "false brothers" (Gal. 2:4). Some interpreters think that Paul is actually speaking of members of the church that are no longer worthy of the name "believer."[3]

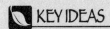 **KEY IDEAS**

If 2 Corinthians 6:14–7:1 belongs at this point in the letter, it implies that some non-Christian influence was pulling the Corinthians away from Paul.

When we read these verses at this point of the text, they become a kind of climax to Paul's previous discussion, perhaps even a real key to what has been going on at Corinth.[4] Some group of "unbelievers"— or of Christians with false ways—becomes responsible for leading the Corinthians astray. It makes sense that the closest relationships of a Christian—the "yoked" kind of relationships—would be with other Christians. Paul explains his reasoning in the next three verses (6:14–16). All the questions in verses 14–15 expect the same basic answer: "none" or "nothing."

Again, in its context, Paul must have particular unbelieving influences on the Corinthians in mind. Perhaps his final question hones in on one of the corrupting influences that had particularly endangered the Corinthians.

LIFE CHANGE

We would expect the closest friends and associates of a Christian to be Christians too, not because we do not love non-Christians or unbelievers, but because we have the most fundamental elements of our life in common with other Christians.

What agreement is there between the temple of God and idols? For we are the temple of the living God (6:16). This comment may hint at the issue over which he and the "sinner" at Corinth have tussled. Perhaps the issue of meat offered to idols continued to vex the community even after they received 1 Corinthians.[5]

Second Corinthians 6:17–7:1 tell us how we should live once we realize how incompatible the world of Belial, or Satan, is with the world of the true God. This name for Satan is unique in both the Old and New Testaments, although it is used of Satan in the Dead Sea Scrolls and in other "apocalyptic" Jewish literature from Paul's day.[6] It evokes images of the ongoing cosmic struggle that is currently taking place between God and the forces of Satan. Satan's influence is nothing with which to trifle. When the influence of unbelievers is leading us astray, we must **come out from them and be separate** (6:17). In the context of the Corinthians, they must leave the temples and idols of Corinth behind them. Whatever their motivation might be for keeping contact, Paul required them to make a clean break with pagan temples and with the "unclean" things of the pagan world.

The final verse to which Paul alludes is actually used of the Messiah elsewhere in the New Testament (Heb. 1:5): **I will be a Father to you, and you will be my sons and daughters, says the Lord Almighty** (6:18 quoting 2 Sam. 7:14). Perhaps Paul also had Isa. 43:6 in mind as he quotes 2 Samuel, for he has changed the verse in a couple ways. The most noticeable way that Paul has changed the quote is by adding the words "and daughters" to it. So, the newer translations such as the *New Living Translation* and *Today's New International Version* certainly have biblical precedence for adding "and sisters" to passages originally addressed to simply "brothers."

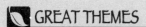

GREAT THEMES

Paul adds the words "and daughters" to his quotation of 2 Samuel 7:14, showing that comments in the Bible directed toward men often applied to women as well.

Paul comes to his final conclusion: **[L]et us purify ourselves** (7:1). So Paul instructs the Corinthians to purify themselves from the influences among them that are contaminating them, that are corrupting God's temple. The application is fairly straightforward. Whatever is contrary to God in our lives, whatever opposes righteousness or furthers disbelief, these are things we must extract from our lives. We must "come out" from these people and things. We must not "touch" these unclean things. Anything that contaminates us and distracts from the fact that we belong to God, that we are "holy" to God, we must separate ourselves from these things.

ENDNOTES

1. Although this theory has some problems. These verses tell the Corinthians not to associate with unbelievers (6:14). But in 1 Corinthians Paul indicates his first letter was about not associating with Christians who were sexually immoral (1 Cor. 5:9–11).

3. For example, R. P. Martin, *2 Corinthians* (Waco: Word, 1986), 194.

4. So S. J. Hafemann, *2 Corinthians*, 277.

5. So G. D. Fee, "II Corinthians vi.14–vii.1 and Food Offered to Idols," *New Testament Studies* 23 (1977): 140–67.

6. Apocalyptic literature is literature of the same flavor as the book of Revelation, writings in which a heavenly messenger brings revelations of what is going on in the invisible, heavenly realm.

8

PAUL RECOUNTS RECENT EVENTS:

PART TWO

2 Corinthians 7:2–16

The long trail that began in 1:12 finally comes to an end in 2 Corinthians 7. The final section begins where 6:13 had left off: **Make room for us in your hearts** (7:2). At the end of chapter 6 he had accused the Corinthians of withholding their affection from him (6:12)—something of which they had accused him (1:24). His heart was wide open to them (6:11). Now he hoped they would make room for him in their hearts.

We have wronged . . . corrupted . . . exploited no one (7:2). Some were accusing Paul of the very things they were thinking and feeling. Of all people to accuse of exploitation, Paul was the one who worked with his own hands rather than rely on their material support (1 Cor. 9:6; 2 Cor. 11:7). Far from corrupting them, Paul was a minister of God's reconciliation who had their ultimate spiritual interests in mind.

But Paul himself maintained a good attitude, and gives a good example to pastors, parents, or other caregivers facing resistance. **[Y]ou have such a place in our hearts that we would live or die with you. I have great confidence in you; I take great pride in you. I am greatly encouraged** (7:3–4). Paul must have found it difficult some times to maintain such a positive attitude toward the Corinthians, just as it is often hard for us to feel this way toward those who are giving us trouble. But love "always protects, always trusts, always hopes, always perseveres" (1 Cor. 13:7). With human beings such an attitude is impossible, but "with God all things are possible" (Matt. 19:26).

Paul now resumes recounting the events leading up to this letter. **[W]hen we came into Macedonia . . . we were harassed at every turn—conflicts on the outside, fears within** (7:5). Paul not only had the external pressures of those persecuting him on the outside; he was troubled inwardly too as he worried about the Corinthians.

But thanks be to God! We have a **God, who comforts the downcast** (7:6). He will not allow us to be tempted or tested beyond what we can bear (1 Cor. 10:13). Paul uses the same word here for comfort that he used in the opening prayer of the letter to express the great comfort we can find in God (*parakaleō*).

LIFE CHANGE

When we feel like our life is nothing but "fightings and fears, within, without," we have a God who comforts the downcast!

Paul was not only comforted by the coming of Titus, **but also by the comfort you had given him** (7:6–7). Apparently all the right things had happened when Titus visited the Corinthians and delivered Paul's harsh letter.

First of all, the community had all the right attitudes toward Paul. Titus **told us about your longing for me, your deep sorrow, your ardent concern for me** (7:7).

If Paul is referring to a time when he was imprisoned at Ephesus, this comment may refer to how much they were concerned about him in his troubles and how much they hoped to see him again soon. Far from wanting Paul to stay away, they were disappointed that Titus had come instead of him. Paul's sorrow turned into incredible joy. Another good aspect of the Corinthians attitude toward Paul was their submission to him. Paul and the Corinthians both found out **how devoted to us you are** (7:12). They had submitted to his authority.

The Corinthians also demonstrated the correct attitude toward God. Someone had done someone else wrong, including the wrong done to Paul by rebellion against his authority (7:12). But this individual had repented (2:7), and the community had repented of not dealing handily with the individual. **Even if I caused you sorrow by my letter, I do not regret it. Though I did regret it—I see that my letter hurt you** (7:8–9).

The most important attitude the community demonstrated was that of *repentance*. Paul was happy, **not because you were made sorry, but because your sorrow led you to repentance** (7:9). Repentance involves a certain sorrow or regret of past deeds, but it is more than just a feeling. True repentance involves change, a change of attitude that leads to a change of behavior. Paul's actions, while they did not feel good to the Corinthians, were ultimately for their betterment, for it led them to change. **Godly sorrow brings repentance that leads to salvation and leaves no regret** (7:10). Certainly this comment is true with regard to becoming a Christian. Peter tells the crowd on the Day of Pentecost that they must "Repent and be baptized, every one of you, in the name of the Lord Jesus Christ for the forgiveness of your sins" (Acts 2:38).

The Corinthians also show us the crucial importance of repentance *in a Christian's* life, after coming to Christ. Here we remember that Paul primarily thinks of salvation as a *future* event that will take place on the Day of Judgment when we *escape* God's wrath by way of Christ (Rom. 5:9). Appropriate repentance throughout our Christian life is the path to our ultimate salvation. In contrast,

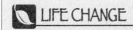

LIFE CHANGE

Appropriate repentance throughout our Christian life is the path to our ultimate salvation.

worldly sorrow brings death (7:10). The person who is sorry that they have not continued in sin, the person who is sorry that they must obey God, this person is on a path for death rather than salvation.

Paul revels in the fruit of repentance in the hearts of the Corinthians: **earnestness . . . eagerness to clear yourselves . . . indignation . . . longing . . . concern, what readiness to see justice done** (7:11). It could have gone the other way. Church confrontations today all too often result in people leaving the church. In our glut of churches, it is all too easy to slip in and out from one to the next.

But the Corinthians proved themselves **to be innocent in this matter** (7:11). They dealt **with the one who did the wrong** (7:12), and he repented (2:7). The community had stood up for justice and had vindicated **the**

injured party (7:12), which also included Paul himself. With regard to Paul, they had demonstrated **how devoted to us you are** (7:12). What was the net result of the conflict? **By all this we are encouraged** (7:13).

We were especially delighted to see how happy Titus was, because his spirit has been refreshed by all of you (7:13). Paul knew there is a point where fresh perspectives and "new blood" are needed to infuse a tense situation. Paul does not send Timothy or any of those who have already been involved with Corinth. Rather he sends in Titus, a new minister.

Paul **had boasted to him about you, and you have not embarrassed me** (7:14). This fact not only is a boost to the Corinthians honor and character, it substantiates the fact that Paul himself is truthful and a good judge of character: **our boasting about you to Titus has proved to be true** (7:14). Paul means all these comments to reinforce the positive behavior the Corinthians have just made Titus' **affection for you is all the greater . . . I am glad I can have complete confidence in you** (7:15–16).

9

THE OFFERING FOR JERUSALEM

2 Corinthians 8:1–9:15

1. OVERVIEW

At first glance, 2 Corinthians 8–9 seem somewhat out of place in the letter up to this point. They appear to deal with an isolated topic that disappears as quickly as it comes. One scholar has actually written a commentary on just these two chapters alone, thinking that each chapter is a different letter Paul sent to Corinth.[1] The topic is the offering Paul raised to take to Jerusalem from his churches.[2]

Paul already mentioned an offering of this sort at the end of 1 Corinthians (refer to our discussion of 1 Cor. 16:1–4 as background to these chapters in 2 Corinthians). Paul does not give us extensive details about this offering he was collecting. It was clearly a gift for the poor in the church of Jerusalem (Rom. 15:26), but we are left to guess whether Jerusalem was in crisis or whether the offering served a number of subsidiary purposes in addition to its most straightforward one to help the poor.

In the first section (8:1–15), Paul uses the generosity of the Macedonian Christians to spur the Corinthians on to give generously as well. He reminds them how eager they had originally been and hopes they will follow through given the way God has blessed them materially. In the second (8:16–9:5), Paul talks about the logistics of sending Titus and two brothers he does not name for some reason. Apparently the Corinthians know who he means. The discussion ends with a reminder of the blessings in store for those who give cheerfully, as well as of the benefit the offering will bring to the relationship between the Corinthians and the Christians in Jerusalem (9:6–15).

2. PAUL ENCOURAGES THE CORINTHIANS TO GIVE (8:1–15)

Paul begins by using the Macedonians as an example for the Corinthians to emulate (8:1–7). He wants them **to know about the grace that God has given the Macedonian churches** (8:1). These churches probably included the churches at Philippi, Thessalonica, and Berea. These churches apparently were undergoing persecution, as we hear in Philippians 1:28–30. Yet they had not failed Paul. **[T]heir overflowing joy and their extreme poverty welled up in rich generosity . . . they gave as much as they were able** (8:2–3).

Paul thus gives us the impression that the churches of Macedonia were not well off materially. Instead, they were givers like the woman who gave two very small copper coins to the temple treasury in Luke. Jesus said that she had "put in more than all the others." The others "gave their gifts out of their wealth; but she out of her poverty put in all she had to live on" (Luke 21:3–4). Both Jesus and Paul clearly did not value so much the amount one gives as much as the generosity of the heart. He thus encouraged each Corinthian to give "in keeping with his income" (1 Cor. 16:2).

The Macedonians had such generosity. **Entirely on their own, they urgently pleaded with us for the privilege of sharing in this service to the saints** (2 Cor. 8:3–4). Given their poverty, Paul apparently had not expected the Macedonians to contribute—**[a]nd they did not do as we expected** (8:5). While they would not have sinned if they had not given, they showed that their priorities were in order: **they gave themselves first to the Lord and then to us in keeping with God's will** (8:5).[3]

Paul uses the example of the Macedonians to push the Corinthians toward giving even more. Apparently the Corinthian church was a prosperous church at the time (8:14), so Paul knew it would not burden them to give since there were apparently a number of wealthy individuals such as Erastus mentioned earlier.[4]

We should reflect carefully before using these kinds of tactics today. Paul's world was an honor-shame world where shaming was a regular motivational technique. Paul uses these kinds of techniques in other places in his writings. While there is certainly nothing wrong with some good natured competition between individuals and churches, our culture works better when all the parties involved create the competition rather than when a leader tries to shame one by comparing it to another.

But shaming was part and parcel of Paul's world. We will find him pouring the shame on later in chapter 9, particularly 9:2–5. This approach also worked well in Paul's letter to Philemon (17).

Paul has less to hold over the Corinthians' head, but he uses some of the same techniques. First there is the Corinthians' new relationship with Titus. **So we urged Titus . . . to bring also to completion this act of grace on your part** (8:6). Paul has bragged on them about how good an impression they had made on Titus (7:13). Anyone in that world would prefer to retain rather than lose such honor.

Then there is their own reputation with Paul himself. **[J]ust as you excel in everything . . . see that you also excel in this grace of giving** (8:7). Paul is really using their worldly values to persuade them in comments like these. He is appealing to their desire for status and honor. But the honor he urges them to pursue is legitimate honor: the honor of helping others in need.

Second Corinthians 8:8 is a test, a classic example of his shaming technique: **I want to test the sincerity of your love by comparing it with the earnestness of others.** If your love is truly sincere, as you have protested it is to Titus, then you will follow us in the matter of this offering as well. Are you as eager to give as those who have far less than you? A bad response would show that you are not as earnestly devoted to Christ as you think you are and claim to be. Throughout this discussion we should remember that Paul was not raising this money for himself. This was no building fund he was creating for his own church or some sale of books he himself had written. He was raising this money for the poor in someone else's church.[5]

The greatest example of selfless giving is Jesus, the greatest example for any of us to strive to emulate. **[Y]ou know the grace of our Lord Jesus Christ** (8:9)—His willingness to give to others without payment. **[T]hough he was rich, yet for your sakes he became poor, so that you**

through his poverty might become rich (8:9). While the Corinthians could not hope to pay Jesus back for what He did for them, they could "pay it forward" in a small way by helping others.

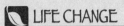

LIFE CHANGE

While we might wish we could pay Jesus back for what He did for us, we can at least "pay it forward" in a small way by helping others.

With these things in mind, Paul encourages the Corinthians to complete the effort they had begun a year previously. **Last year you were the first not only to give but also to have the desire to do so. Now finish the work** (8:10–11). Before the conflict between Paul and the Corinthians had come to a head, they had shown great eagerness to give. Now that the relationship was back on track, as it seemed to be, Paul hoped they would continue with the intentions they had at first.

The remainder of this section makes it clear that Paul is asking **according to your means** (8:11). As with the widow's two copper coins, God is not interested in the amount we give but in our desire to give. **For if the willingness is there, the gift is acceptable according to what one has, not according to what he does not have** (8:12). Many may say they have nothing to give when in fact their priorities are not in order.

Paul also recognized that our ability to give may differ over time. **Our desire is not that others might be relieved while you are hard pressed, but that there might be equality. At the present time your plenty will supply what they need, so that in turn their plenty will supply what you need** (8:13–14). At this particular point in time, the Corinthians were enjoying a greater prosperity than the church at Jerusalem. But all it would take is a well-positioned famine to reverse the situation.

When we are all faithful to what God has given, then **there will be equality, as it is written: "He who gathered much did not have too much, and he who gathered little did not have too little"** (8:14–15). The early Christian community was not one in which individuals hoarded their own property and prosperity to themselves. Rather, "All the believers were together and had everything in common. Selling their possessions and goods, they gave to anyone as he had need" (Acts 2:44–45). While these verses describe the early Jerusalem church, they reflect the principle that the church is more like a family than a group of individuals who happen to come together once or twice a week.

Paul's quotation of Exod. 16:18 evokes the image of the Israelites collecting manna in the wilderness. Each found as much as he or she needed. So Paul says if everyone gives as God blesses them, then everyone in the church will have as much as they need. This aspect of the early church is one that we might profitably revisit today. Do I hoard the material blessings *God* has given to me? What of my "treasure on earth" might better serve some needy part of the body of Christ or serve as an evangelistic tool to the needy of the world?

3. THE LOGISTICS OF THE COLLECTION (8:16–9:5)

Paul gives us a number of hints throughout his writings about the way he handled money in his churches. While he had a right to the support of those to whom he ministered (1 Cor. 9:3–12), he did not take support from a church when he was there with them (1 Cor. 9:12, 15). His reasoning was probably that accepting such help created "strings" of obligation that would only encumber his ministry at a location. How easily could he tell the sinner to repent if the sinner was providing his bread and butter?

Paul also did not want anyone to see him as a "peddler" of the gospel for profit (2 Cor. 2:17). We find hints throughout the New Testament, particularly in the Pastoral Epistles, that traveling teachers and prophets were sometimes a catalyst for false teaching in the church (Matt. 7:21–23; 1 Tim. 1:3–7, 4:1–5, 6:10; 2 Tim. 3:6–9; Titus 1:10–16; 2 Pet. 2:1–3; 3 John 5–8, 10; Jude 4). Paul's "tentmaking" work ensured that no one could accuse him of such motives.

Paul did, however, receive support from churches when he was not ministering directly to them. The Philippian church in particular seems to have supported Paul throughout his ministry. They sent help to him more than once while he was in Thessalonica (Phil. 4:15–16). They showed the same concern again during the imprisonment when he wrote Philippians (Phil. 2:25).

With regard to the offering for Jerusalem, Paul modeled incredible wisdom in the way he orchestrated its logistics. He himself did not carry the money but arranged for each location to send a representative with their offering (1 Cor. 16:3). He would not even travel with the group unless it met with the approval of the parties involved (1 Cor. 16:4). The result was a rather large group of individuals with representatives from locations as wide ranging as Galatia, Berea, Thessalonica, and Asia (Acts 20:4).

Second Corinthians 8:16–9:5 deal with a preparatory visit to shore up the Corinthian part of this collection before Paul's official visit with all these representatives from the other churches. Paul was sending three individuals to prepare the way. The leader of this small delegation was Titus (8:16). When Paul asked Titus to return to Corinth, **Titus not only welcomed our appeal, but he is coming to you with much enthusiasm and on his own initiative** (8:17). This would be Titus' second visit to the church, the first of which was when he delivered Paul's "harsh letter."

But Paul sent with Titus two other unnamed brothers with whom the Corinthians were apparently familiar already. The first was **the brother who is praised by all the churches for his service to the gospel** (8:18). Paul oddly does not mention the brother's name, perhaps to make it clear that Titus was the leader of the delegation.[7] The person's identity would be obvious to the Corinthians, since this person would be in their midst as this part of the letter was read aloud to them. The same is true of a second unnamed brother **who has often proved to us in many ways that he is zealous** (8:22).

The first brother **was chosen by the churches to accompany us as we carry the offering** (8:19). This intentional accountability is **to avoid any criticism of the way we administer this liberal gift** (8:20). It was not enough for Paul to know that everything he was doing was above board. He took pains **to do what is right, not only in the eyes of the Lord but also in the eyes of men** (8:21).

Paul asks the Corinthians to **show these men the proof of your love and the reason for our pride in you, so that the churches can see it** (8:24). On the one hand, Paul does not think there is truly a **need for me to write to you about this service to the saints** (9:1). They were eager a year ago (8:10), and Paul still believes in their **eagerness to help** (9:2). He had even boasted **about it to the Macedonians, telling them that since last year you in Achaia were ready to give** (9:2). If he used the giving of the Macedonians to inspire the Corinthians to give, he had used the earlier enthusiasm of the Corinthians to stir **most of them to action** (9:2). Paul in everything shows himself to be "wise as a serpent" in his motivational techniques.

But despite his protests of confidence, he clearly had doubts as well. He was sending Titus and the two brothers anyway **in order that our boasting about you in this matter should not prove hollow** (9:3). The honor of both Paul and the Corinthians was at stake. Paul had made high claims of the Corinthian generosity to the Macedonians. The Corinthians would not want to feel shamed. Paul also did not want to "lose face" because of the Corinthians. **For if any Macedonians come with me and find you unprepared, we . . . would be ashamed of having been so confident** (9:4).

So Paul's savvy leads him **to urge the brothers to visit you in advance and finish the arrangements** (9:5). Clearly Paul's doubts are greater than we might have thought at the beginning of his discussion. By sending Titus and the brothers ahead, the Corinthians would fulfill both their earlier intentions and Paul's boasts about them. Their offering **will be ready as a generous gift, not as one grudgingly given** (9:5).

4. THE PRINCIPLES BEHIND THE COLLECTION (9:6–15)

The final part of Paul's appeal presents the principles behind giving, as well as its benefits. The first principle is that **[w]hoever sows sparingly will also reap sparingly, and whoever sows generously will also reap generously** (9:6). This principle is obvious in farming, but it is also true in terms of our spiritual investment. We remember the Parable of the Talents (Matt. 25:14–30), where the one who hid his money in the ground received stern condemnation from his master. In contrast, those who invested more, received more in return.

We should not translate Paul's words here into some sort of prosperity gospel in terms of material wealth and possessions. We remember that one of the main themes of 2 Corinthians is encouragement in the midst of suffering, loss, and impoverishment. God does sometimes return material blessing for material investment, but the greater rewards are spiritual. **God** is able to make all *grace* abound to you (9:8, *italics* mine). This grace translates into the fact that in all things at all times, having all that you need, you will abound *in every good work* (9:8, *italics* mine). "God will meet all your needs according to his glorious riches in Christ Jesus" (Phil. 4:19), and He will enlarge the harvest of your righteousness (2 Cor. 9:10).

All that God asks is that we give cheerfully, for God loves a cheerful giver (9:7). Paul tells the Corinthians that [e]ach man should give what he has decided to give, not reluctantly or under compulsion (9:7). Our "cheer" comes from the fact that we love God and want Him to know how thankful we are for all He has given us. Our cheer comes because we love others and want to see their needs met. Sometimes it is difficult on us to give, but God does not ask a particular amount—only that we give what we can cheerfully.

The person who rationalizes what they can give has failed to give cheerfully and so has already left God's will unfulfilled before giving anything. Yet the New Testament does not specify a specific percentage or amount, as the Old Testament did. The Old Testament tithe referred to a tenth of one's harvest, for the culture of the Old Testament was agrarian. The New Testament comes to us from a world that was part agrarian and partially a monetary society, and the church was not yet organized formally enough to specify the recipient of its giving. But the principle of giving to those in need and of supporting those who minister is still clear, as is the principle of giving in proportion to God's blessing.

So the richness that God returns is not primarily material, although it can be material. Paul tells the Corinthians that they will have all that they need (9:8). He will also supply and increase your store of seed and will enlarge the harvest of your righteousness (9:10). Not just in material things, but [y]ou will be made rich in every way so that you can be generous on every occasion (9:11).

Paul ends his appeal by pointing out the benefits of the offering beyond merely sup-

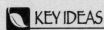

KEY IDEAS

Paul seems to address more directly how a Christian with material means should serve the Lord: such a person must give cheerfully and generously in proportion to the way God has blessed them.

plying the needs of God's people (9:12). It is even more importantly a service **overflowing in many expressions of thanks to God** (9:12). While it is certainly in our own best interest to thank God for the abundance He has given us, our giving leads others to praise God as well **for the obedience that accompanies your confession of the gospel of Christ** (9:13). This thankfulness **for your generosity in sharing with them and with everyone else** (9:13) will lead them to pray for the Corinthians. **And in their prayers for you their hearts will go out to you, because of the surpassing grace God has given you** (9:14). These prayers will complete the cycle of blessing because their prayers will bring spiritual blessing back to the Corinthians for the material gifts they have made. **Thanks be to God for his indescribable gift!** (9:15).

ENDNOTES

1. H. D. Betz, *1 Corinthians 8 and 9: A Commentary on Two Administrative Letters of the Apostle Paul* (Philadelphia: Fortress, 1985).

2. Interestingly, while this offering was clearly of great significance for Paul, Acts does not mention it.

3. The word "then" is not in the Greek original, and it may actually be misleading. Perhaps Paul is not so much comparing himself as second to God who comes first, but to the fact that the Macedonians put God *and* him first next to themselves as second.

4. See the Introduction to 1 Corinthians.

5. It is true that he would gain honor from initiating and effecting the offering.

6. This leads a few scholars to suggest that the person later became a heretic and his name was expunged. This theory seems rather far-fetched.

10

INTRODUCTION TO 2 CORINTHIANS 10–13

We will not read very far into 2 Corinthians 10 before we begin to sense that Paul's tone has changed from the earlier part of the letter. The Corinthians have covered a lot of ground in terms of reconciling, repenting, giving Paul comfort, and giving generously, but clearly they had more ground to cover. For this reason many see 2 Corinthians 10–13 as Paul's address to that part of the community that had not yet submitted to his authority. The first nine chapters address the group loyal to Paul, the last four those still resistant.

Other scholars suggest 2 Corinthians 10–13 are in fact an excerpt from a letter Paul sent to the Corinthians *shortly after* he had sent the first nine chapters with Titus and the two brothers. This position is in fact the one currently held by the majority of Pauline scholars. In this suggestion, Paul sent Titus and the two brothers with 2 Corinthians 1–9 both as a celebration of their reconciliation and in preparation for the offering Paul was about to collect.

But the trip did not go as well as Titus' first one. The latent hostility that some felt toward Paul came to the fore, and some demanded proof of his apostolic authority (13:3). They had come under the influence of certain traveling Christian teachers Paul calls "super apostles" (11:5, 12:11) who themselves questioned Paul's authority.[1] Some criticized Paul for writing heavy letters, but being timid and shy when he was present (10:10). Worst of all, Paul began to doubt whether the sinner in the community had really repented (13:2). He was afraid he would find that all the sins he had addressed in his earlier correspondence would be rampant in the community

(12:21). He is so discouraged that he does not even mention the offering—an issue that may also have been a sore spot to the Corinthians and an excuse for them to accuse him of making money off the gospel (12:14–17).

The differences between the two parts of 2 Corinthians are significant enough to consider strongly that chapters 10–13 was a separate letter. Such a suggestion actually saves us from wondering whether Paul *does* contradict himself in the space of a single letter.

Therefore, while we will keep an open mind to the other possibilities, we will largely read this final section of 2 Corinthians as the bulk of a letter subsequent to 2 Corinthians 1–9. Paul sends 2 Corinthians 1–9 with Titus and the brothers, but they return with disturbing news that leads Paul to send 2 Corinthians 10–13 back to the Corinthians in rather short order. The close relationship between the content of the two letters led to the combining of them together in the early collections of Paul's letters. In this process, perhaps a very brief farewell to 2 Corinthians 1–9 and introduction to 2 Corinthians 10–13 would have been omitted. On the whole this reconstruction seems to make the most sense of the differences between the two sections.

ENDNOTES

1. We can only hope that Paul is not referring to Apollos.

11

PAUL'S APPEAL FOR FULL OBEDIENCE

2 Corinthians 10:1–18

With the beginning of this section, Paul presents new issues that had not surfaced in the previous chapters. In our reconstruction of events, we are now reading part of a letter slightly later in time than the previous chapters, part of a letter Paul wrote after Titus and the two brothers had returned from Corinth with less than optimal news. Nevertheless, nothing in this section could not have come from the same letter as the first nine chapters.[1]

The NIV rightly puts a number of words in quotation marks, indicating that Paul is responding to comments some Corinthians have shared with Titus. **Paul, who am "timid" when face to face with you, but "bold" when away!** (10:1). Paul interestingly shifts from the "we" he has used of himself throughout 2 Corinthians 1–9 to a pointed "I." He singles himself out from Timothy, who was perhaps the co-writer, to confront this group of Corinthians.

In keeping with his theme of strength through weakness, Paul begins his appeal with a reference to the meekness and gentleness of Christ, the ultimate example of strength through weakness. Paul had implied this theme in the earlier section of 2 Corinthians where he spoke of the treasure of the glory of the new covenant housed in our earthly jars of clay (4:7).

I beg you that when I come I may not have to be as bold as I expect to be toward some people who think that we live by the standards of this world (10:2). The Corinthians who oppose Paul continue to criticize him by worldly standards. Paul protests once again that **though we live in the world, we do not wage war as the world does** (10:3). As Paul said in 1 Corinthians, he does not fight with **the weapons of the world** (10:4), things like rhetorical eloquence or philosophical wisdom. He is not interested in talk but in **divine power** (10:4). Way back in 1 Corinthians he had told the Corinthians that when he came he would find out "not only how these arrogant people are talking, but what power they have" (1 Cor. 4:19). Apparently this group had still not submitted to his authority or recognized him as an apostle from God, even after all this time.

In terms of argument and supposed knowledge, Paul could **demolish arguments and every pretension** (10:5). The purpose was to **take captive every thought to make it obedient to Christ** (10:5). What a great goal within the battles of our own heart! Through the power of the Spirit every thought should become an obedient captive to Christ, which is exactly what our holiness heritage understands entire sanctification to be.

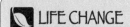

LIFE CHANGE

Through the power of the Spirit our every thought should become obedient to Christ.

So Paul now expects to deal with continued rebellion against him when he arrives in Corinth this third time. **And we will be ready to punish every act of disobedience, once your obedience is complete** (10:6). Again, 2 Corinthians 1–9 would not leave us thinking their obedience was so incomplete that Paul would make a comment like this one (2:9). But apparently the second visit of Titus revealed their continued questions about Paul's authority and doubts about his Christian status.

You are looking only on the surface of things (10:7). They almost seem to question whether Paul is even truly a Christian. **If anyone is confident that he belongs to Christ, he should consider again that we belong to Christ just as much as he** (10:7). Given Paul's dialog with super-apostles in 11:5 and 21–23, some of this questioning may actually originate from what other Christian missionaries were saying about Paul.

We know that such Christian opposition to him was around. We hear about it in Jerusalem in Acts 21:20–21, although it seems doubtful that the super-apostles at Corinth were legalists from the Jerusalem church. Paul's

opponents at Corinth sided with Apollos and seemed to favor secular eloquence rather than Jewish law keeping. Nevertheless, we know that during
the imprisonment when Paul wrote Philippians, some Christians preached in
such a way as to make things harder for him (Phil. 1:15). They probably did
so by emphasizing the radical, revolutionary dimension to his preaching, the
kinds of things that got him into trouble with political authorities.

But Paul claims to belong to Christ just as much as anyone who might
criticize him. He wants them to know that he is not ashamed **even if I
boast somewhat freely about the authority the Lord gave us** (10:8).
Paul has in view here the fact that he has sent to the Corinthians such
"weighty and forceful" letters. His purpose, he wants them to know, is not
to frighten you with my letters (10:9). The purpose of flexing his
authority is to build them up, to bring them into proper relationship with
God and to where they need to be in the faith. His authority is not the
problem. The problem is their refusal to obey God's commands as Paul
has made them clear to the Corinthians. If the disobedience persists, then
**what we are in our letters when we are absent, we will be in our
actions when we are present** (10:11).

Paul's Christian opponents, probably the super-apostles, **measure themselves by themselves and compare themselves with themselves** (10:12).
These individuals **commend themselves** (10:12), using themselves as the
standard. In contrast, Paul does not **dare to classify or compare** himself
with these individuals (10:12), because their measuring rod is set by the
wrong standard. They show their lack of wisdom by not comparing themselves **to the field** or measuring standard **God has assigned** (10:13).

Paul would not have made it as far as Corinth if God had not been on
his side. But Paul did reach the Corinthians—**we did get as far as you
with the gospel of Christ** (10:14). Paul did not conduct missions to
which God had assigned other people. **Neither do we go beyond our
limits by boasting of work done by others** (10:15). But this was exactly
the kind of boasting the "super-apostles" were doing, boasting of their
influence on the Corinthians when in fact God had appointed Paul as
"father" of the community. Paul's philosophy, on the other hand, was "to
preach the gospel where Christ was not known, so that I would not be
building on someone else's foundation" (Rom. 15:20).

315

Paul hoped that Corinth was not the full extent of God's blessing on his ministry. **Our hope is that . . . our area of activity among you will greatly expand** (10:15–16). He hopes eventually to push beyond Corinth to Rome and then to Spain, as he tells the Romans, "I hope to visit you [Romans] while passing through and to have you assist me on my journey there [to Spain]" (Rom. 15:24).

Rather than boast in what God was doing, the traveling super-apostles boasted in their own wisdom and spirituality. But **"Let him who boasts, boast in the Lord." For it is not the one who commends himself who is approved, but the one whom the Lord commends** (10:17–18). The Lord has made such a commendation of Paul in the way He has given him converts and churches from Asia to Macedonia to Greece. The Lord has commended him by helping him escape the persecution of Jews, magistrates, and perhaps even other Christians. The super-apostles had only themselves to boast for them.

ENDNOTES

1. Although the beginning of this chapter sounds similar to something Paul might say in one of his letters just after a greeting and thanksgiving.

PAUL MAKES A FOOL OF HIMSELF BY BOASTING

2 Corinthians 11:1–12:10

Both at the beginning and end of this section, Paul expresses his discomfort at the foolishness in which he now engages. **I hope you will put up with a little of my foolishness** (11:1). The foolishness is his boasting about his own apostolic credentials. He does not want to commend himself or boast about himself (10:18). When God is the One who gives all good things, it is foolish to take the credit for any gifts you have or greatness you demonstrated. Even the non-Christians of Paul's day did not believe in boasting of this sort; the people of that day believed a person who boasted was just tempting the gods to take you down a notch and put you in your place.

But Paul felt that the Corinthians were forcing him to present his spiritual creden-

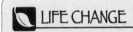

LIFE CHANGE

When God is the one who gives all good things, it is foolish for us to take credit for any gifts we might have.

tials. After all, the "super-apostles" gave theirs (11:18).

Paul compares these teachers to the serpent in the garden: **I am afraid that just as Eve was deceived by the serpent's cunning, you minds may somehow be led astray from your sincere and pure devotion to Christ** (11:3).

317

Paul thus compares the community to Eve, not as a type of *all women*, but the type of a person who is led astray by deceptive forces—a spiritual problem rather than a physical one.

For if someone comes to you and preaches a Jesus other than the Jesus we preached . . . you put up with it easily enough (11:4). This comment confers immense shame on the Corinthian community: they all too easily listen to false teaching. Paul has already asserted his authority in previous letters, yet he still finds a significant part of the community rejecting his preaching in favor of that of the "super-apostles." Paul is forced to defend himself more vigorously than he ever has.

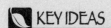 **KEY IDEAS**

Paul's tone in 2 Corinthians 10–13 is more sullen, as if he is losing the battle for the obedience of the Corinthian community.

We hear one of their criticisms in 11:6: **I may not be a trained speaker, but I do have knowledge.** Paul already dealt with this issue in 1 Corinthians 1–4. Some of the Corinthians found secular wisdom and rhetorical eloquence impressive. Paul had made it clear to them that "the message of the cross is foolishness to those who are perishing" (1 Cor. 1:18) and that for Christians it is "Christ the power of God and the wisdom of God" (1 Cor. 1:24). He did not come "with eloquence or superior wisdom" (1 Cor. 2:1).[1] Instead he "resolved to know nothing . . . except Jesus Christ and him crucified" (1 Cor. 2:2).

But apparently the power of suffering and the cross just did not compute to some in the church. Paul had given them the truth; what more could he say if they were not willing to believe and obey?

Paul's detractors also continued to look down on him because he worked to support himself. **Was it a sin for me to lower myself in order to elevate you by preaching the gospel free of charge?** (11:7). The worldly Corinthians took Paul for granted because they did not have to pay for him. How ironic! But unfortunately human nature often works this way, as we value one thing over another simply because it is more expensive. The carnal Corinthians valued the "super-apostles" because they cost more.

In 1 Corinthians 9 he had made it clear that he was worthy of their support, that "those who preach the gospel should receive their living from the gospel" (1 Cor. 9:14). He has "the right to food and drink" (1 Cor. 9:4), just as much as the other apostles, the Lord's brothers, and Cephas (1 Cor. 9:5). To be sure, the Corinthians were obligated to support Paul, but he "did not use this right. On the contrary, we put up with anything rather than hinder the gospel of Christ" (1 Cor. 9:12). As we discussed in our commentary on that passage, Paul probably did not want to have any strings of patronage between himself and the Corinthians. He knew that it would hinder his ability to speak the gospel forthrightly if sinners such as these controlled his purse strings.

Incidentally, we probably should not think of the apostles Paul mentions in 1 Corinthians 9 as the "super-apostles" of 2 Corinthians 11. While individuals like James and Peter (Cephas) no doubt disagreed with Paul on some issues, it is doubtful that the Corinthians would have considered any of them more rhetorically eloquent than Paul.[2] The members of the Sanhedrin consider the disciples "unschooled, ordinary men" (Acts 4:13). The only real name that fits the details of Paul's defense in 2 Corinthians 11 is Apollos, who had been at issue earlier in Paul's relationship with the Corinthians. Nevertheless, Paul speaks of super-apostles in the plural, and let us hope that Apollos was not one of those who was subverting the Corinthians at this point!

Instead of entangling himself with material support from the Corinthians, Paul had taken resources from the faithful Macedonians over and over again, the Philippians in particular. **And when I was with you and needed something, I was not a burden to anyone, for the brothers who came from Macedonia supplied what I needed** (11:9).

The truth was that the Corinthian church owed Paul. While the Corinthians were putting Paul down for working while he was with them, he considered it a matter for boasting. **[N]obody in the regions of Achaia will stop this boasting of mine** (11:10). He would continue to find his support elsewhere, in part because he loved them (11:11) and did not want to be a burden to them (11:9). But by supporting himself he also **cut the ground from under those who want an opportunity to be considered equal with us in the things they boast about** (11:12). Do they think they are really important? Let us see if God will support them without the money of the rich at Corinth!

Paul now draws the line with regard to the teachers whose message is corrupting some of the Corinthians. He places them outside the true faith: **such men are false apostles, deceitful workmen, masquerading as apostles of Christ** (11:13). They called themselves Christians, but their message and manner proved that they were not truly sent and commissioned by God. **Satan himself masquerades as an angel of light. It is not surprising, then, if his servants masquerade as servants of righteousness** (11:14–15).

Paul has now gone far from his tactful rhetoric in 1 Corinthians. In 1 Corinthians he tried to find aspects of his opponents' teaching that he agreed with in order to lead them toward a healthier perspective and course of action. But he now draws the line sharply: those who propagate the thinking of these other teachers are siding with Satan and are destined for judgment. These are frightening words, for these teachers were no doubt counted among the saints by others. We remember that the same types of individuals that Acts is willing to call "believers who belonged to the party of the Pharisees" (Acts 15:5), Paul considers to be "false brothers" who had "infiltrated our ranks to spy on the freedom we have in Christ Jesus" (Gal. 2:4).

LIFE CHANGE

If God's Spirit inhabits the body of Christ, the church, then the more Christians we are in communion with, the more likely it is that we will know the mind of the Spirit.

Only fools like the superapostles would boast in this way, so Paul tells them to **receive me just as you would a fool** (11:16). Throughout, he is mindful that he is **not talking as the Lord would, but as a fool** (11:17). All these remarks are not so thinly veiled sarcasm of the false apostles. **Since many are boasting in the way the world does, I too will boast** (11:18). The foolish Corinthians have once again taken the signals that should have led them to reject these masqueraders and mistaken them for true spiritual clout.

Paul's sarcasm deepens. **In fact, you even put up with anyone who enslaves you and pushes himself forward or slaps you in the face** (11:20). Even if the Corinthians did not, we feel the embarrassment and shame they should have. They thought they were getting gems of truth and wisdom when in fact someone was simply taking their money. The false apostles were taking advantage of them, and they were thanking them for it.

What anyone else dares to boast about—I am speaking as a fool— I also dare to boast about. Are they Hebrews? So am I (11:21–22). Paul was no Gentile. He was born into the Jewish race, the people of God. Did they boast about their birth? Paul could too, although he did not ultimately think any qualification of this sort mattered in Christ (Phil. 3:13).

Are they Israelites? So am I. Are they Abraham's descendents? So am I. None of these things matter in Christ. "[W]hatever was to my profit I now consider loss for the sake of Christ. What is more, I consider everything a loss compared to the surpassing greatness of knowing Christ Jesus my Lord, for whose sake I have lost all things. I consider them rubbish, that I may gain Christ" (Phil. 3:7–8). That the false apostles would take stock in such things only showed how misguided their thinking was.

Are they servants of Christ? (11:23). Now Paul was getting serious, for this characteristic did matter. While Paul felt **out of my mind to talk like this** (11:23), it was overwhelmingly clear that he had lived a life of ministry that did far more service to Christ than perhaps any other Christian, including the original disciples. **I have worked much harder** than any of the apostles the Corinthians admired (11:23).

We now get a precious list of the kinds of things that Paul had endured for the sake of the gospel. These include

1. **Been in prison more frequently**
2. **Been flogged more severely**
3. **Been exposed to death again and again** (11:23)
4. **Five times I received from the Jews the forty lashes minus one** (11:24)
5. **Three times I was beaten with rods**
6. **Once I was stoned**
7. **Three times I was shipwrecked, I spent a night and a day in the open sea** (11:25)

Because God preserved the book of Acts for us, we can picture a number of the sufferings Paul mentions. Clement of Rome, writing some forty years later, was aware of seven times Paul had been imprisoned.[3] At least two of these took place after Paul wrote 2 Corinthians.[4]

The Jews only gave thirty-nine lashes because of Deut. 25:3, which forbade a judge from having a fellow Jew flogged more than forty times. Since this punishment was specifically Jewish, Paul must have received it either in Judea or in a synagogue. Paul does indeed mention being driven from Jerusalem (1 Thess. 2:15). By contrast, the Romans used rods in their floggings (Acts 16:22–23). Acts records Paul's stoning while he was in Lystra (Acts 14:19). But the shipwreck in Acts actually took place after Paul had written 2 Corinthians (Acts 27:27–44). So we know of at least four shipwrecks Paul endured in the course of his ministry.

Surely no other apostle—true or false—came close to enduring what Paul had endured for the sake of the gospel. Even the mention of a few of Paul's efforts must have made any competitor seem silly. Paul had invested his whole life in his mission. He gave everything to the ministry of reconciling the world to God. While the false apostles were wining and dining off of foolish Christians, Paul was

8. Constantly on the move
9. In danger from rivers, bandits, countrymen, Gentiles
10. In danger in the city, in the country, at sea, from false brothers (11:26)

Travel was a lot more dangerous in Paul's day. While the emperor Augustus did a great deal to make travel safer, the mugging of the Parable of the Good Samaritan was an all too real possibility in Paul's world. What is more discouraging is that Paul faced danger from fellow Jews and even people claiming to be Christians. While Paul was imprisoned and writing Philippians, he mentioned Christians who must have taken "pot shots" at him while they were presenting the gospel (Phil. 1:15–16).

11. I have labored and toiled
12. Often gone without sleep
13. I have known hunger and thirst and have often gone without food

14. I have been cold and naked (11:27).

Anyone who has ever gone hiking with inadequate clothing (which is the meaning of "naked" here) or preparation can picture a bit of what Paul is saying here. There must have been many occasion on Paul's trips over mountains and other long distances that he found himself in hazardous conditions.

In prison there were no cafeterias or state system to feed you. If you did not have resources or someone on the outside to support you, you could starve to death before your trial even if you were innocent. In short, Paul's mission work was a big deal. He had sacrificed everything for his ministry. Who would volunteer for such a lifestyle?

To top it all off . . .

15. I face daily the pressure of my concern for all the churches (11:28).

These included immense struggles with carnal Christians like those at Corinth. Paul gives two examples of how this concern impacted him. **Who is weak, and I do not feel weak?** (11:29). Some of those in his churches had what Paul referred to as a "weak" conscience. Their consciences were bothered by things that Paul's was not. To the weak, Paul became weak, that he might win the weak for Christ (1 Cor. 9:22). This was one of the pressures Paul faced in his ministry: to care for those who did not feel the freedom in the Lord that he did.

But Paul balances out this concern with the pressure of those who "scandalized" the weak (*skandalizō*): **Who is led into sin [who is scandalized], and I do not inwardly burn?** (11:29). There is perhaps a not so thinly veiled warning here to the "strong" party at Corinth. I

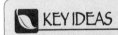 **KEY IDEAS**

Paul felt the pressure both of caring for those who did not feel the freedom in the Lord that he did and of dealing with those whose freedom led others into sin.

may have to care for those whose faith is weak, the people that some of you feel so superior to. But I also have to deal with those that lead others into sin—and that makes me burn. Some of *you* make me burn.

In the end, the game of boasting is a farce. The honest person eventually comes to realize his or her ultimate dependence on God for strength and power. **If I must boast, I will boast of the things that show my weakness.** (11:30). These kinds of things put the emphasis where it should be, namely, on the **God and Father of the Lord Jesus** (11:31). He is the One to whom we should draw our attention, not to ourselves. As Jesus had revealed to Paul, "My power is made perfect in weakness" (12:9).

Paul ends this sub-section (11:16–33) with an illustration of an incident where he was forced to rely on God. **In Damascus the governor under King Aretas had the city of the Damascenes guarded in order to arrest me. But I was lowered in a basket from a window in the wall and slipped through his hands** (11:32–33). We hear of this incident in Acts 9:23–25, although in typical fashion Acts only tells us about the Jewish opposition to Paul. Paul himself makes it clear that some secular authorities were after him as well, including the "governor under King Aretas."[5]

Paul now begins the final section of his boasting (12:1–10): **I must go on boasting . . . I will go on to visions and revelations from the Lord** (12:1). We remember that some Corinthians apparently boasted in their ability to speak in tongues (1 Cor. 14:12, 26, 37). Paul told them that he spoke "in tongues more than all of you" (1 Cor. 14:18), but pushed them to use spiritual gifts in the church that build up others.

Now Paul finds himself defending his connection to the heavenly realm. Were the tongues of which he spoke his ability to speak in many different languages? Did they criticize him for not speaking in tongues like they did—or not as much as they did? It is hard to know exactly what he meant when he claimed to speak in more tongues than them. At the very least it seems that they did not think he was as spiritually gifted as they were. So Paul tells them of a mystical vision he had, the likes of which they could not boast. He is so uncomfortable boasting about such a vision that he speaks of himself in the third person: as a "he" rather than "I."

I know a man in Christ who fourteen years ago was caught up to the third heaven (12:2). While at first we wonder if Paul is talking about someone else, 12:7 makes it clear that Paul was indeed referring to himself. He is so uncomfortable boasting about the spectacular experiences

God has graciously given him that he cannot even bring himself to say "*I was caught up to heaven.*" It is hard to date Paul's ministry with precision. But if he refers straightforwardly to a period of fourteen years, then he may have had this experience during the period of time after his conversion when he was back home in Tarsus (Acts 9:30, 11:25–26). Other scholars see the number fourteen as somewhat symbolic (two sevens) and think Paul refers here to his conversion, over twenty years previous.

We should not be surprised or troubled that Paul expressed this religious experience in terms of the way he pictured the world: "the third heaven." We have examples of other Jewish literature from this time that speak of a multilayered heaven or sky above the earth, with God in the highest layer. The Ascension of Isaiah, a Jewish work, thinks of the sky in terms of seven layers. The Testament of Levi thinks of three layers of sky, just as Paul does. Just as I am not really talking about cosmology when I speak of the "sunrise" or "sunset," Paul was simply using a certain Jewish way of referring to God's location. In other words, Paul's statement that he was taken up into "paradise" or the "third heaven" is his way of saying that he went into the presence of God.

Paul is unclear whether this heavenly journey took place **in the body or out of the body** (12:2). Paul repeats this uncertainty in the next verse: **whether in the body or apart from the body I do not know—God knows** (12:3). But whether he took this trip in the body or out, he knows that **this man . . . was caught up to paradise** (12:4), which almost certainly is another way of thinking about the third heaven where God's presence is. There Paul **heard inexpressible things, things that man is not permitted to tell** (12:4). It is not clear whether Paul has in mind the same kinds of sounds that he mentions in Rom. 8:26, where the Spirit intercedes with "groans that words cannot express." But such revelations seem one step "more spiritual" than tongues, for tongues *are* expressed by way of human voice. The things Paul heard were unspeakable. If the Corinthians did think of Paul as inferior to them on the playing field of tongues, Paul clearly trumped them with his heavenly journey.

I will boast about a man like that, but I will not boast about myself, except about my weaknesses (12:5). Paul is ashamed to be boasting the way he is. He is not really a fool to boast about such things, because they really happened: he was **speaking the truth** (12:6). But he does not want their respect and loyalty because of things of this sort. He wants no one to **think more of me than is warranted by what I do or say** (12:6). Anyone can make up stories about visions or things that are un-interpreted or in the past. But what are those people *doing* in front of you? What are they *saying* now? Do they have the power Paul has?

A person's ego could easily become inflated with the kinds of revelations Paul experienced. But **[t]o keep me from becoming conceited . . . there was given me a thorn in my flesh** (12:7). We do not know exactly what this burden in Paul's life was. It obviously troubled him greatly. Various individuals have made different suggestions. The fact that it was a thorn in his "flesh" likely refers either to a physical problem or perhaps to a temptation of "flesh" understood in spiritual terms, a besetting sin with which he continuously struggled. Since Paul speaks of the flesh as something from which Christ frees us when we receive the Spirit, it does not seem likely that Paul was speaking of sinful flesh (Rom. 8:1–8). He consistently taught that a Christian will have victory over this kind of flesh (Gal. 5:16; 1 Cor. 10:13).

It seems more likely that Paul refers to a literal physical malady. Paul does mention problems with his eyes in Galatians (4:13, 15), and Acts tells us Paul went blind for a time when he first saw the risen Christ (Acts 9:9). All in all, this is the only real hint Paul gives us about what this "thorn" might be. Whatever the thorn in the flesh was, **Three times I pleaded with the Lord to take it away from me** (12:8). But the Lord did not grant Paul his request, nor does God always say "yes" in answer to our prayers. To be sure, God did not chastise Paul for asking again and again—three times in all. Nevertheless, once Paul had a sense of God's answer, he stopped begging. God invites us to ask repeatedly, like the persistent widow of Jesus' parable (Luke 18:1–8). But there is also a time when we must accept God's answer and rely on His strength in our weakness.

The Lord's answer was that Paul needed to rely on him. Christ said to him, **My grace is sufficient for you, for my power is made perfect in weakness** (12:9). God would get glory through Paul by way of Paul's reliance on Christ for strength. This is the paradox that Paul has tried to show the Corinthians all along. God is not to be found in the worldly wise or the worldly rich. God is not to be found in the worldly eloquent or worldly powerful. God shows His strength the most by taking the weak and making them strong (1 Cor. 1:26–31).

Therefore I will boast all the more gladly about my weaknesses, so that Christ's power may rest on me (12:9).

GREAT THEMES

God shows His strength the most by taking the weak and making them strong.

The super-apostles and their deceived followers in Corinth could only glory in themselves and in their limited abilities. Such boasting begins and ends with yourself and is thus incredibly small in its scope. True greatness is to be connected to the cosmic power source of the universe, whose resources and strength are without measure. **For when I am weak, then I am strong** (12:10). Our human weakness

LIFE CHANGE

There is a time when we must accept God's no answer and simply rely on His strength in our weakness.

and difficulty only give us a chance to turn to God's power. When God turns on the power, it brings a voltage far greater than anything we could produce on our own.

ENDNOTES

1. Many Pauline scholars now believe that Paul may actually have had some secular rhetorical training. See M. M. Mitchell, *Paul and the Rhetoric of Reconciliation: An Exegetical Investigation of the Language and Composition of 1 Corinthians* (Louisville: Westminster John Knox, 1991) and F. J. Long, *Ancient Rhetoric and Paul's Apology: The Compositional Unity of 2 Corinthians* (SNTSMS 131; Cambridge: Cambridge University, 2004).

2. Although Paul does refer to them somewhat sarcastically in Galatians: "those who seemed to be leaders" (Gal. 2:2) and "those who seemed to be important—whatever they were makes no difference to me; God does not judge by external appearance" (Gal. 2:6).

3. 1 Clement 5:6.

4. In Caesarea (Acts 24:27) and Rome (Acts 28:30).

5. This event is thought to have taken place around the years A.D. 36–37.

FINAL REMARKS AND FAREWELL

2 Corinthians 12:11–13:14

1. WORRY ABOUT HIS THIRD VISIT (12:11–13:10)

He begins these near-closing remarks with a reminder of how foolish and shameful it is that he has had to boast about himself to them, to this church of which he was the father, to this church with which he had spent so much time. **I have made a fool of myself . . . I ought to have been commended by you** (12:11).

What a sad day for Paul! At this low point of his relationship with the Corinthians Paul serves as an encouragement for those who find themselves leaving a church wronged or with unfulfilled dreams. If it could happen to the apostle Paul, who are we to think we are immune to discouragement and defeat in ministry? In times like these we remember that God gives the increase and that we are, in the end, only His servants called to ministry.

Paul, again defending his apostleship, gives us his understanding of the true signs of apostleship in 12:12: **The things that mark an apostle—signs, wonders and miracles—were done among you with great perseverance.** The super-apostles did not do these kinds of things; they were just smooth talkers, "wise guys." Had Paul's ministry to them made them inferior to any other church with any other apostle or teacher, **except that I was never a burden to you? Forgive me this wrong!** (12:13). Paul's sarcasm again is clear. I guess I should have taken advantage of you and defrauded you so that you would feel more important!

Now I am ready to visit you for the third time (12:14). The first was when he founded the church and stayed for about a year and a half (Acts 18:1–18). Then there was his painful visit that was full of conflict and that included some rejection of his authority (2 Cor. 2:1). Paul would write Romans on his third stay there (Rom. 16:1, 23), the one that he is anticipating here in 2 Cor. 12:14 and 13:1.

If in fact Titus had taken 1 Corinthians 1–9 and received a negative response to Paul's instructions on the offering (2 Cor. 8–9), that would explain what Paul says next. **I will not be a burden to you, because what I want is not your possessions but you** (12:14). He makes no mention of the offering any more. That is no longer important. Paul only wants reconciliation. He will not burden the Corinthians with the issue of money. It is sad that no individuals from Corinth are mentioned in the list of Paul's traveling companions in Acts 20:4.

After all, children should not have to save up for their parents, but parents for their children (12:14). If they thought he was just after their money, they were wrong. Forget the offering and any support he might deserve. **I will very gladly spend for you everything I have and expend myself as well** (12:15). As Paul wrote in 2 Cor. 7:3, "you have such a place in our hearts that we would live or die with you."

But as is often the case, the more love you are willing to give, the easier it is for the beloved to take your love for granted. **If I love you more, will you love me less?** (12:15). The super-apostles made the Corinthians feel like they had to pay for them, so the Corinthians were deceived into thinking them more valuable. How ironic then that they would think Paul was trying to take advantage of them when he did not take money or support from them? He was **not a burden** to them (12:16).

But then there was the offering. Perhaps someone was accusing him of getting his due through the backdoor, through the offering. Was Paul finally taking advantage of them through his offering, **crafty fellow that I am, I caught you by trickery**? (12:16). Preposterous, Paul implies, the kind of thing a guilty person projects on someone who is innocent.

Did I exploit you through any of the men I sent you? (12:17). In our reconstruction, this is a reference to Titus and the two brothers' trip to Corinth to prepare for the coming offering (2 Cor. 8:16–9:5), a trip that apparently did not go well. Had they tried to take advantage of the Corinthians financially? **I urged Titus to go to you and I sent our brother with him.**[1] **Titus did not exploit you, did he?** (12:18). The patent answer was no. This accusation was nothing but an embarrassing attempt to find some fault in Paul. But Paul had conducted the affairs in relation to the offering with the highest degree of circumspection. His accusers should have felt foolish.

As Paul brings his boasting to an end, he reiterates why he has taken so much time giving reasons for them to have confidence in him and his apostolicity. He has not done it for himself but because they need him. If they choose the super-apostles over him, they are running the risk of destruction. **We have been speaking in the sight of God as those in Christ; and everything we do, dear friends, is for your strengthening** (12:19). If it was only a question of Paul himself, it would not be necessary for him to bolster their opinion of him. But their own faith was at stake in the mix, and it was worth him playing the fool to try to get them back on track.

Although Paul had confidence in them when he wrote 2 Cor. 7:16, Titus' shaky trip over the offering had brought back all his earlier fears. **I am afraid that when I come I may not find you as I want you to be** (12:20). If that is the case, then **you will not find me as you want me to be. I fear that there may be quarreling, jealousy, outbursts of anger, factions, slander, gossip, arrogance and disorder** (12:20). These are all the same issues he has so painstakingly and carefully addressed in his earlier correspondence. First Corinthians 1–4 thoroughly corrected their arrogance and factions. Paul's discussion of the Lord's Supper in 1 Corinthians 10 also dealt with their factions, and no doubt so many of the questions Paul answered related to quarreling and the like. First Corinthians 14 addressed the disorder of their worship in very careful terms. Now Paul worries that his words have not affected them at all.

How discouraging! **I am afraid that . . . I will be grieved over many who have sinned earlier and have not repented** (12:21). Here are more of the issues Paul already addressed in 1 Corinthians, particularly in chapters 5 and 7. Has Paul now discovered that the sinner he thought had repented (2 Cor. 2:5–7; 7:12) really had not? If so, it is no wonder that

Paul wrote the Romans from Corinth that "there is no more place for me to work in these regions" (Rom. 15:23).

So Paul was bracing himself for a showdown. **This will be my third visit to you,** he says again (13:1). If some have grievances with others, Paul will follow the Old Testament rule that **"Every matter must be established by the testimony of two or three witnesses"** (13:1). We find Paul saying the same things again that he must have said in his earlier harsh letter.[2] **I already gave you a warning when I was with you the second time** (13:2), on the painful visit (2:1).

He would now come and make sure that those who wronged others were punished. **On my return I will not spare those who sinned earlier or any of the others** (13:2–3). This comment once again contrasts sharply with the fact that the chief sinner of the community was thought to be repentant when 2 Corinthians 1–9 was written. Verse 3 reminds us why Paul has so vehemently defended himself in 11:1–12:10.

Although Christ's strength is made perfect in our weakness, the Corinthians should make no mistake. Christ **is not weak in dealing with you** or your sin, **but is powerful among you** (13:3). He may have been **crucified in weakness, yet he lives by God's power** (13:4). So Paul, who has been boasting of his own weakness, **by God's power . . . will live with him to serve you.** Despite Paul's own weakness, God will demonstrate His power once again to the Corinthians through Paul when he arrives.

The bottom line is similar to what Paul said in 2 Cor. 5:20 when he said, "Be reconciled to God." **Examine yourselves to see whether you are in the faith,** whether you truly have faith in what God has done and will do through Jesus Christ. **Do you not realize that Christ Jesus is in you—unless, of course, you fail the test?** (13:5). The way to show that they are in the faith is to repent of the kinds of behavior Paul has catalogued in 12:20–21. If they have no desire to follow God's will, then they will fail this test, and there is no way that Christ Jesus is truly in them.

Unfortunately, some have accused Paul of failing the test. Apparently they have seriously misjudged his attempt to raise the offering for Jerusalem, and they are calling his motives into question. Barely any of us will escape the misjudging of our motives at one point or another. When we are falsely accused, our first inclination may be to lash out in self-defense.

But Paul is well beyond any reaction of that sort. At this point he has two simple responses. First, he affirms that his motives are in fact pure: **I trust that you will discover that we have not failed the test** (13:6). If they do not believe him, he cannot do any more than maintain his innocence. But in the meantime, **we pray to God that you will not do anything wrong** (13:7). If the offering stands behind this whole sequence of thought, no doubt Paul hopes that they will still give toward the offering, even if they do not trust him. It is also possible that Paul has in mind sins that the false apostles are allowing them to continue doing.

In the end, it is the second hope that is most important. It is ultimately not important **that people will see that we have stood the test** (13:7). What is important to Paul is that **you will do what is right even though we may seem to have failed**. What an incredible model for us when we are falsely accused! Paul certainly wants to clear himself, but he is far more concerned with furthering true understanding and behavior that is true to God. **For we cannot do anything against the truth, but only for the truth** (13:8).

So let him be weak and thought a failure, as long as **you are strong** (13:9). The goal, **our prayer is for your perfection**, or better yet, their mending (13:9). The word Paul uses here has the connotations of something that needs

LIFE CHANGE

While Paul wants to clear himself, he is far more concerned with furthering true understanding and behavior that is true to God. May God help us to have the same attitude when we are wrongly treated in the church!

to be repaired and mended, like a net that has ripped. The Corinthians have such a long way to go, and they seem to have regressed back to their lowest point. But Paul has not given up or abandoned hope. He writes them one last time before he comes, so **that when I come I may not have to be harsh in my use of authority** (13:10). After all, the main purpose behind the authority God gave Paul was **for building you up, not for tearing you down** (13:10).

2. FAREWELL (13:11-14)

Paul does not need a long farewell—he will be with them in person very soon. He sends this letter as a last ditch effort in hope that his visit will be edifying rather than punitive. He reiterates his main admonition for them: **Aim for perfection** (13:11), or better yet, be mended. He has made a final appeal, and asks them to **listen to** it.

Throughout his earnest appeal, there have no doubt been those faithful to him in the background, in the back of his mind. The tension between some Corinthians and him no doubt existed similarly between various members of the church. It is no wonder he prays for them to be mended. As he encouraged the Philippians (Phil. 2:2), he tells the Corinthians to **be of one mind** and to **live in peace** (2 Cor. 13:11). The potential pay-off was great: **And the God of love and peace will be with you** (13:11), words that are easy to understand—too easy. We should linger on every word until the depth of this promise sinks into our deepest soul.

Now come some of Paul's standard closing remarks. He encourages them to **greet one another with a holy kiss** (13:12), a sign of the fact that the church is a family. How hard it must have been to greet with a kiss someone you were slandering or backbiting! Despite the Corinthian problems, the churches of Macedonia still **send their greetings** (13:13). So we do well to do the loving thing even while those to whom we show love are hurting us.

It is unfortunate that Paul's correspondence with the Corinthians seems to close on such an uncertain note. We know that Paul went on to Corinth and wrote Romans from there. He mentions the hospitality of some of its patrons (Rom. 16:23). On the whole, Romans does not give us any hints of conflict at the place from which he writes. However, he no longer feels any room to minister in Greece and the east any more (Rom. 15:23). He now looks west toward Spain.

But 2 Timothy gives us a glimpse of hope. If it was written much later, after Paul had been to Rome, we learn that Paul may have made one more trip to Corinth. Second Timothy 4:20 tells us that Erastus stayed at Corinth while Paul went on to stand trial. If this Erastus is the same person we hear of in Rom. 16:23, then at least some Corinthians went on to follow and even assist Paul in the continuation of his ministry.

Paul closes with a benediction that is so majestic, so spiritual, so uplifting that it became the standard benediction of the church throughout the centuries. It incorporates all the members of the Trinity, even if Paul and the early Christians had not yet worked out the details of how they all fit together. Each thing for which Paul gives thanks indicates a key dimension of each divine person.

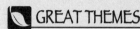 GREAT THEMES

Second Corinthians closes with a benediction that is so majestic, so spiritual, so uplifting that it has been a standard benediction throughout the centuries.

May the grace of the Lord Jesus Christ, and the love of God, and the fellowship of the Holy Spirit be with you all (13:14).

ENDNOTES

1. In our reconstruction, this is the anonymous brother mentioned in 2 Cor. 8:22–24. A slight problem for this theory is the absence of the other anonymous brother who was sent by the churches (2 Cor. 8:18–19). But this individual was not so much a representative of Paul as a representative of the other churches. Paul did not send him but the other churches did.

2. This section would make a lot of sense as an excerpt from the harsh letter, but Paul's mention of Titus's trip in 12:18 makes this almost impossible. Titus had not made a previous trip for Paul to refer to at that time.